5 $\mathcal{S}$
D0853156

THE IRISH ❧ FAIRY BOOK

THE IRISH FAIRY BOOK

by Alfred Perceval Graves
illustrated by George Denham

GREENWICH HOUSE
Distributed by Crown Publishers, Inc.   New York

Copyright © 1983 by Arlington House, Inc
All rights reserved.

This 1983 edition is published by Greenwich House,
a division of Arlington House, Inc.,
distributed by Crown Publishers, Inc.
One Park Avenue, New York, New York, 10016

Manufactured in the United States of America

Library of Congress Cataloging in Publication Data
Main entry under title:

The Irish Fairy Book.
    1. Fairy tales—Ireland.   I. Graves, Alfred
Perceval, 1846-1931.   II. Denham, George.
GR153.5.I72   1983   398.2'1'09415   83-14082
ISBN 0-517-421593

h g f e d c b a

A Faery Song

Sung by the people of faery over Diarmuid
and Grania, who lay in their bridal sleep
under a Cromlech.

WE who are old, old and gay,
  O so old!
 Thousands of years, thousands of years,
  If all were told:

 Give to these children, new from the
   world,
  Silence and love;
And the long dew-dropping hours of the night,
  And the stars above:

 Give to these children, new from the world,
  Rest far from men.
Is anything better, anything better?
  Tell us it then:

Us who are old, old and gay,
  O so old!
Thousands of years, thousands of years,
  If all were told.

      W. B. YEATS.

vii

Contents

Contents

* From " Hero Tales of Ireland."

Contents

Foreword

In Ireland, the fairy tale was one of many vehicles the storyteller used to convey the legend and lore of a country rich in culture and tradition. The storyteller, also known in Gaelic as the *Shanachie*, would gather his listeners around the open hearth to retell the stories of long ago. He would enchant and amuse his audience with tales about pookas, leprechauns, mischievous elves and fairy-eating giants. In the old and medieval Irish period of literature, traditional tales of kings and heroes were also very popular among the *Shanachies*.

Fairy tales are traditional narratives that have been passed on from person to person by word of mouth. These fanciful tales were passed on from generation to generation until collectors of such lore began to put them down on paper. Yet the magic of these tales has not been lost just because they have gone from oral to written form. The stories collected here have been set down with accuracy and good faith, just as if they had been gathered from the lips of the storyteller only yesterday.

The Irish Fairy Book is an enchanting collection of tales and poems that have been written down true to the native dialect of the Irish people. Gaelic is the official language of Erin; however, it no longer is spoken that frequently among the Irish people. Yet certain terms and expressions still live on, such as *slānlate* (goodbye) and *tīrna nōg* (land of the young). Much of the work here has been written in narrative form taken down first hand from the inhabitants of the Irish countryside. The Irish people have a long oral tradition.

Fairy tales were originally written as a form of entertainment for adults. These stories served as a source of information concerning the history and culture of the Emerald Isle. Modern day forms of communication, such as television and radio, have replaced storytelling

Foreword

as an important origin for information and entertainment. Thus, the art of storytelling has been preserved mainly in authentic collections such as this one.

The Irish have been known to be a superstitious race (although they no longer place much store in the powers of wee elves and twinkling fairies). So, even though many Irish fairy tales do not actually contain fairies, a magical or supernatural element is always present. In this delightful collection, inanimate objects take on human qualities and old women possess magical powers. An aura of mysticism pervades each charming story.

The Irish Fairy Book will warm the hearts of any Irishman and everyone else who enjoys the merriment and wit that is an integral part of Irish folklore. Each contributor here shares a common love for the Irish people and their land and culture. This book will delight and entertain anyone with a fondness for Ireland and her people.

KAREN BURKE

New York City
1984

Preface

IRISH Fairy Lore has well been called by Mr. Alfred Nutt, one of the leading authorities on the subject, "As fair and bounteous a harvest of myth and romance as ever flourished among any race," and Dr. Joyce, the well-known Irish scholar and historian, states : "that it is very probable that the belief in the existence of fairies came in with the earliest colonists that entered Ireland, and that this belief is recorded in the oldest of native Irish writings in a way that proves it to have been, at the time treated of, long established and universally received."

Colgan himself supplies us with the name and derivation of the Irish word for fairy, Sidh (shee), still used throughout the country. "Fantastical spirits," he writes, "are by the Irish called men of the Sidh, because they are seen, as it were, to come out of the beautiful hills to infest men, and hence the vulgar belief that they reside in certain subterranean habitations; and sometimes the hills themselves are called by the Irish Sidhe or Siodha."

In Colgan's time, then, the fairy superstition had passed from the upper classes, gradually disenthralled of it by the influence of Christianity to the common people, among whom it is still rife. But it is clear that in the time of St. Patrick a belief in a world of fairies existed even in the King's household, for it is recorded that "when the two daughters of King Leary of Ireland, Ethnea the fair and Fedelma the ruddy, came early one morning to the well of Clebach to wash, they found there a synod of holy bishops with Patrick. And they knew not whence they came, or in what form, or from what people, or from what country; but they supposed them to be Duine Sidh, or gods of the earth, or a phantasm."

As suggested, the belief of the Princesses obtains to this very day amongst the peasantry of remote districts in Ireland, who still maintain that the fairies inhabit the Sidhe, or hills, and record instances of relations and friends being transported into their underground palaces.

The truth is that the Gaelic peasant, Scotch and Irish, is a mystic, and believes not only in this world, and the world to come, but in that other world which is the world of Faery, and which exercises an extraordinary influence upon many actions of his life.

We see in the well-known dialogue between Oisin (Ossian) and St. Patrick, and in other early Irish writers, how potent an influence Druidism, with its powers of concealing and changing, of paralysing and cursing, had been held to be in the days when the Irish worshipped no hideous idols, but adored Beal and Dagdae, the Great or the Good God, and afterwards Aine, the Moon, Goddess of the Water and of Wisdom, and when their minor Deities were Mananan Mac Lir, the Irish Neptune, whose name is still to be found in the Isle of *Man*; Crom, who corresponded to Ceres; Iphinn, the benevolent, whose relations to the Irish Oirfidh resembled those of Apollo towards Orpheus. The ancient Irish owed allegiance also to the Elements, to the Wind, and to the Stars.

Besides these Pagan Divinities, however, and quite apart from them, the early Irish believed in a hierarchy of fairy beings, closely analagous to us " humans," supposed to people hill and valley, old road and old earth-mound, lakes and rivers, and there to exercise a constant, if occult, influence upon mankind.

Various theories have been advanced to account for their origin. Some call these fairies angels outcast from heaven for their unworthiness, yet not evil enough for hell, and who, therefore, occupy intermediate space.

Others suggest that they are the spirits of that mysterious early

Preface

Irish race, the Tuatha da Danann, who were driven by their conquerors, the Milesians, to become "men of the hills," if not "cave" and "lake dwellers," in order to avoid the extermination that ultimately awaited them. Their artistic skill and superior knowledge evidenced to this day by remarkable sepulchral mounds, stone-inscribed spiral ornamentation, and beautiful bronze spearheads, led them to be accounted magicians, and Mr. Yeats and others of his school favour the idea that the minor deities of the early Irish above referred to were the earliest members of the Tuatha da Danann dynasty, and that we here have a form of that ancestor worship now met with amongst the Chinese and Japanese.

Dr. Joyce does not hold, however, that the subjugation of the Tuatha da Dananns, with the subsequent belief regarding them, was the origin of Irish fairy mythology.

"The superstition, no doubt, existed long previously; and this mysterious race, having undergone a gradual deification, became confounded and identified with the original local gods, and ultimately superseded them altogether."

But whatever their origin, supernatural powers evil and beneficent were supposed to attach to them such as the power of spiriting away young married women to act as fairy nurses, and their infants to replace fairy weaklings, or again the power of conferring wealth, health, and prosperity where a certain ritual due to them had been performed by their human allies.

The injurious powers of malevolently disposed fairies can only be met, according to popular belief, by wizards and wise women, who still exercise their arts in remote districts of Gaelic-speaking Ireland and Scotland.

These fairies are supposed to be life-sized, but there was another class of diminutive preternatural beings who came into close touch with man.

Amongst these were the Luchryman (Leith-phrogan) or *brogue* (shoe) maker, otherwise known as Lepracaun. He is always found mending or making a shoe, and if grasped firmly and kept constantly in view will disclose hid treasure to you or render up his *sporan na sgillinge* or purse of the (inexhaustible) shilling. He could only be bound by a plough chain or woollen thread. He is the type of industry which, if steadily faced, leads to fortune, but, if lost sight of, is followed by its forfeiture.

Love in idleness is personified by another pigmy, the *Gean-canach* (love-talker). He does not appear like the Luchryman, with a purse in one of his pockets but with his hands in both of them and a DUDEEN (ancient Irish pipe) in his mouth as he lazily strolls through lonely valleys making love to the foolish country lasses and " gostering " with the idle " boys."

To meet him meant bad luck, and whoever was ruined by ill-judged love was said to have been with the Gean-canach.

Another evil sprite was the *Clobher-ceann*, " a jolly, red-faced drunken little fellow," always " found astride on a wine-butt " and drinking and singing from a full tankard in a hard drinker's cellar, and bound by his appearance to bring its owner to speedy ruin.

Then there were the Leannan-sighe, or native Muses, to be found in every place of note to inspire the local bard, and the *Bean-sighes* (Banshees, fairy women) attached to each of the old Irish families and giving warning of the death of one of its members with piteous lamentations.

Black Joanna of the Boyne *(Siubhan Dubh na Boinne)* appeared on Hallowe'en in the shape of a great black fowl, bringing luck to the house whose *Vanithee* (woman of the house) kept it constantly clean and neat.

The Pooka, who appeared in the shape of a horse, and whom Shakespeare has adapted as " Puck," was a goblin who combined " horse-play " with viciousness.

The *dullaghan* was a churchyard demon whose head was of a

movable kind, and Dr. Joyce writes : " You generally meet him with his head in his pocket, under his arm, or absent altogether; or if you have the fortune to light upon a number of *dullaghans*, you may see them amusing themselves by flinging their heads at one another or kicking them for footballs."

An even more terrible churchyard demon is the beautiful phantom that waylays the widower at his wife's very tomb and poisons him by her kiss when he has yielded to her blandishments.

Of monsters the Irish had, and still believe in, the *Piast* (Latin *bestia*), a huge dragon or serpent confined to lakes by St. Patrick till the day of judgment, but still occasionally seen in their waters.

In Fenian times the days of Finn and his companion knights, the Piast, however, roamed the country, devouring men and women and cattle in large numbers, and some of the early heroes are recorded to have been swallowed alive by them and then to have hewed their way out of their entrails.

The Merrow, or Mermaid, is also still believed in, and many Folk Tales exist describing their intermarriage with mortals.

According to Nicholas O'Kearney—" It is the general opinion of many old persons versed in native traditional lore, that, before the introduction of Christianity, all animals possessed the faculties of human reason and speech; and old story-tellers will gravely inform you that every beast could speak before the arrival of St. Patrick, but that the Saint having expelled the demons from the land by the sound of his bell, all the animals that, before that time, had possessed the power of foretelling future events, such as the Black Steed of Binn-each-labhra, the Royal Cat of Clough-magh-righ-cat (Clough), and others, became mute; and many of them fled to Egypt and other foreign countries."

Cats are said to have been appointed to guard hidden treasures; and there are few who have not heard old Irish peasants tell about a strange meeting of cats and a violent battle fought by them in his neighbourhood. " It was believed," adds O'Kearney, " that

Preface

an evil spirit in the shape of a cat assumed command over these animals in various districts, and that when those wicked beings pleased they could compel all the cats belonging to their division to attack those of some other district. The same was said of rats; and rat-expellers, when commanding a colony of those troublesome and destructive animals to emigrate to some other place, used to address their 'billet' to the infernal rat supposed to hold command over the rest. In a curious pamphlet on the power of bardic compositions to charm and expel rats, lately published, Mr. Eugene Curry states that a degraded priest, who was descended from an ancient family of hereditary bards, was enabled to expel a colony of rats by the force of satire ! "

Hence, of course, Shakespeare's reference to rhyming Irish rats to death.

A few words upon the writers in this collection. Of Folk Tale collectors the palm must be given to Dr. Douglas Hyde, whose great knowledge of Irish, combined with a fine literary faculty, has enabled him to present the stories he has generously granted me the use of, in a manner which combines complete fidelity to his original, with true artistic feeling.

Dr. Joyce has not only granted the use of his fine Heroic Tale of the Pursuit of the Gilla Dacker, but had the honour of supplying Alfred, Lord Tennyson, the late Poet Laureate, with the subject of his " Voyage of Maeldune " in a story of that name, adapted into English in his " Old Celtic Romances." The Laureate acted on my suggestion that he should found a poem upon one of the romances in that book ; and to that circumstance I owe the kind permission by his son and Messrs. Macmillan to republish it at length in this volume.

Besides Dr. Hyde and Dr. Joyce I have been enabled, through the friendly leave of Messrs. Macmillan and Elliot and Stock, to use Mr. Jeremiah Curtin's and Mr. Larminie's excellently told Irish Fairy Tales. These two latter Folk Tale collectors have

Preface

worked upon Dr. Hyde's plan of taking down their tales from the lips of the peasants, and reproducing them, whether from their Irish or Hiberno-Irish, as clearly as they were able to do so. The recent death of both of these writers is a serious loss to Irish Folk Lore.

Obligations are due to Miss Hull for two hitherto unpublished and fine Folk Tales, to Lady Gregory for the use of her " Birth of Cuchulain," to Standish James O'Grady for his " Boyish Exploits of Cuchulain and The Coming of Finn," to the late Mrs. Ewing for " The Hill-man and the House-wife," to Mrs. William Allingham for the use of two of her husband's poems, to Mr. D. J. Donoghue for a poem by Mr. Thomas Boyd, and Mr. Chesson for one of his wife's (Nora Hopper), to Mrs. Shorter (Dora Sigerson) for a poem, and to Mr. Joseph Campbell for another, and finally to Mr. W. B. Yeats for his two charming Fairy Poems, " The Stolen Child " and " Faery Song."

ALFRED PERCEVAL GRAVES.

Erinfa, Harlech, N. Wales,

THE COMING OF FINN

The Coming of Finn

IT was the Eve of Samhain, which we Christians call All Hallows' Eve.

The King of Ireland, Conn, the Hundred - Fighter, sat at supper in his palace at Tara. All his chiefs and mighty men were with him. On his right hand was his only son, Art the Solitary, so called because he had no brothers. The sons of Morna, who kept the boy Finn out of his rights and were at the time trying to kill him if they could, were here too. Chief amongst them was Gaul mac Morna, a huge and strong warrior, and Captain of all the Fians ever since that battle in which Finn's father had been killed.

And Gaul's men were with him. The great long table was spread for supper. A thousand wax candles shed their light through the chamber, and caused the vessels of gold, silver, and bronze to shine. Yet, though it was a great feast, none of these warriors seemed to care about eating or drinking; every face was sad, and there was little conversation, and no music. It seemed as if they were expecting some calamity. Conn's sceptre, which was a plain staff of silver, lay beside him on the table, and there was a canopy of bright bronze over his head. Gaul mac Morna, Captain of the Fians, sat at the other end of the long table. Every warrior wore a bright banqueting mantle of silk or satin, scarlet or crimson, blue, green, or purple, fastened on the breast either with a great brooch or with a pin of gold or silver. Yet, though their raiment was bright and gay, and though all the usual instruments of festivity were there, and a thousand tall candles shed their light over the scene, no one looked happy.

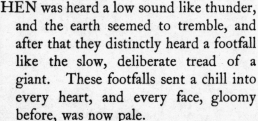 HEN was heard a low sound like thunder, and the earth seemed to tremble, and after that they distinctly heard a footfall like the slow, deliberate tread of a giant. These footfalls sent a chill into every heart, and every face, gloomy before, was now pale.

The King leaned past his son Art the Solitary, and said to a certain Druid who sat beside Art, " Is this the son of Midna come before his time? " " It is not," said the Druid, " but it is the man who is to conquer Midna. One is coming to Tara this night before whose glory all other glory shall wax dim."

Shortly after that they heard the voices of the doorkeepers raised in contention, as if they would repel from the hall someone who wished to enter, then a slight scuffle, and after that a strange figure entered the chamber. He was dressed in the skins of wild beasts, and wore over his shoulders a huge thick cloak of wild boars' skins, fastened on the breast with a white tusk of the same animal. He wore a shield and two spears. Though of huge stature his face was that of a boy, smooth on the cheeks and lips. It was white and ruddy, and very handsome. His hair was like refined gold. A light seemed to go out from him, before which the candles burned dim. It was Finn.

He stood in the doorway, and cried out in a strong and sonorous, but musical, voice:

"O CONN the Hundred-Fighter, son of Felimy, the righteous son of Tuthal the legitimate, O King of the Kings of Erin, a wronged and disinherited youth, possessing nowhere one rood of his patrimony, a wanderer and an outlaw, a hunter of the wildernesses and mountains, claims hospitality of thee, illustrious prince, on the eve of the great festival of Samhain."

"Thou art welcome whoever thou art," answered the King, "and doubly welcome because thou art unfortunate. I think, such is thy face and form, that thou art the son of some mighty king on whom disaster has fallen undeserved. The high gods of Erin grant thee speedy restoration and strong vengeance of thy many wrongs. Sit here, O noble youth, between me and my only son, Art, heir to my kingdom."

An attendant took his weapons from the youth and hung them on the wall with the rest, and Finn sat down between the King of Ireland and his only son. Choice food was set before him, which he ate, and old ale, which he drank. From the moment he entered no one thought of anything but of him. When Finn had made an end of eating and drinking, he said to the King:

3

"O illustrious prince, though it is not right for a guest to even seem to observe aught that may be awry, or not as it should be, in the hall of his entertainer, yet the sorrow of a kindly host is a sorrow, too, to his guest, and sometimes unawares the man of the house finds succour and help in the stranger. There is sorrow in this chamber of festivity. If anyone who is dear to thee and thy people happens to be dead, I can do nothing. But I say it, and it is not a vain boast, that even if a person is at the point of death, I can restore him to life and health, for there are marvellous powers of life-giving in my two hands."

ONN the Hundred-Fighter answered, "Our grief is not such as you suppose; and why should I not tell a cause of shame, which is known far and wide? This, then, is the reason of our being together, and the gloom which is over us. There is a mighty enchanter whose dwelling is in the haunted mountains of Slieve Gullion in the north. His name is Allen, son of Midna, and his enmity to me is as great as his power. Once every year, at this season, it is his pleasure to burn Tara. Descending out of his wizard haunts, he standeth over against the city and shoots balls of fire out of his mouth against it, till it is consumed. Then he goes away mocking and triumphant. This annual building of Tara, only to be annually consumed, is a shame to me, and till this enchanter declared war against me, I have lived without reproach."

"But," said Finn, "how is it that thy young warriors, valiant and swift, do not repel him, or kill him?"

"Alas!" said Conn, "all our valour is in vain against

4

this man. Our hosts encompass Tara on all sides, keeping watch and ward when the fatal night comes. Then the son of Midna plays on his Druidic instrument of music, on his magic pipe and his magic lyre, and as the fairy music falls on our ears, our eyelids grow heavy, and soon all subside upon the grass in deep slumber. So comes this man against the city and shoots his fire-balls against it, and utterly consumes it. Nine years he has burnt Tara in that manner, and this is the tenth. At midnight to-night he will come and do the same. Last year (though it was a shame to me that I, who am the high King over all Ireland, should not be able myself to defend Tara) I summoned Gaul mac Morna and all the Fians to my assistance. They came, but the pipe and lyre of the son of Midna prevailed over them too, so that Tara was burned as at other times. Nor have we any reason to believe that the son of Midna will not burn the city again to-night, as he did last year. All the women and children have been sent out of Tara this day. We are only men of war here, waiting for the time. That, O noble youth, is why we are sad. The ' Pillars of Tara ' are broken, and the might of the Fians is as nought before the power of this man."

" What shall be my reward if I kill this man and save Tara? " asked Finn.

"Thy inheritance," answered the King, " be it great or small, and whether it lies in Ireland or beyond Ireland; and for securities I give you my son Art and Gaul mac Morna and the Chief of the Fians."

Gaul and the captains of the Fianna consented to that arrangement, though reluctantly, for their minds misgave them as to who the great youth might be.

After that all arose and armed themselves and ringed Tara round with horse and foot, and thrice Conn the Hundred-Fighter raised his awful regal voice, enjoining vigilance upon his people, and thrice Gaul mac Morna did the same, addressing the Fians, and after that they filled their ears with wax and wool, and kept a stern and fierce watch, and many of them thrust the points of their swords into their flesh.

 OW Finn was alone in the banqueting chamber after the rest had gone out, and he washed his face and his hands in pure water, and he took from the bag that was at his girdle the instruments of divination and magic, which had been his father's, and what use he made of them is not known; but ere long a man stood before him, holding a spear in one hand and a blue mantle in the other. There were twenty nails of gold of Arabia in the spear. The nails glittered like stars, and twinkled with live light as stars do in a frosty night, and the blade of it quivered like a tongue of white fire. From haft to blade-point that spear was alive. There were voices in it too, and the war-tunes of the enchanted races of Erin, whom they called the Tuatha De Danan, sounded from it. The mantle, too, was a wonder, for innumerable stars twinkled in the blue, and the likeness of clouds passed through it. The man gave these things to Finn, and when he had instructed him in their use, he was not seen.

Then Finn arose and armed himself, and took the magic spear and mantle and went out. There was a ring of flame round Tara that night, for the Fians and the warriors of Conn had torches in their hands, and all the royal buildings of Tara showed clear in the light, and also the dark serpentine course of the Boyne, which flowed past Tara on the north; and there, standing silent and alert, were the innumerable warriors of all Erin, with spear and shield, keeping watch and ward against the son of Midna, also the Four Pillars of Tara in four dense divisions around the high King, even Conn the Hundred-Fighter.

Finn stood with his back to the palace, which was called the House-of-the-going-round-of-Mead, between the palace and Conn, and he grasped the magic spear strongly with one hand and the mantle with the other.

S midnight drew nigh, he heard far away in the north, out of the mountains of Slieve Gullion, a fairy tune played, soft, low, and slow, as if on a silver flute; and at the same time the roar of Conn the Hundred-Fighter, and the voice of Gaul like thunder, and the responsive shouts of the captains, and the clamour of the host, for the host shouted all together, and clashed their swords against their shields in fierce defiance, when in spite of all obstructions the fairy music of the enchanter began to steal into their souls. That shout was heard all over Ireland, echoing from sea to sea, and the hollow buildings of Tara reverberated to the uproar. Yet through it all could be heard the low, slow, delicious music that came from Slieve Gullion. Finn put the point of the spear to his forehead. It burned him like fire, yet his stout heart did not fail. Then the roar of the host slowly faded away as in a dream, though the captains were still shouting, and two-thirds of the torches fell to the ground. And now, succeeding the flute music,

7

sounded the music of a stringed instrument exceedingly sweet. Finn pressed the cruel spear-head closer to his forehead, and saw every torch fall, save one which wavered as if held by a drunken man, and beneath it a giant figure that reeled and tottered and strove in vain to keep its feet. It was Conn the Hundred-Fighter. As he fell there was a roar as of many waters; it was the ocean mourning for the high King's fall. Finn passed through the fallen men and stood alone on the dark hill-side. He heard the feet of the enchanter splashing through the Boyne, and saw his huge form ascending the slopes of Tara. When the enchanter saw that all was silent and dark there he laughed and from his mouth blew a red fire-ball at the Teck-Midcuarta, which he was accustomed first to set in flames. Finn caught the fire-ball in the magic mantle. The enchanter blew a second and a third, and Finn caught them both. The man saw that his power over Tara was at an end, and that his magic arts had been defeated. On the third occasion he saw Finn's face, and recognised his conqueror. He turned to flee, and though slow was his coming, swifter than the wind was his going, that he might recover the protection of his enchanted palace before the "fair-faced youth clad in skins" should overtake him. Finn let fall the mantle as he had been instructed, and pursued him, but in vain. Soon he perceived that he could not possibly overtake the swift enchanter. Then he was aware that the magic spear struggled in his hand like a hound in a leash. "Go, then, if thou wilt," he said, and, poising, cast the spear from him. It shot through the dark night hissing and screaming. There was a track of fire behind it. Finn followed, and on the threshold of the enchanted palace he found the body of Midna. He was quite dead, with the blood pouring through a wound in the middle of his back; but the spear was gone. Finn drew his sword and cut off the enchanter's head, and returned with it to Tara. When he came to the spot where he had dropped the mantle it was not seen, but smoke and flame issued there from a hole in the ground. That hole was twenty feet deep in the earth, and at the bottom of it there was a fire always from that night, and it was never extinguished. It was called the fire of the son of Midna. It was in a depression on the north side of the hill of Tara, called the Glen of the Mantle, Glen-a-Brat.

FINN, bearing the head, passed through the sleepers into the palace and spiked the head on his own spear, and drove the spear-end into the ground at Conn's end of the great hall. Then the sickness and faintness of death came upon Finn, also a great horror and despair overshadowed him, so that he was about to give himself up for utterly lost. Yet he recalled one of his marvellous attributes, and approaching a silver vessel, into which pure water ever flowed and which was always full, he made a cup with his two hands and, lifting it to his mouth, drank, and the blood began to circulate in his veins, and strength returned to his limbs, and the cheerful hue of rosy health to his cheeks.

Having rested himself sufficiently he went forth and shouted to the sleeping host, and called the captains by their names, beginning with Conn. They awoke and rose up, though dazed and stupid, for it was difficult for any man, no matter how he had stopped his ears, to avoid hearing

9

Finn when he sent forth his voice of power. They were astonished to find that Tara was still standing, for though the night was dark, the palaces and temples, all of hewn timber, were brilliantly coloured and of many hues, for in those days men delighted in splendid colours.

When the captains came together Finn said, " I have slain Midna." " Where is his head? " they asked, not because they disbelieved him, but because the heads of men slain in battle were always brought away for trophies. " Come and see," answered Finn. Conn and his only son and Gaul mac Morna followed the young hero into the Teck-Midcuarta, where the spear-long waxen candles were still burning, and when they saw the head of Midna impaled there at the end of the hall, the head of the man whom they believed to be immortal and not to be wounded or conquered, they were filled with great joy, and praised their deliverer and paid him many compliments.

"HO art thou, O brave youth? " said Conn. " Surely thou art the son of some great king or champion, for heroic feats like thine are not performed by the sons of inconsiderable and unknown men."

Then Finn flung back his cloak of wild boars' skins, and holding his father's treasure-bag in his hand before them all, cried in a loud voice:

" I am Finn, the son of Cool, the son of Trenmor, the son of Basna; I am he whom the sons of Morna have been seeking to destroy from the time that I was born; and here to-night, O King of the Kings of Erin, I claim the fulfilment of thy promise, and the restoration of my inheritance, which is the Fian leadership of Fail. Thereupon Gaul mac Morna put his right hand into Finn's, and became his man. Then his brothers and his sons, and the sons of his brothers, did so in succession, and after that all the chief men of the Fians did the same, and that night Finn was solemnly and surely installed in the Fian leadership of Erin, and put in possession of all the woods and forests and waste places, and all the hills and mountains and promontories, and all the streams and rivers of Erin, and the harbours and estuaries and the harbour-dues of the merchants, and all ships and boats and galleys with their mariners, and all that pertained of old time to the Fian leadership of Fail.

STANDISH JAMES O'GRADY.

The Three Crowns

(Told in the Wexford Peasant Dialect.)

HERE was once a king, some place or other, and he had three daughters. The two eldest were very proud and uncharitable, but the youngest was as good as they were bad. Well, three princes came to court them, and two of them were the *moral* of the two eldest ladies, and one was just as lovable as the youngest. They were all walking down to a lake one day that lay at the bottom of the lawn, just like the one at Castleboro', and they met a poor beggar. The King wouldn't give him anything, and the eldest princes wouldn't give him anything, nor their sweethearts; but the youngest daughter and her true love did give him something, and kind words along with it, and that was better *nor* all.

When they got to the edge of the lake, what did they find but the beautifulest boat you ever saw in your life; and says the eldest, " I'll take a sail in this fine boat; " and says the second eldest, " I'll take a sail in this fine boat; " and says the youngest, " I won't take a sail in that fine boat, for I'm afraid it's an enchanted one." But the others over-persuaded her to go in, and her father was just going in after her, when up sprung on the deck a little man only seven inches high, and he ordered him to stand back. Well, all the men put their hands to their *soords*; and if the same soords were only thraneens they weren't able to draw them, for all *sthrenth* was left their arms. *Seven Inches* loosened the silver chain that fastened the boat and pushed away; and after grinning at the four men, says he to them: " Bid your daughters and your brides farewell for awhile. That wouldn't have happened you three, only for your want of charity. You," says he to the youngest, " needn't fear; you'll recover your princess all in good time, and you and she will be as happy as the day is long. Bad people, if they were rolling stark naked in gold, would not be rich. *Banacht lath!* " Away they sailed, and the ladies stretched out their hands, but weren't able to say a word.

WELL, they were crossin' the lake while a cat'd be lickin' her ear, and the poor men couldn't stir hand nor foot to follow them. They saw *Seven Inches* handing the three princesses out of the boat, and letting them down by a nice basket and *winglas* into a draw-well that was convenient, but king nor princes never saw an opening before in the same place. When the last lady was out of sight the men found the strength in their arms and legs again. Round the lake they ran, and never drew rein till they came to the well and windlass, and there was the silk rope rolled on the axle, and the nice white basket hanging to it. " Let me down," says the youngest prince; " I'll die or recover them again." "No," says the second daughter's sweetheart, "I'm entitled to my turn before you." "And," says the other, "I must get first turn, in right of my bride." So they gave way to him, and in he got into the basket, and down they let him. First they lost sight of him, and then, after winding off a hundred perches of the silk rope, it slackened, and they stopped turning. They waited two hours, and then they went to dinner, because there was no chuck made at the rope.

GUARDS were set till morning, and then down went the second prince, and, sure enough, the youngest of all got himself let down on the third day. He went down perches and perches, while it was as dark about him as if he was in a big pot with the cover on. At last he saw a glimmer far down, and in a short time he felt the ground. Out he came from the big lime-kiln, and lo and behold you, there was a wood and green fields, and a castle in a lawn, and a bright sky over all. "It's in Tir-na-n Oge I am," says he. "Let's see what sort of people are in the castle." On he walked across fields and lawn, and no one was there to keep him out or let him into the castle; but the big hall door was wide open. He went from one fine room to another that was finer, and at last he reached the handsomest of all, with a table in the middle; and such a dinner as was laid upon it! The prince was hungry enough, but he was too mannerly to go eat without being invited. So he sat by the fire, and he did not wait long till he heard steps, and in came *Seven Inches* and the youngest sister by the hand. Well, prince and princess flew into one another's arms, and says the little man, says he, "Why aren't you eating?" "I think, sir," says he, "it was only good manners to wait to be asked." "The other princes didn't think so," says he. "Each of them fell to without leave nor license, and only gave me the rough side o' his tongue when I told them they were making more free than welcome. Well, I don't think they feel much hunger now. There they are, good *marvel* instead of flesh and blood," says he, pointing to two statues, one in one corner and the other in the other corner of the room. The prince was frightened, but he was afraid to say anything, and *Seven Inches* made him sit down to dinner between himself and his bride, and he'd be as happy as the day is long, only for the sight of the stone men in the corner. Well, that day went by, and when the next came, says *Seven Inches to* him, "Now, you'll have to set out that way," pointing to the sun, "and you'll find the second princess in a giant's castle this evening, when you'll be tired and hungry, and the eldest princess to-morrow evening; and you may as well bring them here with you. You need not ask leave of their masters; they're only house-keepers with the big fellows. I suppose, if they ever get home, they'll look on poor people as if they were flesh and blood like themselves."

Away went the prince, and bedad it's tired and hungry he was when he reached the first castle at sunset. Oh, wasn't the second princess glad to see him! And if she didn't give him a good supper it's a wonder. But she heard the giant at the gate, and she hid the prince in a closet. Well, when he came in, he snuffed, and he snuffed, an' says he, "*Be* (by) the life, I smell fresh mate." "Oh," says the princess, "it's only the calf I got killed to-day." "Ay, ay," says he, "is supper ready?" "It is," says she; and before he ruz from the table he hid three-quarters of the calf and a kag of wine. "I think," says he, when all was done, "I smell fresh mate still." "It's sleepy you are," says she; "go to bed." "When will you marry me?" says the giant; you're puttin' me off too long." "St. Tibb's Eve," says she. "I wish I knew how far off that is," says he; and he fell asleep with his head in the dish.

EXT day he went out after breakfast, and she sent the prince to the castle where the eldest sister was. The same thing happened there; but when the giant was snoring, the princess wakened up the prince, and they saddled two steeds in the stables, and *magh go bragh* (the field for ever) with them. But the horses' heels struck the stones outside the gate, and up got the giant, and after them he made. He roared, and he shouted, and the more he shouted the faster ran the horses; and just as the day was breaking he was only twenty perches behind. But the prince didn't leave the Castle of *Seven Inches* without being provided with something good. He reined in his steed, and flung a short, sharp knife over his shoulder, and up sprung a thick wood between the giant and themselves. They caught the wind that blew before them, and the wind that blew behind them did not catch them. At last they were near the castle where the other sister lived; and there she was, waiting for them under a high hedge, and a fine steed under her.

But the giant was now in sight, roaring like a hundred lions, and the other giant was out in a moment, and the chase kept on. For every two springs the horses gave the giants gave three, and at last they were only seventy perches off. Then the prince stopped again and flung the second skian behind him. Down went all the flat field, till there was a quarry between them a quarter of a mile deep, and the bottom filled with black water; and before the giants could get round it the prince and princesses were inside the domain of the great magician, where the high thorny hedge opened of itself to everyone that he chose to let in.

Well, to be sure, there was joy enough between the three sisters till the two eldest saw their lovers turned into stone. But while they were shedding tears for them *Seven Inches* came in and touched them with his rod. So they were flesh and blood and life once more, and there was great hugging and kissing, and all sat down to a nice breakfast, and *Seven Inches* sat at the head of the table.

When breakfast was over he took them into another room, where there was nothing but heaps of gold and silver and diamonds, and silks and satins; and on a table there was lying three sets of crowns: a gold crown was in a silver crown, and that was lying in a copper crown. He took up one set of crowns and gave it to the eldest princess; and another set, and gave it to the second princess; and another set, and gave it to the youngest princess of all; and says he, " Now you may all go to the bottom of the pit, and you have nothing to do but stir the basket, and the people that are watching above will draw you up, princesses first, princes after. But remember, ladies, you are to keep your crowns safe, and be married in them all the same day. If you be married separately, or if you be married without your crowns, a curse will follow—mind what I say."

So they took leave of him with great respect, and walked arm-in-arm to the bottom of the draw-well. There was a sky and a sun over them and a great high wall, and the bottom of the draw-well was inside the arch. The youngest pair went last, and says the princess to the prince, " I'm sure the two princes don't mean any good to you. Keep these crowns under your cloak, and if you are obliged to stay last, don't get into the basket, but put a big stone, or any heavy thing, inside, and see what will happen."

O when they were inside the dark cave they put in the eldest princess first, and she stirred the basket and up she went, but first she gave a little scream. Then the basket was let down again, and up went the second princess, and then up went the youngest; but first she put her arms round her prince's neck and kissed him, and cried a little. At last it came to the turn of the youngest prince, and well became him—instead of going into the basket he put in a big stone. He drew on one side and listened, and after the basket was drawn up about twenty perch down came itself and the stone like thunder, and the stone was made *brishe* of on the flags.

Well, my poor prince had nothing for it but to walk back to the castle; and through it and round it he walked, and the finest of eating and drinking he got, and a bed of bog-down to sleep on, and fine walks he took through gardens and lawns, but not a sight could he get, high or low, of *Seven Inches*. Well, I don't think any of *us* would be tired of this way of living for ever! Maybe we would. Anyhow, the prince got tired of it before a week, he was so lonesome for his true love; and at the end of a month he didn't know what to do with himself.

One morning he went into the treasure room and took notice of a beautiful snuff-box on the table that he didn't remember seeing there before. He took it in his hands and opened it, and out *Seven Inches* walked on the table. " I think, prince," says he, "you're getting a little tired of my castle?" "Ah!" says the other, " if I had my princess here, and could see you now and then, I'd never see a dismal day." " Well, you're long enough here now, and you're wanting there above. Keep your bride's crowns safe, and whenever you want my help open this snuff-box. Now take a walk down the garden, and come back when you're tired."

ELL, the prince was going down a gravel walk with a quick-set hedge on each side and his eyes on the ground, and he thinking on one thing and another. At last he lifted his eyes, and there he was outside of a smith's bawn gate that he had often passed before, about a mile away from the palace of his betrothed princess. The clothes he had on him were as ragged as you please, but he had his crowns safe under his old cloak.

So the smith came out, and says he, " It's a shame for a strong big fellow like you to be on the *sthra*, and so much work to be done. Are you any good with hammer and tongs? Come in and bear a hand, and I'll give you diet and lodging and a few thirteens when you earn them. "Never say't twice," says the prince; " I want nothing but to be employed." So he took the sledge and pounded away at the red-hot bar that the smith was turning on the anvil to make into a set of horse-shoes.

Well, they weren't long powdhering away, when a *stronshuch* (idler) of a tailor came in; and when the smith asked him what news he had, he got the handle of the bellows and began to blow to let out all he had heard for the last two days. There were so many questions and answers at first that, if I told them all, it would be bed-time before I'd be done. So here is the substance of the discourse; and before he got far into it the forge was half filled with women knitting stockings and men smoking.

YOUS all heard how the two princesses were unwilling to be married till the youngest would be ready with her crowns and her sweetheart. But after the windlass loosened *accidentally* when they were pulling up her bridegroom that was to be, there was no more sign of a well or a rope or a windlass than there is on the palm of your hand. So the buckeens that were coortin' the eldest ladies wouldn't give peace nor ease to their lovers nor the King till they got consent to the marriage, and it was to take place this morning. Myself went down out of curiosity; and to be sure I was delighted with the grand dresses of the two brides and the three crowns on their heads—gold, silver, and copper—one inside the other. The youngest was standing by, mournful enough, in white, and all was ready. The two bridegrooms came walking in as proud and grand as you please, and up they were walking to the altar rails when, my dear, the boards opened two yards wide under their feet, and down they went among the dead men and the coffins in the vaults. Oh, such screeching as the ladies gave! and such running and racing and peeping down as there was; but the clerk soon opened the door of the vault, and up came the two heroes, and their fine clothes covered an inch thick with cobwebs and mould."

So the King said they should put off the marriage, "For," says he, "I see there is no use in thinking of it till my youngest gets her three crowns and is married along with the others. I'll give my youngest daughter for a wife to whoever brings three crowns to me like the others; and if he doesn't care to be married, some other one will, and I'll make his fortune." "I wish," says the smith, "I could do it; but I was looking at the crowns after the princesses got home, and I don't think there's a black or a white smith on the face of the earth could imitate them." "Faint heart never won fair lady," says the prince. "Go to the palace, and ask for a quarter of a pound of gold, a quarter of a pound of silver, and a quarter of a pound of copper. Get one crown for a pattern, and my head for a pledge, and I'll give you out the very things that are wanted in the morning." "Ubba-bow," says the smith, "are you in earnest?" "Faith, I am so," says he. "Go! Worse than lose you can't."

O make a long story short, the smith got the quarter of a pound of gold, and the quarter of a pound of silver, and the quarter of a pound of copper, and gave them and the pattern crown to the prince. He shut the forge door at nightfall, and the neighbours all gathered in the bawn, and they heard him hammering, hammering, hammering, from that to daybreak, and every now and then he'd pitch out through the window bits of gold, silver, or copper; and the idlers scrambled for them, and cursed one another, and prayed for the good luck of the workman.

Well, just as the sun was thinking to rise he opened the door and brought the three crowns he got from his true love, and such shouting and huzzaing as there was! The smith asked him to go along with him to the palace, but he refused; so off set the smith, and the whole townland with him; and wasn't the King rejoiced when he saw the crowns! "Well," says he to the smith, "you're a married man, and what's to be done?" "Faith, your majesty, I didn't make them crowns at all; it was a big shuler (vagrant) of a fellow that took employment with me yesterday." "Well, daughter, will you marry the fellow that made these crowns?" "Let me see them first, father." So when she examined them she knew them right well, and guessed it was her true love that had sent them. "I will marry the man that these crowns came from," says she.

"WELL," said the King to the eldest of the two princes, "go up to the smith's forge, take my best coach, and bring home the bridegroom." He was very unwilling to do this, he was so proud, but he did not wish to refuse. When he came to the forge he saw the prince standing at the door, and beckoned him over to the coach. "Are you the fellow," says he, "that made them crowns?" "Yes," says the other. "Then," says he, "maybe you'd give yourself a brushing, and get into that coach; the King wants to see you. I pity the princess." The young prince got into the carriage, and while they were on the way he opened the snuff-box, and out walked *Seven Inches*, and stood on his thigh. "Well," says he, "what trouble is on you now?" "Master," says the other, "please to let me back in my forge, and let this carriage be filled with paving-stones." No sooner said than done. The prince was sitting in his forge, and the horses wondered what was after happening to the carriage.

When they came to the palace yard the King himself opened the carriage door to pay respect to the new son-in-law. As soon as he turned the handle a shower of stones fell on his powdered wig and his silk coat, and down he fell under them. There was great fright, and some tittering, and the King, after he wiped the blood from his forehead, looked very cross at the eldest prince. "My liege," says he, "I'm very sorry for this *accidence*, but I'm not to blame. I saw the young smith get into the carriage, and we never stopped a minute since." "It's uncivil you were to him. Go," says he to the other prince, " and bring the young prince here, and be polite." "Never fear," says he.

BUT there's some people that couldn't be good-natured if they were to be made heirs of Damer's estate. Not a bit civiller was the new messenger than the old, and when the King opened the carriage door a second time it's a shower of mud that came down on him; and if he didn't fume and splutter and shake himself it's no matter. "There's no use," says he, " going on this way. The fox never got a better messenger than himself."

So he changed his clothes and washed himself, and out

he set to the smith's forge.   Maybe he wasn't polite to the
young prince, and asked him to sit along with himself.   The
prince begged to be allowed to sit in the other carriage, and
when they were half-way he opened his snuff-box.
" Master," says he, " I'd wished to be dressed now according
to my rank."   "You shall be that," says *Seven Inches*.
" And now I'll bid you farewell.   Continue as good and kind
as you always were; love your wife, and that's all the advice
I'll give you."   So *Seven Inches* vanished; and when the
carriage door was opened in the yard, out walks the prince,
as fine as hands and pins could make him, and the first thing
he did was to run over to his bride and embrace her very
heartily.

Everyone had great joy but the two other princes.   There
was not much delay about the marriages that were all cele-
brated on the same day, and the youngest prince and princess
were the happiest married couple you ever heard of in a
story.   PATRICK KENNEDY.

The Grateful Beasts

HERE was once a young man on his
way to a fair with five shillings in his
pocket. As he went he saw some little
boys beating a poor mouse they had
just caught.

"Come, boys," says he, "do not be
so cruel. Sell me your mouse for sixpence, and go off and buy some sweets."

They gave him the mouse, and he let the poor little beast
go. He had not gone far when he met a fresh set of boys
teasing the life out of a poor weasel.

Well, he bought him off for a shilling and let him go. The
third creature he saved, from a crowd of cruel young men,
was an ass, but he had to give a whole half-crown to get him
off. "Now," says poor Neddy, "you may as well take me

25

with you. I'll be of some use, I think, for when you are tired you can get up on my back." "With all my heart," said Jack, for that was the young man's name.

The day was very hot, and the boy sat under a tree to enjoy the shade. As soon as he did he fell asleep, but he was soon awakened by a wicked-looking giant and his two servants. "How dare you let your ass trespass in my field," cried he, "and do such mischief." "I had no notion that he had done anything of the kind." "No notion? I'll notion you, then. Bring out that chest," said he to one of his servants, and before you could wink they had tied the poor boy, hand and foot, with a stout rope, thrown him into the chest, and tossed the chest into the river. Then they all went away but poor Neddy, till who should come up but the weasel and the mouse, and they asked him what was the matter. So the ass told them his story.

"H," said the weasel, "he must be the same boy that saved the mouse and myself. Had he a brown patch in the arm of his coat?" "The very same." "Come, then," said the weasel, "and let us try and get him out of the river." "By all means," said the others. So the weasel got on the ass's back and the mouse got into his ear, and away they went. They had not gone far when they saw the chest, which had been stopped among the rushes at the end of a little island.

In they went, and the weasel and the mouse gnawed the rope till they had set their master free.

Well, they were all very glad, and were having a great talk about the giant and his men, when what should the weasel spy but an egg, with the most lovely colours on the shell, lying down in the shallow water. It was not long before he had fished it out, and Jack kept turning it round and round and praising it.

" Oh, my dear friends," said he to the ass, the mouse, and the weasel, " how I wish it was in my power to thank you as I should like. How I wish I had a fine house and grounds to take you to where you could live in peace and plenty."

The words were hardly out of his mouth when he and the beasts found themselves standing on the steps of a grand castle, with the finest lawn before it that you ever saw. There was no one inside or outside it to keep it from them, so in they went, and there they lived as happy as kings.

Jack was standing at his gate one day as three merchants were passing by with their goods packed on the backs of horses and mules.

" Bless our eyes," cried they, " what does this mean? There was no castle or lawn here when we went by last time."

" That is true," cried Jack, " but you shall not be the worse for it. Take your beasts into the yard at the back of the house and give them a good feed, and if you can spare the time stay and take a bit of dinner with me."

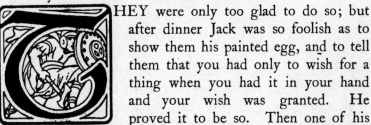

HEY were only too glad to do so; but after dinner Jack was so foolish as to show them his painted egg, and to tell them that you had only to wish for a thing when you had it in your hand and your wish was granted. He proved it to be so. Then one of his guests put a powder into Jack's next glass of wine, and when he awoke he found himself in the island again, with his patched coat on him, and his three friends in front of him, all looking very downhearted. "Ah, Master," said the weasel, "you will never be wise enough for the tricky people that are in the world."

"Where did these thieves say they lived, and what names did they say they were called by?" Jack scratched his head, and after a while was able to tell them.

"Come, Neddy," says the weasel, "let us be jogging. It would not be safe for the master to go with us; but if we have luck we will bring him the egg back after all."

So the weasel got on the ass's back and the mouse got into his ear, and away they went till they reached the house of the head rogue. The mouse went in, and the ass and the weasel hid themselves in a copse outside.

THE mouse soon came back to them. "Well, what news?" said they. "Dull news enough; he has the egg in a low chest in his bedroom, and the door is strongly locked and bolted, and a pair of cats with fiery eyes are chained to the chest watching it night and day."

"Let us go back," said the ass; "we can do nothing." "Wait!" said the weasel.

When bedtime came, said the weasel to the mouse: "Go in at the keyhole and get behind the rogue's head, and stay there two or three hours sucking his hair."

"What good would there be in that?" asked the ass. "Wait, and you'll know!" said the weasel.

Next morning the merchant was quite mad to find the state his hair was in.

"But I'll be a match for you to-night, my fine mouse,"

said he. So he unchained the cats next night and made them sit by his bedside and watch.

Just as he was dropping asleep the weasel and the mouse were outside the door, and gnawing away till they had scooped out a hole in the bottom of it. In went the mouse, and it was not long before he had the egg quite safe.

They were soon on the road again; the mouse in the ass's ear, the weasel on his back, and the egg in the weasel's mouth.

When they came to the river, and were swimming across, the ass began to bray. "Hee-haw, hee-haw," cried he. "Is there anyone like me in all the world? I am carrying the mouse and the weasel and the great enchanted egg that can do anything. Why do you not praise me?"

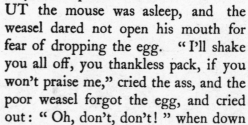

BUT the mouse was asleep, and the weasel dared not open his mouth for fear of dropping the egg. "I'll shake you all off, you thankless pack, if you won't praise me," cried the ass, and the poor weasel forgot the egg, and cried out: "Oh, don't, don't!" when down went the egg into the deepest pool in the river. "Now you have done it," said the weasel, and you may be sure the ass looked very foolish.

"Oh, what are we to do?" groaned he. "Keep a good heart," said the weasel. Then looking down into the deep water, he cried: "Hear! all you frogs and fish. There is a great army of storks and cranes coming to take you all out and eat you up red-raw. Make haste! Make haste!" "Oh, and what can we do?" cried they, coming up to the top. "Gather up the stones from below and hand them to us, and we'll build a big wall on the bank to defend you." So the fish and frogs fell to work like mad, and were at it hard and fast, reaching up all the stones and pebbles they found at the bottom of the pool.

At last a big frog came up with the egg in his mouth, and when the weasel had hold of it he climbed into a tree and cried out, "That will do; the army has got a great fright at our walls, and they are all running away." So the poor things were greatly relieved.

You may be sure that Jack jumped for joy to see his friends and the egg again. They were soon back in their castle, and when Jack began to feel lonely he did not find it hard to find a pretty lady to marry him, and then they two and the three grateful beasts were as happy as the days were long.

PATRICK KENNEDY.

The Lepracaun or Fairy Shoemaker

I.

LITTLE Cowboy, what have you heard,
    Up on the lonely rath's green mound?
Only the plaintive yellow bird
    Sighing in sultry fields around,
Chary, chary, chary, chee-ee!—
Only the grasshopper and the bee?—
    "Tip-tap, rip-rap,
    Tick-a-tack-too!
Scarlet leather, sewn together,
    This will make a shoe.
Left, right, pull it tight;
    Summer days are warm;
Underground in winter,
    Laughing at the storm!"
Lay your ear close to the hill.
Do you not catch the tiny clamour,
Busy click of an elfin hammer,

Voice of the Lepracaun singing shrill
  As he merrily plies his trade?
      He's a span
      And a quarter in height.
Get him in sight, hold him tight,
      And you're a made
      Man!

II.

You watch your cattle the summer day,
Sup on potatoes, sleep in the hay;
  How would you like to roll in your carriage,
  Look for a Duchess's daughter in marriage?
Seize the Shoemaker—then you may!
    " Big boots a-hunting,
      Sandals in the hall,
    White for a wedding-feast,
      Pink for a ball.
    This way, that way,
      So we make a shoe;
    Getting rich every stitch,
      Tick-tack-too! "
Nine-and-ninety treasure-crocks
This keen miser-fairy hath,
Hid in mountains, woods, and rocks,
Ruin and round-tow'r, cave and rath,
  And where the cormorants build;
      From times of old
      Guarded by him;
      Each of them fill'd
      Full to the brim
        With gold!

III.

I caught him at work one day, myself,
  In the castle-ditch, where foxglove grows—
A wrinkled, wizen'd, and bearded Elf,
  Spectacles stuck on his pointed nose,
  Silver buckles to his hose,
  Leather apron—shoe in his lap—
    " Rip-rap, tip-tap,
    Tick-tack-too!
  (A grasshopper on my cap!
    Away the moth flew!)
  Buskins for a fairy prince,
    Brogues for his son—
  Pay me well, pay me well,
    When the job is done! "
The rogue was mine, beyond a doubt.
I stared at him; he stared at me;
" Servant, Sir! "   " Humph! " says he,
  And pulled a snuff-box out.
He took a long pinch, look'd better pleased,
  The queer little Lepracaun;
Offer'd the box with a whimsical grace—
Pouf! he flung the dust in my face,
    And, while I sneezed,
      Was gone!

WILLIAM ALLINGHAM.

Daniel O'Rourke

Daniel O'Rourke

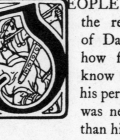

P EOPLE may have heard of the renowned adventures of Daniel O'Rourke, but how few are there who know that the cause of all his perils, above and below, was neither more nor less than his having slept under the walls of the Pooka's Tower. I knew the man well. He lived at the bottom of Hungry Hill, just at the right-hand side of the road as you go towards Bantry. An old man was he at the time he told me the story, with grey hair and a red nose; and it was on the 25th of June, 1813, that I heard it from his own lips, as he sat smoking his pipe under the old poplar tree, on as fine an evening as ever shone from the sky. I was going to visit the caves in Dursey Island, having spent the morning at Glengariff. "I am often axed to tell it, sir," said he, "so that this is not the first time. The master's son, you see, had come from beyond foreign parts in France and Spain, as young gentlemen used to go before Buonaparte or any such was heard of; and, sure enough, there was a dinner given to all the people on the ground, gentle and simple, high and low, rich and poor. The *ould* gentlemen were the gentlemen, after all, saving your honour's presence. They'd swear at a body a little, to be sure, and, maybe, give one a cut of a whip now and then, but we were no losers by it in the end; and they were so easy and civil, and kept such rattling houses, and thousands of welcomes; and there was no grinding for rent, and there was hardly a tenant on the estate that did not taste of his landlord's bounty often and often in a year; but now it's another thing. No matter for that, sir, for I'd better be telling you my story.

WELL, we had everything of the best, and plenty of it; and we ate, and we drank, and we danced, and the young master, by the same token, danced with Peggy Barry, from the Bohereen—a lovely young couple they were, though they are both low enough now. To make a long story short, I got, as a body may say, the same thing as tipsy almost, for I can't remember, ever at all, no ways, how it was I left the place; only I did leave it, that's certain. Well, I thought, for all that, in myself, I'd just step to Molly Cronohan's, the fairy woman, to speak a word about the bracket heifer that was bewitched; and so, as I was crossing the stepping-stones of the ford of Ballyashenogh, and was looking up at the stars, and blessing myself—for why? it was Lady-day—I missed my foot, and souse I fell into the water. ' Death alive! ' thought I, ' I'll be drowned now! '

However, I began swimming, swimming, swimming away for dear life, till at last I got ashore, somehow or other, but never the one of me can tell how, upon a *dissolute* island.

" I wandered and wandered about there, without knowing where I wandered, until at last I got into a big bog. The moon was shining as bright as day, or your fair lady's eyes, sir (with your pardon for mentioning her), and I looked east and west, north and south, and every way, and nothing did I see but bog, bog, bog. I could never find out how I got into it; and my heart grew cold with fear, for sure and certain I was that it would be my *berrin'* place. So I sat upon a stone, which, as good luck would have it, was close by me, and I began to scratch my head, and sing the ULLAGONE —when all of a sudden the moon grew black, and I looked up and saw something for all the world as if it was moving down between me and it, and I could not tell what it was. Down it came with a pounce, and looked at me full in the face; and what was it but an eagle?—as fine a one as ever flew from the kingdom of Kerry! So he looked at me in the face, and says he to me, 'Daniel O'Rourke,' says he, ' how do you do?' 'Very well, I thank you, sir,' says I; 'I hope you're well'; wondering out of my senses all the time how an eagle came to speak like a Christian. 'What brings you here, Dan?' says he. 'Nothing at all, sir,' says I, ' only I wish I was safe home again.' 'Is it out of the island you want to go, Dan?' says he. ''Tis, sir,' says I; so I up and told him how I had taken a drop too much, and fell into the water; how I swam to the island; and how I got into the bog and did not know my way out of it. 'Dan,' says he, after a minute's thought, 'though it is very improper of you to get drunk on a Lady-day, yet, as you are a decent sober man, who 'tends mass well, and never fling stones at me or mine, nor cries out after one in the field, my life for yours,' says he; ' so get up on my back, and grip me well for fear you'd fall off, and I'll fly you out of the bog.' ' I am afraid,' says I, ' your honour's making game of me; for whoever heard of riding a-horseback on an eagle before?' ' 'Pon the honour of a gentleman,' says he, putting his right foot on his breast, ' I am quite in earnest; and so now either take my offer or starve in the bog—besides I see that your weight is sinking the stone.'

" IT was true enough, as he said, for I found the stone every minute going from under me. I had no choice; so, thinks I to myself, faint heart never won fair lady, and this is fair persuadance. ' I thank your honour,' says I, ' for the loan of your civility; and I'll take your kind offer.' I therefore mounted on the back of the eagle, and held him tight enough by the throat, and up he flew in the air like a lark. Little I knew the trick he was going to serve me. Up, up, up—God knows how far he flew. ' Why, then,' said I to him—thinking he did not know the right road home—very civilly, because why? I was in his power entirely; ' sir,' says I, ' please your honour's glory, and with humble submission to your better judgment, if you'd fly down a bit, you're now just over my cabin, and I could be put down there, and many thanks to your worship.'

" ' *Arrah*, Dan,' says he, ' do you think me a fool? Look down in the next field, and don't you see two men and a gun? By my word, it would be no joke to shoot this way, to oblige a drunken blackguard that I picked up off a *could* stone in a bog.' 'Bother you,' says I to myself, but I did not speak out, for where was the use? Well, sir, up he kept flying, flying, and I asking him every minute to fly down, and all to no use. 'Where in the world are you going, sir?' says I to him. 'Hold your tongue, Dan,' says he, 'and mind your own business, and don't be interfering with the business of other people.' 'Faith, this is my business, I think,' says I. 'Be quiet, Dan!' says he: so I said no more.

"At last, where should we come to but to the moon itself. Now, you can't see it from this, but there is, or there was in my time, a reaping-hook sticking out of the side of the moon, this way (drawing the figure thus on the ground with the end of his stick).

"'D AN,' says the eagle, I'm tired with this long fly; I had no notion 'twas so far.' 'And my lord, sir,' says I, 'who in the world *axed* you to fly so far—was it I? Did not I beg and pray and beseech you to stop half an hour ago?' 'There's no use talking, Dan,' said he; 'I'm tired bad enough, so you must get off, and sit down on the moon until I rest myself.' 'Is it sit down on the moon?' said I; 'is it upon that little round thing, then? Why, then, sure, I'd fall off in a minute, and be *kilt* and spilt, and smashed all to bits; you are a vile deceiver—so you are.' 'Not at all, Dan,' says he; 'you can catch fast hold of the reaping-hook that's sticking out of the side of the moon, and 'twill keep you up.' 'I won't, then,' said I. 'Maybe not,' said he, quite quiet. 'If you don't, my man, I shall just give you a shake, and one slap of my wing, and send you down to the ground, where every bone in your body will be smashed as small as a drop of dew on a cabbage-leaf in the morning.' 'Why, then, I'm in a fine way,' said I to myself, 'ever to have come along with the likes of you'; and so, giving him a hearty curse in Irish, for fear he'd know what I said, I got off his back with a heavy heart, took hold of the reaping-hook and sat down upon the moon, and a mighty cold seat it was, I can tell you that.

"When he had me there fairly landed, he turned about on me, and said, 'Good morning to you, Daniel O'Rourke,' said he; 'I think I've nicked you fairly now. You robbed my nest last year' ('twas true enough for him, but how he found it out is hard enough to say), 'and in return you are freely welcome to cool your heels dangling upon the moon like a cockthrow.'

" 'IS that all, and is this how you leave me, you brute, you,' says I. 'You ugly unnatural *baste*, and is this the way you serve me at last? Bad luck to yourself, with your hook'd nose, and to all your breed, you blackguard.' 'Twas all to no manner of use; he spread out his great big wings, burst out a laughing, and flew away like lightning. I bawled after him to stop; but I might have called and bawled for ever, without his minding me. Away he went, and I never saw him from that day to this—sorrow fly away with him! You may be sure I was in a disconsolate condition, and kept roaring out for the bare grief, when all at once a door opened right in the middle of the moon, creaking on its hinges as if it had not been opened for a month before—I suppose they never thought of greasing them—and out there walks—who do you think but the man in the moon himself? I knew him by his bush.

"'Good morrow to you, Daniel O'Rourke,' says he, 'how do you do?' 'Very well, thank your honour,' says I. 'I hope your honour's well.' 'What brought you here, Dan?' said he. So I told him how I was a little overtaken in liquor at the master's, and how I was cast on a *dissolute* island, and how I lost my way in the bog, and the thief of an eagle promised to fly me out of it, and how, instead of that, he had fled me up to the moon.

"'DAN,' said the man in the moon, taking a pinch of snuff, when I was done, 'you must not stay here.' 'Indeed, sir,' says I, ''tis much against my will that I'm here at all; but how am I to go back?' 'That's your business,' said he; 'Dan, mine is to tell you that you must not stay, so be off in less than no time.' 'I'm doing no harm,' said I, 'only holding on hard by the reaping-hook lest I fall off.' 'That's what you must not do, Dan,' says he. 'Pray, sir,' says I, 'may I ask how many you are in family that you would not give a poor traveller lodging? I'm sure 'tis not often you're troubled with strangers coming to see you, for 'tis a long way.' 'I'm by myself, Dan,' says he, 'but you'd better let go the reaping-hook.' 'Faith, and with your leave,' says I, 'I'll not let go the grip, and the more you bids me the more I won't let go—so I will.' 'You had better, Dan,' says he again. 'Why, then, my little fellow,' says I, taking the whole weight of him with my eye from head to foot, 'there are two words to that bargain; and I'll not budge—you may, if you like.' 'We'll see how that is to be,' says he; and back he went, giving the door such a great bang after him (for it was plain he was huffed), that I thought the moon and all would fall down with it.

"Well, I was preparing myself to try strength with him, when back he comes, with the kitchen cleaver in his hand, and without saying a word he gives two bangs to the handle of the reaping-hook that was holding me up, and *whap*, it came in two. 'Good morning to you, Dan,' says the spiteful little blackguard, when he saw me cleanly falling down with a bit of the handle in my hand; 'I thank you for your visit, and fair weather after you, Daniel.' I had no time to make any answer to him, for I was tumbling over and over, and rolling and rolling, at the rate of a fox-hunt. 'God help me!' says I, 'but this is a pretty pickle for a decent man to be seen in at this time of the night. I am now sold fairly.' The word was not out of my mouth, when, whiz! what should fly by close to my ear but a flock of wild geese, all the way from my own bog of Ballyasheenagh, else how should they know *me*? The *ould* gander, who was their general, turning about his head, cried out to me, 'Is that you, Dan?' 'The same,' said I, not a bit daunted now at what he said, for I was by this time used to all kinds of *bedivilment*, and, besides, I knew him of *ould*. 'Good morrow to you,' says he, 'Daniel O'Rourke; how are you in health this morning?' 'Very well, sir,' says I, 'thank you kindly,' drawing my breath, for I was mightily in want of some, 'I hope your honour's the same.' 'I think 'tis falling you are, Daniel,' says he. 'You may say that, sir,' says I. 'And where are you going all the way so fast?' said the gander. So I told him how I had taken the drop, and how I came on the island, and how I lost my way in the bog, and how the thief of an eagle flew me up to the moon, and how the man in the moon turned me out. 'Dan,' said he, 'I'll save you; put out your hand and catch me by the leg, and I'll fly you home.' 'Sweet is your hand in a pitcher of honey, my jewel,' says I, though all the time I thought within myself that I don't much trust you; but there was no help, so I caught the gander by the leg, and away I and the other geese flew after him as fast as hops.

" We flew, and we flew, and we flew, until we came right over the wide ocean. I knew it well, for I saw Cape Clear to my right hand, sticking up out of the water. 'Ah, my lord,' said I to the goose, for I thought it best to keep a civil tongue in my head anyway, 'fly to land, if you please.' 'It is impossible, you see, Dan,' said he, 'for a while, because, you see, we are going to Arabia.' 'To Arabia!' said I, 'that's surely some place in foreign parts, far away. Oh! Mr. Goose, why, then, to be sure, I'm a man to be pitied among you.'

" 'WHIST, whist, you fool,' said he, 'hold your tongue; I tell you Arabia is a very decent sort of place, as like West Carbery as one egg is like another, only there is a little more sand there.'

" Just as we were talking a ship hove in sight, sailing so beautiful before the wind. 'Ah, then, sir,' said I, 'will you drop me on the ship, if you please?' 'We are not fair over it,' said he; 'if I dropped you now you would go splash into the sea.' 'I would not,' says I, 'I know better than that, for it is just clean under us, so let me drop now at once.'

" 'If you must, you must,' said he; 'there, take your own way'; and he opened his claw, and, faith, he was right—

sure enough, I came down plump into the very bottom of the salt sea! Down to the very bottom I went, and I gave myself up, then, for ever, when a whale walked up to me, scratching himself after his night's sleep, and looked me full in the face, and never the word did he say, but, lifting up his tail, he splashed me all over again with the cold salt water till there wasn't a dry stitch upon my whole carcass! And I heard somebody saying—'twas a voice I knew too—'Get up, you drunken brute, off o' that'; and with that I woke up, and there was Judy with a tub full of water, which she was splashing all over me—for, rest her soul, though she was a good wife, she could never bear to see me in drink, and had a bitter hand of her own.

" ' Get up,' said she again; ' and of all places in the parish, would no place *sarve* your turn to lie down upon but under the *ould* walls of Carrigapooka? An uneasy resting I am sure you had of it.' And, sure enough, I had, for I was fairly bothered out of my senses with eagles, and men of the moons, and flying ganders, and whales, driving me through bogs and up to the moon, and down to the bottom of the green ocean. If I was in drink ten times over, long would it be before I'd lie down in the same spot again, I know that! "

T. Crofton Croker.

CUCHULAIN OF MUIRTHEMNE

(The Birth of Cuchulain.)

IN the long time ago, Conchubar, son of Ness, was King of Ulster, and he held his court in the palace of Emain Macha. And this is the way he came to be King. He was but a young lad, and his father was not living, and Fergus, son of Rogh, who was at that time King of Ulster, asked his mother Ness in marriage.

Now Ness, that was at one time the quietest and kindest of the women of Ireland, had got to be unkind and treacherous because of an unkindness that had been done to her, and she planned to get the kingdom away from Fergus for her own son. So she said to Fergus, "Let Conchubar hold the kingdom for a year, so that his children after him may be called the children of a king; and that is the marriage portion I will ask of you."

"You may do that," the men of Ulster said to him; "for even though Conchubar gets the name of being king, it is yourself that will be our King all the time." So Fergus agreed to it, and he took Ness as his wife, and her son Conchubar was made King in his place.

But all through the year Ness was working to keep the kingdom for him, and she gave great presents to the chief

45

men of Ulster to get them on her side. And though Conchubar was but a young lad at the time, he was wise in his judgments and brave in battle, and good in shape and in form, and they liked him well. And at the end of the year, when Fergus asked to have the kingship back again, they consulted together; and it is what they agreed, that Conchubar was to keep it. And they said, "It is little Fergus thinks about us, when he was so ready to give up his rule over us for a year; and let Conchubar keep the kingship," they said, " and let Fergus keep the wife he has got."

NOW, it happened one day that Conchubar was making a feast at Emain Macha for the marriage of his sister Dechtire with Sualtim, son of Roig. And at the feast Dechtire was thirsty, and they gave her a cup of wine, and as she was drinking it a mayfly flew into the cup, and she drank it down with the wine. And presently she went into her sunny parlour, and her fifty maidens along with her, and she fell into a deep sleep. And in her sleep Lugh of the Long Hand appeared to her, and he said, " It is I myself was the mayfly that came to you in the cup, and it is with me you must come away now, and your fifty maidens along with you." And he put on them the appearance of a flock of birds, and they went with him southward till they came to Brugh na Boinne, the dwelling-place of the Sidhe. And no one at Emain Macha could get tale or tidings of them, or know where they had gone, or what had happened them.

It was about a year after that time there was another feast in Emain, and Conchubar and his chief men were sitting at the feast. And suddenly they saw from the window a great flock of birds, that lit on the ground and began to eat up everything before them, so that not so much as a blade of grass was left.

The men of Ulster were vexed when they saw the birds destroying all before them, and they yoked nine of their chariots to follow after them. Conchubar was in his own chariot, and there were following with him Fergus, son of Rogh, and Laegaire Buadach the Battle-Winner, and Celthair, son of Uithecar, and many others, and Bricriu of the bitter tongue was along with them.

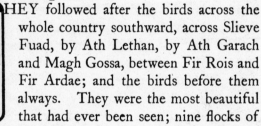

THEY followed after the birds across the whole country southward, across Slieve Fuad, by Ath Lethan, by Ath Garach and Magh Gossa, between Fir Rois and Fir Ardae; and the birds before them always. They were the most beautiful that had ever been seen; nine flocks of them there were, linked together two-and-two with a chain of silver, and at the head of every flock there were two birds of different colours, linked together with a chain of gold; and there were three birds that flew by themselves, and they all went before the chariots to the far end of the country, until the fall of night, and then there was no more seen of them.

And when the dark night was coming on, Conchubar said to his people, " It is best for us to unyoke the chariots now, and to look for some place where we can spend the night."

Then Fergus went forward to look for some place, and what he came to was a very small poor-looking house. A man and a woman were in it, and when they saw him they said, "Bring your companions here along with you, and they will be welcome." Fergus went back to his companions

and told them what he had seen. But Bricriu said : " Where
is the use of going into a house like that, with neither room
nor provisions nor coverings in it; it is not worth our while
to be going there."

Then Bricriu went on himself to the place where the house
was. But when he came to it, what he saw was a grand,
new, well-lighted house; and at the door there was a young
man wearing armour, very tall and handsome and shining.
And he said, "Come into the house, Bricriu; why are you
looking about you?" And there was a young woman
beside him, fine and noble, and with curled hair, and she
said, "Surely there is a welcome before you from me."
"Why does she welcome me?" said Bricriu. "It is on
account of her that I myself welcome you," said the young
man. "And is there no one missing from you at Emain?"
he said. "There is, surely," said Bricriu. "We are
missing fifty young girls for the length of a year." "Would
you know them again if you saw them?" said the young
man. "If I would not know them," said Bricriu, "it is
because a year might make a change in them, so that I would
not be sure." "Try and know them again," said the man,
"for the fifty young girls are in this house, and this woman
beside me is their mistress, Dechtire. It was they themselves, changed into birds, that went to Emain Macha to
bring you here." Then Dechtire gave Bricriu a purple
cloak with gold fringes; and he went back to find his companions. But while he was going he thought to himself,
"Conchubar would give great treasure to find these fifty
young girls again, and his sister along with them. I will
not tell him I have found them. I will only say I have found
a house with beautiful women in it, and no more than that."

When Conchubar saw Bricriu he asked news of him. "What news do you bring back with you, Bricriu?" he said. "I came to a fine well-lighted house," said Bricriu; "I saw a queen, noble, kind, with royal looks, with curled hair; I saw a troop of women, beautiful, well dressed; I saw the man of the house, tall and open-handed and shining." "Let us go there for the night," said Conchubar. So they brought their chariots and their horses and their arms; and they were hardly in the house when every sort of food and of drink, some they knew and some they did not know, was put before them, so that they never spent a better night. And when they had eaten and drunk and began to be satisfied, Conchubar said to the young man, "Where is the mistress of the house that she does not come to bid us welcome?" "You cannot see her to-night," said he, "for she is in the pains of childbirth."

S O they rested there that night, and in the morning Conchubar was the first to rise up; but he saw no more of the man of the house, and what he heard was the cry of a child. And he went to the room it came from, and there he saw Dechtire, and her maidens about her, and a young child beside her. And she bade Conchubar welcome, and she told him all that had happened her, and that she had called him there to bring herself and the child back to Emain Macha. And Conchubar said, "It is well you have done by me, Dechtire; you gave shelter to me and to my chariots; you kept the cold from my horses; you gave food to me and my people, and now you have given us this good gift. And let our sister, Finchoem, bring up the child," he said. "No, it is not for her to bring him up, it is for me," said Sencha, son of Ailell, chief judge and chief poet of Ulster. "For I am skilled; I am good in disputes; I am not forgetful; I speak before anyone at all in the presence of the King; I watch over what he says; I give judgment in the quarrels of kings; I am judge of the men of Ulster; no one has a right to dispute my claim, but only Conchubar."

"If the child is given to me to bring up," said Blai, the distributor, "he will not suffer from want of care or from forgetfulness. It is my messages that do the will of Conchubar; I call up the fighting men from all Ireland; I am well able to provide for them for a week, or even for ten days; I settle their business and their disputes; I support their honour; I get satisfaction for their insults."

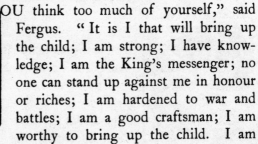

"YOU think too much of yourself," said Fergus. "It is I that will bring up the child; I am strong; I have knowledge; I am the King's messenger; no one can stand up against me in honour or riches; I am hardened to war and battles; I am a good craftsman; I am worthy to bring up the child. I am the protector of all the unhappy; the strong are afraid of me; I am the helper of the weak."

"If you will listen to me at last, now you are quiet," said Amergin, "I am able to bring up a child like a king. The people praise my honour, my bravery, my courage, my wisdom; they praise my good luck, my age, my speaking, my name, my courage, and my race. Though I am a fighter, I am a poet; I am worthy of the King's favour; I overcome all the men who fight from their chariots; I owe thanks to no one except Conchubar; I obey no one but the King."

Then Sencha said, "Let Finchoem keep the child until we come to Emain, and Morann, the judge, will settle the question when we are there."

So the men of Ulster set out for Emain, Finchoem having the child with her. And when they came there Morann gave his judgment. "It is for Conchubar," he said, "to help the child to a good name, for he is next of kin to him; let Sencha teach him words and speaking; let Fergus hold him on his knees; let Amergin be his tutor." And he said, "This child will be praised by all, by chariot drivers and fighters, by kings and by wise men; he shall be loved by many men; he will avenge all your wrongs; he will defend your fords; he will fight all your battles."

And so it was settled. And the child was left until he should come to sensible years with his mother Dechtire and with her husband Sualtim. And they brought him up upon the plain of Muirthemne, and the name he was known by was Setanta, son of Sualtim.

The boyhood of Cuchulain

ECTERA, one of the sisters of Conchubar Mac Nessa, married a prince whose patrimony lay along the shores of the Muirnict, and whose capital was Dun Dalgan. They had one child, a boy, whom they named Setanta.

As soon as Sentata was able to understand the stories and conversation of those around him, he evinced a passion for arms and the martial life, which was so premature and violent as to surprise all who knew him. His thoughts for ever ran on the wars and achievements of the Red Branch. He knew all the knights by name, the appearance and bearing of each, and what deeds of valour they had severally performed. Emain Macha, the capital of the Clanna Rury, was never out of his mind. He saw for ever before his mind its moats and ramparts, its gates and bridges, its streets filled with martial men, its high-raised Duns and Raths, its branching roads, over which came the tributes of wide Ulla to the High King. He had seen his father's tribute driven thither, and had even longed to be one of the four-footed beasts that he beheld wending their way to the wondrous city. But, above all, he delighted to be told of the great school where the young nobles of Ulster were taught martial exercises and the military art, under the superintendence of chosen knights and of the High King himself. Of the several knights he had his own opinion, and had already resolved to accept no one as his instructor save Fergus Mac Roy, tanist of Ulster.

F his father he saw little. His mind had become impaired, and he was confined in a secluded part of the Dun. But whenever he spoke to Dectera of what was nearest his heart, and his desire to enter the military school at Emain Macha, she laughed, and said that he was not yet old enough to endure that rough life. But secretly she was alarmed, and formed plans to detain him at home altogether. Then Setanta concealed his desire, but enquired narrowly concerning the partings of the roads on the way to Emania.

At last, when he was ten years old, selecting a favourable night, Setanta stole away from his father's Dun, and before morning had crossed the frontier. He then lay down to rest and sleep in a wood. After this he set out again, travelling quickly, lest he should be met by any of his father's people. On his back was strapped his little wooden shield, and by his side hung a sword of lath. He had brought his ball and hurle of red-bronze with him, and ran swiftly along the road, driving the ball before him, or throwing up his javelin into the air, and running to meet it ere it fell.

In the afternoon of that day Fergus Mac Roy and the King sat together in the part that surrounded the King's palace. A chessboard was between them, and their attention was fixed on the game.

At a distance the young nobles were at their sports, and the shouts of the boys and the clash of the metal hurles resounded in the evening air.

UDDENLY the noise ceased, and Fergus and the King looked up. They saw a strange boy rushing backwards and forwards through the crowd of young nobles, urging the ball in any direction that he pleased, as if in mockery, till none but the very best players attempted to stop him, while the rest stood about the ground in groups. Fergus and the King looked at each other for a moment in silence.

After this the boys came together into a group and held a council. Then commenced what seemed to be an attempt to force him out of the ground, followed by a furious fight. The strange boy seemed to be a very demon of war; with his little hurle grasped, like a war-mace, in both hands, he laid about him on every side, and the boys were tumbling fast. He sprang at tall youths, like a hound at a stag's throat. He rushed through crowds of his enemies like a hawk through a flock of birds. The boys, seized with a panic, cried out that it was one of the Tuatha from the fairy hills

of the Boyne, and fled right and left to gain the shelter of the trees. Some of them, pursued by the stranger, ran round Conchubar Mac Nessa and his knight. The boy, however, running straight, sprang over the chess table; but Conchubar seized him deftly by the wrist and brought him to a stand, but with dilated eyes and panting.

" Why are you so enraged, my boy ? " said the King, " and why do you so maltreat my nobles? "

" Because they have not treated me with the respect due to a stranger," replied the boy.

" Who are you yourself? " said Conchubar.

" I am Setanta, the son of Sualtim, and Dectera, your own sister, is my mother; and it is not before my uncle's palace that I should be insulted and dishonoured."

 HIS was the début and first martial exploit of the great Cuculain, type of Irish chivalry and courage, in the bardic firmament a bright and particular star of strength, daring, and glory, that will not set nor suffer aught but transient obscuration till the extinction of the Irish race; Cuculain, bravest of the brave, whose glory affected even the temperate-minded Tierna, so that his sober pen has inscribed, in the annals of ancient Erin, this testimony: " *Cuculain, filius Sualtam fortissimus heros Scotorum.*"

After this Setanta was regularly received into the military school, where, ere long, he became a favourite both with old and young. He placed himself under the tuition of Fergus Mac Roy, who, each day, grew more and more proud of his pupil, for while still a boy his fame was extending over Ulla.

It was not long after this that Setanta received the name by which he is more generally known. Culain was chief of the black country of Ulla, and of a people altogether given up to the making of weapons and armour, where the sound of the hammer and husky bellows were for ever heard. One day Conchubar and some of his knights, passing through the park to partake of an entertainment at the house of the armourer, paused awhile, looking at the boys at play. Then, as all were praising his little nephew, Conchubar called to him, and the boy came up, flushed and shy, for there were with the King the chief warriors of the Red Branch. But Conchubar bade him come with them to the feast, and the knights around him laughed, and enumerated the good things which Culain had prepared for them. But when Setanta's brow fell, Conchubar bade him finish his game, and after that proceed to Culain's house, which was to the west of Emain Macha, and more than a mile distant from the city. Then the King and his knights went on to the feast, and Setanta returned joyfully to his game.

Now, when they were seen afar upon the plain the smith left his workshop and put by his implements, and having washed from him the sweat and smoke, made himself ready to receive his guests; but the evening fell as they were coming into the liss, and all his people came in also, and sat at the lower table, and the bridge was drawn up and the door was shut for the night, and the candles were lit in the high chamber.

Then said Culain, " Have all thy retinue come in, O Conchubar? " And when the King said that they were all there, Culain bade one of his apprentices go out and let loose the great mastiff that guarded the house. Now, this mastiff was as large as a calf and exceedingly fierce, and he guarded all the smith's property outside the house, and if anyone approached the house without beating on the gong, which was outside the foss and in front of the drawbridge, he was accustomed to rend him. Then the mastiff, having been let loose, careered three times round the liss, baying dreadfully, and after that remained quiet outside his kennel, guarding his master's property. But, inside, they devoted themselves to feasting and merriment, and there were many jests made concerning Culain, for he was wont to cause laughter to Conchubar Mac Nessa and his knights, yet he was good to his own people and faithful to the Crave Rue, and very ardent and skilful in the practice of his art. But as they were amusing themselves in this manner, eating and drinking, a deep growl came from without, as it were a note of warning, and after that one yet more savage; but where he sat in the champion's seat, Fergus Mac Roy struck the table with his hand and rose straightway, crying out, " It is Setanta." But ere the door could be opened they heard the boy's voice raised in anger and the fierce yelling of the dog, and a scuffling in the bawn of the liss. Then they rushed to the door in great fear, for they said that the boy was torn in pieces; but when the bolts were drawn back and they sprang forth, eager to save the boy's life, they found the dog dead, and Setanta standing over him with his hurle, for he had sprung over the foss, not fearing the dog. Forthwith, then, his tutor, Fergus Mac Roy, snatched him up on his shoulder, and returned with great joy into the banquet hall, where all were well pleased at the preservation of the boy, except Culain himself, who began to lament over the death of his dog and to enumerate all the services which he rendered to him.

58

"Do not grieve for thy dog, O Culain," said Setanta, from the shoulder of Fergus, "for I will perform those services for you myself until a dog equally good is procured to take the place of him I slew."

Then one jesting, said, "Cu-culain!" (Hound of Culain) and thenceforward he went by this name.

STANDISH O'GRADY.

The Legend of Knockgrafton

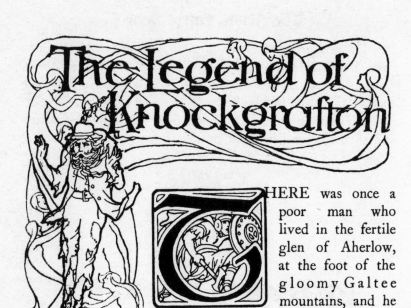

THERE was once a poor man who lived in the fertile glen of Aherlow, at the foot of the gloomy Galtee mountains, and he had a great hump on his back; he looked just as if his body had been rolled up and placed upon his shoulders; and his head was pressed down with the weight so much that his chin, when he was sitting, used to rest upon his knees for support. The country people were rather shy of meeting him in any lonesome place, for though, poor creature, he was as harmless and as inoffensive as a new-born infant, yet his deformity was so great that he scarcely appeared to be a human creature, and some ill-minded persons had set strange stories about him afloat. He was said to have a great knowledge of herbs and charms; but certain it was that he had a mighty skilful hand in plaiting straws and rushes into hats and baskets, which was the way he made his livelihood.

Lusmore, for that was the nickname put upon him, by

reason of his always wearing a sprig of the fairy cap, or
lusmore (the foxglove), in his little straw hat, would ever
get a higher penny for his plaited work than anyone else,
and perhaps that was the reason why someone, out of envy,
had circulated the strange stories about him. Be that as it
may, it happened that he was returning one evening from
the pretty town of Cahir towards Cappagh, and as little
Lusmore walked very slowly, on account of the great hump
upon his back, it was quite dark when he came to the old
moat of Knockgrafton, which stood on the right-hand side
of the road. Tired and weary was he, and no ways comfortable in his own mind at thinking how much farther he
had to travel, and that he should be walking all the night;
so he sat down under the moat to rest himself, and began
looking mournfully enough upon the moon, which—

> Rising in clouded majesty at length
> Apparent Queen, unveil'd her peerless light,
> And o'er the dark her silver mantle threw.

Presently there arose a wild strain of unearthly melody upon
the ear of little Lusmore. He listened, and he thought that
he had never heard such ravishing music before. It was
like the sound of many voices, each mingling and blending
with the others so strangely that they seemed to be one,
though all singing different strains, and the words of the
songs were these:

> Da Luan, Da Mort, Da Luan, Da Mort, Da Luan, Da Mort,
> Da Luan, Da Mort;

when there would be a moment's pause, and then the round
of melody went on again.

Lusmore listened attentively, scarcely drawing his breath,

lest he might lose the slightest note. He now plainly perceived that the singing was within the moat; and though
at first it had charmed him much, he began to get tired of
hearing the same round sung over and over so often without
any change; so, availing himself of the pause when Da Luan,
Da Mort, had been sung three times, he took up the tune,
and raised it with the words augus Da Dardeen, and then
went on singing with the voices inside of the moat, Da Luan,
Da Mort, finishing the melody, when the pause came again,
with augus Da Dardeen.

 HE fairies within Knockgrafton, for the
song was a fairy melody, when they
heard this addition to the tune, were
so much delighted that with instant
resolve it was determined to bring the
mortal among them whose musical skill
so far exceeded theirs, and little
Lusmore was conveyed into their company with the eddying
speed of a whirlwind.

Glorious to behold was the sight that burst upon him as
he came down through the moat, twirling round and round,
with the lightness of a straw, to the sweetest music, that
kept time to his motion. The greatest honour was then
paid him, for he was put above all the musicians, and he had
servants tending upon him and everything to his heart's
content, and a hearty welcome to all; and, in short, he was
made as much of as if he had been the first man in the land.

Presently Lusmore saw a great consultation going on
among the fairies, and, notwithstanding all their civility, he
felt very much frightened, until one, stepping out from the
rest, came up to him and said:

Lusmore ! Lusmore !
Doubt not, nor deplore,
For the hump which you bore
On your back is no more ;
Look down on the floor,
And view it, Lusmore !

HEN these words were said, poor little Lusmore felt himself so light and so happy that he thought he could have bounded at one jump over the moon, like the cow in the history of the cat and the fiddle; and he saw, with inexpressible pleasure, his hump tumble down upon the ground from his shoulders. He then tried to lift up his head, and did so with becoming caution, fearing that he might knock it against the ceiling of the great hall where he was. He looked round and round again with the greatest wonder and delight upon everything, which appeared more and more beautiful; and, overpowered at beholding such a resplendent scene, his head grew dizzy and his eyesight grew dim. At last he fell into a sound sleep, and when he awoke he found that it was broad daylight, the sun shining brightly, and the birds singing sweetly, and that he was lying just at the foot of Knockgrafton, with the cows and sheep grazing peaceably about him. The first thing Lusmore did, after saying his prayers, was to put his hand behind to feel for his hump, but no sign of one was there on his back, and he looked at himself with great pride, for he had now become a well-shaped, dapper little fellow, and, more than that, found himself in a full suit of new clothes, which he concluded the fairies had made for him.

Towards Cappagh he went, stepping out as lightly and

springing up at every step as if he had been all his life a dancing-master. Not a creature who met Lusmore knew him without his hump, and he had a great work to persuade everyone that he was the same man—in truth he was not as far as the outward appearance went.

Of course it was not long before the story of Lusmore's hump got about, and a great wonder was made of it. Through the country for miles round it was the talk of everyone, high and low.

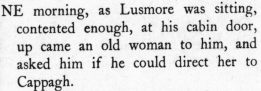

NE morning, as Lusmore was sitting, contented enough, at his cabin door, up came an old woman to him, and asked him if he could direct her to Cappagh.

"I need give you no directions, my good woman," said Lusmore, "for this is Cappagh. And whom may you want here?"

"I have come," said the woman, "out of Decies country, in the county of Waterford, looking after one Lusmore, who, I have heard tell, had his hump taken off by the fairies; for there is a son of a gossip of mine who has got a hump on him that will be his death; and, maybe, if he could use the same charm as Lusmore the hump may be taken off him. And now I have told you the reason of my coming so far; 'tis to find out about this charm if I can."

Lusmore, who was ever a good-natured little fellow, told the woman all the particulars, how he had raised the tune for the fairies at Knockgrafton, how his hump had been removed from his shoulders, and how he had got a new suit of clothes into the bargain.

The woman thanked him very much and then went away,

quite happy and easy in her own mind. When she came back to her gossip's house, in the county of Waterford, she told her everything that Lusmore had said, and they put the little hump-backed man, who was a peevish and cunning creature from his birth, upon a car, and took him all the way across the country. It was a long journey, but they did not care for that, so the hump was taken from off him; so they brought him just at nightfall, and left him under the old moat of Knockgrafton.

Jack Madden, for that was the humpy man's name, had not been sitting there long when he heard the tune going on within the moat much sweeter than before; for the fairies were singing it the way Lusmore had settled their music for them, and the song was going on, Da Luan, Da Mort, Da Luan, Da Mort, Da Luan, Da Mort, augus Da Dardeen, without ever stopping. Jack Madden, who was in a great hurry to get quit of his hump, never thought of waiting till the fairies had done, or watching for a fit opportunity to raise the tune higher than Lusmore had; so, having heard them sing it over seven times without stopping, out he bawls, never minding the time or the humour of the tune, or how he could bring his words in properly, augus Da Dardeen, augus Da Hena, thinking that if one day was good two were better, and that, if Lusmore had one suit of clothes given him, he should have two.

No sooner had the words passed his lips than he was taken up and whisked into the moat with prodigious force, and the fairies came crowding round about him with great anger, screeching and screaming, and roaring out, " Who spoiled our tune? Who spoiled our tune? " And one stepped up to him above all the rest and said :

65

Jack Madden ! Jack Madden !
Your words came so bad in
The tune we felt glad in ;—
This castle you're had in,
That your life we may sadden ;
Here's two humps for Jack Madden !

And twenty of the strongest fairies brought Lusmore's hump
and put it down upon poor Jack's back, over his own, where
it became fixed as firmly as if it was nailed on with twelve-
penny nails by the best carpenter that ever drove one.
Out of their castle they then kicked him; and in the morning,
when Jack Madden's mother and her gossip came to look
after their little man, they found him half dead, lying at the
foot of the moat, with the other hump upon his back.   Well,
to be sure, how they did look at each other, but they were
afraid to say anything lest a hump might be put upon their
shoulders. Home they brought the unlucky Jack Madden with
them, as downcast in their hearts and their looks as ever two
gossips were; and what through the weight of his other hump
and the long journey he died soon after, leaving, they say,
his heavy curse to anyone who would go to listen to fairy
tunes again.

T. Crofton Croker.

The Stolen Child

HERE dips the rocky highland
Of Sleuth Wood in the lake,
There lies a leafy island,
Where flapping herons wake
The drowsy water rats;
There we've hid our faery vats,
Full of berries,
And of reddest stolen cherries.
Come away, O human child!
To the waters and the wild
With a faery, hand in hand,
For the world's more full of weeping than
    you can understand.

Where the wave of moonlight glosses
The dim gray sands with light,

Far off by furthest Rosses
We foot it all the night,
Weaving olden dances,
Mingling hands and mingling glances,
Till the moon has taken flight;
To and fro we leap
And chase the frothy bubbles,
While the world is full of troubles
And is anxious in its sleep.
Come away, O human child!
To the waters and the wild
With a faery, hand in hand,
For the world's more full of weeping than
    you can understand.

Where the wandering water gushes
From the hills above Glen-Car,
In pools among the rushes
That scarce could bathe a star,
We seek for slumbering trout,
And whispering in their ears
Give them unquiet dreams;
Leaning softly out
From ferns that drop their tears
Over the young streams.
Come away, O human child!
To the waters and the wild
With a faery, hand in hand,
For the world's more full of weeping than
    you can understand.

Away with us he's going,
The solemn-eyed :
He'll hear no more the lowing
Of the calves on the warm hillside;
Or the kettle on the hob
Sing peace into his breast,
Or see the brown mice bob
Round and round the oatmeal-chest.
For he comes, the human child!
To the waters and the wild
With a faery, hand in hand,
From a world more full of weeping than
       he can understand.

                    W. B. YEATS.

LAY OF OISIN ON THE LAND OF YOUTH

Lay of Oisin on the Land of Youth

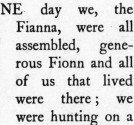

NE day we, the Fianna, were all assembled, generous Fionn and all of us that lived were there; we were hunting on a misty morning nigh the bordering shores of Loch Lein, where through fragrant trees of sweetest blossoms, and the mellow music of birds at all times, we aroused the hornless deer of the best bounding, course, and agility; our hounds and all our dogs were close after in full chase.

'Twas not long till we saw, westwards, a fleet rider advancing towards us, a young maiden of most beautiful appearance, on a slender white steed of swiftest power. We all ceased from the chase on seeing the form of the royal maid; 'twas a surprise to Fionn and the Fianns, they never beheld a woman equal in beauty. A royal crown was on her head, and a brown mantle of precious silk, spangled with stars of red gold, covering her shoes down to the grass. A gold ring was hanging down from each yellow curl of her golden hair; her eyes were blue, clear, and cloudless, like a dewdrop on the top of the grass. Redder were her cheeks than the rose, fairer was her visage than the swan upon the wave, and more sweet was the taste of her balsam lips than honey mingled through red wine. A garment, wide, long, and smooth, covered the white steed; there was a comely saddle of red gold, and her right hand held a bridle with a golden bit. Four shoes, well shaped, were under him, of the yellow gold of the purest quality; a silver wreath was on the back of his head, and there was not in the world a steed better.

HE came to the presence of Fionn, and spoke with a voice sweet and gentle, and she said, " O King of the Fianna, long and distant is my journey now."

" Who art thou thyself, O youthful princess! of fairest form, beauty, and countenance? Relate to us the cause of thy story, thine own name and thy country."

" Golden-headed Niamh is my name, O sage Fionn of the great hosts. Beyond the women of the world I have won esteem; I am the fair daughter of the King of Youth."

" Relate to us, O amiable princess, what caused thee to come afar across the sea—is it thy consort has forsaken thee, or what is the affliction that is on thyself? "

" 'Tis not my husband that went from me; and as yet I have not been spoken of with any man, O King of the Fianna of highest repute; but affection and love I have given to thy son."

"Which of my children is he, O blooming daughter, to whom thou hast given love, or yet affection? Do not conceal from us now the cause, and relate to us thy case, O woman."

"I will tell thee that, O Fionn! Thy noble son of the well-tempered arms, high-spirited Oisin of the powerful hands, is the champion that I am now speaking of."

"What is the reason that thou gavest love, O beautiful daughter of the glossy hair, to my own son beyond all, and multitudes of high lords under the sun?"

 "'IS not without cause, O King of the Fianna! I came afar for him—but reports I heard of his prowess, the goodness of his person and his mien.

"Many a son of a king and a high chief gave me affection and perpetual love; I never consented to any man till I gave love to noble Oisin."

"By that hand on thee, O Patrick, though it is not shameful to me as a story, there was not a limb of me but was in love with the beautiful daughter of the glossy hair."

I, Oisin, took her hand in mine, and said in speech of sweetest tone, "A true, gentle welcome before thee, O young princess, to this country! 'Tis thou art the brightest and the fairest of form, 'tis thee I prefer as wife, thou art my choice beyond the women of the world, O mild star of loveliest countenance!"

"Obligations unresisted by true heroes, O generous Oisin, I put upon thee to come with myself now upon my steed

till we arrive at the ' Land of Youth.' It is the most delightful country to be found, of greatest repute under the sun,
trees drooping with fruit, and blossom and foliage growing
on the tops of boughs. Abundant, there, are honey and
wine and everything that eye has beheld; there will not
come decline on thee with lapse of time; death or decay
thou wilt not see. Thou wilt get feasts, playing, and drink;
thou wilt get melodious music on the harp strings; thou
wilt get silver and gold; thou wilt get also many jewels.
Thou wilt get the royal diadem of the ' King of Youth,'
which he never yet gave to any person under the sun; 'twill
protect thee both night and day, in battle, in tumult, and
in rough conflict. Thou wilt get a fitting coat of protecting
mail, and a gold-headed sword apt for strokes, from which
no person ever escaped alive who once saw the sharp weapon.
Thou wilt get everything I promised thee, and delights, also,
which I may not mention; thou wilt get beauty, srtength,
and power, and I myself will be thy wife."

"No refusal will I give from me," said I, "O charming
queen of the golden curls! Thou art my choice above the
women of the world, and I will go with willingness to the
' Land of Youth.' "

On the back of the steed we went together. Before me
sat the virgin; she said, "Oisin, let us remain quiet till we
reach the mouth of the great sea."

Then arose the steed swiftly; when we arrived on the
borders of the strand he shook himself then to pace forward,
and neighed three times aloud.

When Fionn and the Fianna saw the steed travelling
swiftly, facing the great tide, they raised three shouts of
mourning and grief.

"O Oisin!" said Fionn slowly and sorrowfully, "woe it is to me that thou art going from me; I have not a hope that thou wilt ever again come back to me victorious."

His form and beauty changed, and showers of tears flowed down, till they wet his breast and his bright visage, and he said, "My woe art thou, O Oisin, in going from me!"

PATRICK, 'twas a melancholy story our parting from each other in that place, the parting of the father from his own son—'tis mournful, weak, and faint to be relating it! I kissed my father sweetly and gently, and the same affection I got from him. I bade adieu to all the Fianna, and the tears flowed down my cheeks. We turned our backs to the land and our faces directly due west; the smooth sea ebbed before us and filled in billows after us. We saw wonders in our travels, cities, courts, and castles, lime-white mansions and fortresses, brilliant summer-houses and palaces. We also saw, by our sides, a hornless fawn leaping nimbly, and a red-eared white dog, urging it boldly in the chase. We beheld also, without fiction, a young maid on a brown steed, a golden apple in her right hand, and she going on the top of the waves. We saw after her a young rider on a white steed, under a purple, crimson mantle of satin, and a gold-headed sword in his right hand.

"Who are yon two whom I see, O gentle princess? Tell me the meaning, of that woman of most beautiful countenance and the comely rider of the white steed."

"Heed not what thou wilt see, O gentle Oisin, nor what thou hast yet seen; there is in them but nothing, till we reach the land of the 'King of Youth.'"

We saw from us afar a sunny palace of beautiful front; its form and appearance were the most beauteous that were to be found in the world.

"What exceeding fine royal mansion, and also the best that eye hath seen, is this that we are travelling near to, or who is high chief of that place?"

"The daughter of the King of the 'Land of Life' is Queen, yet in that fortress she was taken by Fomhor Builleach, of Dromloghach, with violent strength of arms and activity. Obligation she put upon the brave never to make her a wife till she got a champion or true hero to stand battle with him hand to hand."

"AKE success and blessings, O golden-headed Niamh. I have never heard better music than the gentle voice of thy sweet mouth; great grief to us is a woman of her condition. I will go now to visit her to the fortress, and it may be for us it is fated that that great hero should fall by me, in feats of activity as is wont to me."

We went then into the fortress. To us came the youthful Queen. Equal in splendour was she to the sun, and she bade us a hundred welcomes.

There was apparel of yellow silk on the Queen of excellent beauty. Her chalk-white skin was like the swan on the wave, and her cheeks were of the colour of the rose. Her hair was of a golden hue, her blue eyes clear and cloudless; her honey lips of the colour of the berries, and her slender brows of loveliest form.

Then we there sat down, each of us on a chair of gold. There was laid out for us abundance of food and drinking-horns filled with beer. When we had taken a sufficiency of food and much sweet drinking wines, then spoke the mild young princess, and thus said he, "Hearken to me awhile." She told us the knowledge and cause of her tale, and the tears flowed down her cheeks. She said, "My return is not to my own country whilst the great giant shall be alive."

"Be silent, O young princess! Give o'er thy grief and do not mourn, and I give to thee my hand that the giant of slaughter shall fall by me!"

"There's not a champion now to be found of greatest repute under the sun to give battle hand to hand to the bold giant of the hard blows."

 "I TELL to thee, O gentle queen, I am not daunted at his coming to meet me. Unless he fall by me, by the strength of my arms, I will fall myself in thy defence."

'Twas not long till we saw approaching the powerful giant that was most repulsive. A load was on him of the skins of deer, and an iron bar in his hand. He did not salute or bow to us, but looked into the countenance of the young maiden, proclaimed battle and great conflict, and I myself went to meet him. During three nights and three days we were in the great contest; though powerful was he, the valiant giant, I beheaded him without delay.

When the two young maidens saw the great giant lying motionless, weak and low, they uttered three joyful cries, with great boasting and merriment.

We then went to the fortress, and I was bruised, weak,

and feeble, shedding blood in great abundance coming
closely out of my wounds. The daughter of the "King of
the Living" came in truth to relieve myself. She put balm
and balsam in my wounds, and I was whole after her.

We consumed our feast with pleasure, and then we were
merry after. In the fortress were prepared for us warm beds
of the down of birds. We buried the great man in a deep
sod-grave, wide and clear. I raised his flag and monument,
and I wrote his name in Ogham Craobh.

On the morrow, at the appearance of day, we awoke out
of our slumbers. "It is time for us," said the daughter of
the King, "to go without delay to our own land."

WE prepared ourselves without a stay, and
we took our leave of the virgin. We
were sorrowful and sad after her, and
not less after us was the refulgent maid.

We turned our backs on the fortress,
and our horse under us in full speed,
and swifter was the white steed than
March wind on the mountain summit. Ere long the sky
darkened and the wind arose in every point, the great sea
lit up strongly, and sight of the sun was not to be found.
We gazed awhile on the clouds and on the stars that were
under gloom. The tempest abated and the wind, and
Phœbus brightened o'er our heads.

We beheld by our side a most delightful country, under full
bloom, and plains, beautiful, smooth, and fine, and a royal
fortress of surpassing beauty. Not a colour that eye has
beheld of rich blue, green, and white, or purple, crimson,
and of yellow, but was in this royal mansion that I am
describing. There were at the other side of the fortress

radiant summer-houses and palaces made, all of precious stones, by the hands of skilful men and great artists.

Ere long we saw approaching from the fortress to meet us three fifties of champions of best agility, appearance, fame, and of highest repute.

"What beauteous country is that, O gentle daughter of the golden locks? Of best aspect that the eye has seen; or is it the 'Land of Youth'?"

"It is, truly, O generous Oisin! I have not told you a lie concerning it; there is nothing I promised thyself but is manifest to thee for ever."

O us came after that a hundred maids of exquisite beauty, under-garments of silk filled with gold, welcoming me to their own country. We saw again approaching a multitude of glittering bright hosts, and a noble, great, and powerful King of matchless grace, form, and countenance. There was a yellow shirt of silken satin and a bright golden garment over it; there was a sparkling crown of gold, radiant and shining, upon his head. We saw coming after him the young Queen of highest repute, and fifty virgins sweet and mild, of most beautiful form, in her company. When all arrived in one spot, then courteously spoke the "King of Youth," and said, "This is Oisin, the son of Fionn, the gentle consort of 'Golden-headed Niamh'!"

He took me then by the hand and said aloud to the hearing of the host, "O brave Oisin! O son of the King! A hundred thousand welcomes to you! This country into which thou comest, I'll not conceal its tidings from you, in

truth, long and durable is your life, and thou thyself shalt
be ever young. There's not a delight on which the heart
hath mused but is in this land awaiting thee. O Oisin!
believe me in truth, for I am King of the 'Land of
Youth'! This is the gentle Queen and my own daughter,
the Golden-headed Niamh, who went over the smooth seas
for thee to be her consort for ever."

I gave thanks to the King and I bowed down to the gentle
Queen; nor stayed we there, but proceeded soon, till we
reached the royal mansion of the "King of Youth." There
came the nobles of the fine fortress, both men and women,
to meet us; there was a feast and banquet continuously there
for ten nights and ten days.

 ESPOUSED "Golden-headed Niamh,"
O Patrick from Rome of white croziers!
That is how I went to the "Land of
Youth," tho' woeful and grievous to
me to relate. I had, by Golden-headed
Niamh, of children of surpassing
beauty and bloom, of best form, shape,
and countenance, two young sons and a gentle daughter. I
spent a time protracted in length, three hundred years and
more, until I thought 'twould be my desire to see Fionn
and the Fianna alive. I asked leave of the King and of my
kind spouse, Golden-headed Niamh, to go to Erin back
again to see Fionn and his great host.

"Thou wilt get leave from me," said the gentle daughter,
"though 'tis a sorrowful tale to me to hear you mention it,
lest thou mayest not come again in your life to my own land,
O victorious Oisin!"

"What do we dread, O blooming Queen? Whilst the

white steed is at my service he will teach me the way with ease, and will return safe back to thyself."

"Remember, O Oisin! what I am saying. If thou layest foot on level ground thou shalt not come again for ever to this fine land in which I am myself. I say to thee again without guile, if thou alightest once off the white steed thou wilt never more come to the 'Land of Youth,' O golden Oisin of the warlike arms! I say to thee for the third time, if thou alightest off the steed thyself thou wilt be an old man, withered and blind, without activity, without pleasure, without run, without leap. 'Tis a woe to me, O loving Oisin, that thou ever goest to green Erin; 'tis not now as it has been; and thou never shalt see Fionn of the hosts. There is not now in all Erin but a father of orders and hosts of saints. O loving Oisin, here is my kiss; thou wilt never return to the 'Land of Youth'!"

 I LOOKED up into her countenance with compassion, and streams of tears ran from my eyes. O Patrick! thou wouldst have pitied her tearing the hair off the golden head. She put me under strict injunctions to go and come without touching the lea, and said to me, by virtue of their power, if I broke them that I'd never return safe. I promised her each thing, without a lie, that I would fulfil what she said to me. I went on the back of the white steed and bade farewell to the people of the fortress. I kissed my gentle consort, and sorrowful was I in parting from her; my two sons and my young daughter were under grief, shedding tears. I prepared myself for travelling, and I turned my back on the "Land of Youth." The steed ran

swiftly under me, as he had done with me and "Golden-headed Niamh."

On my coming, then, into the country, I looked closely in every direction. I thought then, in truth, that the tidings of Fionn were not to be found. 'Twas not long for me, nor tedious, till I saw from the west approaching me a great troop of mounted men and women, and they came into my presence. They saluted me kindly and courteously, and surprise seized every one of them on seeing the bulk of my own person, my form, my appearance, and my countenance. I myself asked then of them, did they hear if Fionn was alive, or did anyone else of the Fianna live, or what disaster had swept them away?

E have heard tell of Fionn, for strength, for activity, and for prowess, that there never was an equal for him in person, in character, and in mien. There is many a book written down by the melodious sweet sages of the Gaels which we, in truth, are unable to relate to thee, of the deeds of Fionn and of the Fianna. We heard that Fionn had a son of brightest beauty and form; that there came a young maiden for him, and that he went with her to the 'Land of Youth.'"

When I myself heard that announcement that Fionn did not live, or any of the Fianna, I was seized with weariness and great sorrow, and I was full of melancholy after them! I did not stop on my course, quick and smart without any delay, till I set my face straightforward to Almhuin of great exploits in broad Leinster. Great was my surprise there that I did not see the court of Fionn of the hosts; there was not in its place, in truth, but weeds, chick-weeds, and nettles. Alas, O Patrick! and alas, my grief! A miserable journey it was to me, without the tidings of Fionn or the Fianna; it left me through life under pain. After I left Almhuin of Leinster, there was not a residence where the Fianna had been, but I searched accurately without any delay. On my passing through the Glen of the Thrushes I saw a great assembly there, three hundred men and more were before me in the glen. One of the assembly spoke, and he said with a loud voice, "Come to our relief, O kingly champion, and deliver us from difficulty!"

I THEN came forward, and the host had a large flag of marble; the weight of the flag was down on them, and to uphold it they were unable! Those that were under the flag below were being oppressed, weakly; by the weight of the great load many of them lost their senses. One of the stewards spoke and said, "O princely young hero, forthwith relieve my host, or not one of them will be alive!" 'Tis a shameful deed that it should now be said, and the number of men that is there, that the strength of the host is unable to lift the flag with great power. If Oscur, the son of Oisin, lived, he would take this flag in his right hand; he would fling it in a throw over the host. It is not my custom to speak falsehood.

I lay upon my right breast and I took the flag in my hand; with the strength and activity of my limbs I sent it seven perches from its place! With the force of the very large flag the golden girth broke on the white steed; I came down full suddenly on the soles of my two feet on the lea. No sooner did I come down than the white steed took fright. He went then on his way, and I stood in sorrow, both weak and feeble. I lost the sight of my eyes, my form, my countenance, and my vigour; I was an old man, poor and blind, without strength, understanding, or esteem. Patrick! there is to thee my story, as it occurred to myself, without a lie, my going and my adventures in certain, and my returning from the "Land of Youth."

From "Ossianic Poems."
Edited by JOHN O'DALY.

Adventures of Gilla na Chreck an Gour

(*Told in the Wexford Peasant Dialect.*)

LONG ago a poor widow woman lived down by the iron forge near Enniscorthy, and she was so poor, she had no clothes to put on her son; so she used to fix him in the ash-hole, near the fire, and pile the warm ashes about him; and, accordingly, as he grew up, she sunk the pit deeper. At last, by hook or by crook, she got a goat-skin, and fastened it round his waist, and he felt quite grand, and took a walk down the street. So says she to him next morning, "Tom, you thief, you never done any good yet, and six-foot high, and past nineteen: take that rope and bring me a *bresna* from the wood." "Never say't twice, mother," says Tom; "here goes."

When he had it gathered and tied, what should come up but a big *joiant*, nine-foot high, and made a lick of a club at him. Well become Tom, he jumped a-one side and picked up a ram-pike; and the first crack he gave the big fellow he made him kiss the clod. "If you have e'er a prayer," says Tom, "now's the time to say it, before I make *brishe* of you." "I have no prayers," says the giant, "but if you spare my life I'll give you that club; and as long as you keep from sin you'll win every battle you ever fight with it."

Tom made no bones about letting him off; and as soon as he got the club in his hands he sat down on the bresna and gave it a tap with the kippeen, and says, "Bresna, I had a great trouble gathering you, and run the risk of my life for you; the least you can do is to carry me home." And, sure enough, the wind of the word was all it wanted. It went off through the wood, groaning and cracking till it came to the widow's door.

ELL, when the sticks were all burned Tom was sent off again to pick more; and this time he had to fight with a giant with two heads on him. Tom had a little more trouble with him— that's all; and the prayers *he* said was to give Tom a fife that nobody could help dancing when he was playing it. *Begonies*, he made the big faggot dance home, with himself sitting on it. Well, if you were to count all the steps from this to Dublin, dickens a bit you'd ever arrive there. The next giant was a beautiful boy with three heads on him. He had neither prayers nor catechism no more *nor* the others; and so he gave Tom a bottle of green ointment that wouldn't let you be burned, nor scalded, nor wounded. "And now," says he, "there's no more of us. You may come and gather sticks here till little *Lunacy Day* in harvest without giant or fairy man to disturb you."

Well, now, Tom was prouder nor ten paycocks, and used to take a walk down street in the heel of the evening; but some of the little boys had no more manners nor if they were Dublin jackeens, and put out their tongues at Tom's club and Tom's goat-skin. He didn't like that at all, and it would be mean to give one of them a clout. At last, what should come through the town but a kind of bellman, only it's a big bugle he had, and a huntsman's cap on his head, and a kind of painted shirt. So this—he wasn't a bellman, and I don't know what to call him—bugleman, maybe—proclaimed that the King of Dublin's daughter was so melancholy that she didn't give a laugh for seven years, and that her father would grant her in marriage to whoever would make her laugh three times. "That's the very thing for me to try," says Tom; and so, without burning any more daylight, he kissed his mother, curled his club at the little boys, and he set off along the yalla highroad to the town of Dublin.

At last Tom came to one of the city gates, and the guards laughed and cursed at him instead of letting him through. Tom stood it all for a little time, but at last one of them—out of fun, as he said—drove his *bagnet* half an inch or so into his side. Tom did nothing but take the fellow by the scruff of his neck and the waistband of his corduroys and fling him into the canal. Some ran to pull the fellow out, and others to let manners into the vulgarian with their swords and daggers; but a tap from his club sent them headlong into the moat or down on the stones, and they were soon begging him to stay his hands.

So at last one of them was glad enough to show Tom the way to the palace yard; and there was the King and the

Queen, and the princess in a gallery, looking at all sorts of wrestling and sword-playing, and *rinka-fadhas* (long dances) and mumming, all to please the princess; but not a smile came over her handsome face.

ELL, they all stopped when they seen the young giant, with his boy's face and long black hair, and his short curly beard —for his poor mother couldn't afford to buy *razhurs*—and his great strong arms and bare legs, and no covering but the goat-skin that reached from his waist to his knees. But an envious wizened *basthard* of a fellow, with a red head, that wished to be married to the princess, and didn't like how she opened her eyes at Tom, came forward, and asked his business very snappishly. " My business," says Tom, says he, " is to make the beautiful princess, God bless her, laugh three times." "Do you see all them merry fellows and skilful swordsmen," says the other, "that could eat you up with a grain of salt, and not a mother's soul of 'em ever got a laugh from her these seven years ? " So the fellows gathered round Tom, and the bad man aggravated him till he told them he didn't care a pinch of snuff for the whole bilin' of 'em; let 'em come on, six at a time, and try what they could do. The King, that was too far off to hear what they were saying, asked what did the stranger want. " He wants," says the red-headed fellow, " to make hares of your best men." "Oh! " says the King, "if that's the way, let one of 'em turn out and try his mettle." So one stood forward, with *soord* and pot-lid, and made a cut at Tom. He struck the fellow's elbow with the club, and up over their heads flew the sword, and down went the owner of it on the gravel from a thump he got on the helmet. Another took his place, and another, and another, and then half a dozen at once, and Tom sent swords, helmets, shields, and bodies rolling over and over, and themselves bawling out that they were kilt, and disabled, and damaged, and rubbing their poor elbows and hips, and limping away. Tom contrived not to kill anyone; and the princess was so amused that she let a great sweet laugh out of her that was heard all over the yard. "King of Dublin," says Tom, "I've quarter of your daughter." And the King didn't know whether he was glad or sorry, and all the blood in the princess's heart run into her cheeks.

O there was no more fighting that day, and Tom was invited to dine with the royal family. Next day Redhead told Tom of a wolf, the size of a yearling heifer, that used to be *serenading* (sauntering) about the walls, and eating people and cattle; and said what a pleasure it would give the King to have it killed. "With all my heart," says Tom. "Send a jackeen to show me where he lives, and we'll see how he behaves to a stranger." The princess was not well pleased, for Tom looked a different person with fine clothes and a nice green *birredh* over his long, curly hair; and besides, he'd got one laugh out of her. However, the King gave his consent; and in an hour and a half the horrible wolf was walking in the palace yard, and Tom a step or two behind, with his club on his shoulder, just as a shepherd would be walking after a pet lamb. The King and Queen and princess were safe up in their gallery, but the officers and people of the court that were *padrowling*

about the great bawn, when they saw the big baste coming
in gave themselves up, and began to make for doors and
gates; and the wolf licked his chops, as if he was saying,
"Wouldn't I enjoy a breakfast off a couple of yez!" The
King shouted out, "O Gilla na Chreck an Gour, take away
that terrible wolf, and you must have all my daughter."
But Tom didn't mind him a bit. He pulled out his flute
and began to play like vengeance; and dickens a man or boy
in the yard but began shovelling away heel and toe, and the
wolf himself was obliged to get on his hind legs and dance
Tatther Jack Walsh along with the rest. A good deal of
the people got inside and shut the doors, the way the hairy
fellow wouldn't pin them; but Tom kept playing, and the
outsiders kept shouting and dancing, and the wolf kept
dancing and roaring with the pain his legs were giving him:
and all the time he had his eyes on Redhead, who was shut
out along with the rest. Wherever Redhead went the wolf
followed, and kept one eye on him and the other on Tom,
to see if he would give him leave to eat him. But Tom
shook his head, and never stopped the tune, and Redhead
never stopped dancing and bawling and the wolf dancing
and roaring, one leg up and the other down, and he ready
to drop out of his standing from fair tiresomeness.

When the princess seen that there was no fear of anyone
being kilt she was so divarted by the stew that Redhead was
in that she gave another great laugh; and well become Tom,
out he cried, "King of Dublin, I have two quarters of your
daughter." "Oh, quarters or alls," says the King, "put away
that divel of a wolf and we'll see about it." So Gilla put
his flute in his pocket, and says he to the baste that was
sittin' on his currabingo ready to faint, "Walk off to your

Adventures of
Gilla na Chreck an gour

mountains, my fine fellow, and live like a respectable baste; and if ever I find you come within seven miles of any town——" He said no more, but spit in his fist, and gave a flourish of his club. It was all the poor divel wanted: he put his tail between his legs and took to his pumps without looking at man nor mortial, and neither sun, moon, nor stars ever saw him in sight of Dublin again.

AT dinner everyone laughed but the foxy fellow; and, sure enough, he was laying out how he'd settle poor Tom next day. "Well, to be sure!" says he, "King of Dublin, you are in luck. There's the Danes moidhering us to no end. D—— run to Lusk wid 'em! and if anyone can save us from 'em it is this gentleman with the goat-skin. There is a flail hangin' on the collar-beam in Hell, and neither Dane nor Devil can stand before it." "So," says Tom to the King, "will you let me have the other half of the princess if I bring you the flail?" "No, no," says the princess, "I'd rather never be your wife than see you in that danger."

But Redhead whispered and nudged Tom about how shabby it would look to reneague the adventure. So he asked him which way he was to go, and Redhead directed him through a street where a great many bad women lived, and a great many shibbeen houses were open, and away he set.

Well, he travelled and travelled till he came in sight of the walls of Hell; and, bedad, before he knocked at the gates, he rubbed himself over with the greenish ointment. When he knocked a hundred little imps popped their heads out through the bars, and axed him what he wanted. "I want to speak to the big divel of all," says Tom: "open the gate."

It wasn't long till the gate was *thrune* open, and the Ould Boy received Tom with bows and scrapes, and axed his business. "My business isn't much," says Tom. "I only came for the loan of that flail that I see hanging on the collar-beam for the King of Dublin to give a thrashing to the Danes." "Well," says the other, "the Danes is much better customers to me; but, since you walked so far, I won't refuse. Hand that flail," says he to a young imp; and he winked the far-off eye at the same time. So while some were barring the gates, the young devil climbed up and took down the iron flail that had the handstaff and booltheen both made out of red-hot iron. The little vagabond was grinning to think how it would burn the hands off of Tom, but the dickens a burn it made on him, no more nor if it was a good oak sapling. "Thankee," says Tom; now would you open the gate for a body and I'll give you no more trouble." "Oh, tramp!" says Ould Nick, is that the way? It is easier getting inside them gates than getting out again. Take that tool from him, and give him a dose of the oil of stirrup." So one fellow put out his claws to seize on the flail, but Tom gave him such a welt of it on the side of his head that he broke off one of his horns, and made him roar like a divel as he was. Well, they rushed at Tom, but he gave them, little and big, such a thrashing as they didn't forget for a while. At last says the ould thief of all, rubbing his elbows, "Let the fool out; and woe to whoever lets him in again, great or small."

So out marched Tom and away with him, without minding

the shouting and cursing they kept up at him from the tops of the walls. And when he got home to the big bawn of the palace, there never was such running and racing as to see himself and the flail. When he had his story told he laid down the flail on the stone steps, and bid no one for their lives to touch it. If the King and Queen and princess made much of him before they made ten times as much of him now; but Redhead, the mean scruff-hound, stole over, and thought to catch hold of the flail to make an end of him. His fingers hardly touched it, when he let a roar out of him as if heaven and earth were coming together, and kept flinging his arms about and dancing that it was pitiful to look at him. Tom run at him as soon as he could rise, caught his hands in his own two, and rubbed them this way and that, and the burning pain left them before you could reckon one. Well, the poor fellow, between the pain that was only just gone, and the comfort he was in, had the comicalest face that ever you see; it was such a mixerum-gatherum of laughing and crying. Everyone burst out a laughing—the princess could not stop no more than the rest —and then says Gilla, or Tom, " Now, ma'am, if there were fifty halves of you I hope you'll give me them all." Well, the princess had no mock modesty about her. She looked at her father, and, by my word, she came over to Gilla and put her two delicate hands into his two rough ones, and I wish it was myself was in his shoes that day!

Tom would not bring the flail into the palace. You may be sure no other body went near it; and when the early risers were passing next morning they found two long clefts in the stone where it was, after burning itself an opening downwards, nobody could tell how far. But a messenger came in at noon and said that the Danes were so frightened when they heard of the flail coming into Dublin that they got into their ships and sailed away.

Well, I suppose before they were married Gilla got some man like Pat Mara of Tomenine to larn him the "principles of politeness," fluxions, gunnery, and fortifications, decimal fractions, practice, and the rule-of-three direct, the way he'd be able to keep up a conversation with the royal family. Whether he ever lost his time larning them sciences, I'm not sure, but it's as sure as fate that his mother never more saw any want till the end of her days.

PATRICK KENNEDY.

The Hill-man and the Housewife

IT is well known that the good people cannot stand mean ways. Now, there once lived a house-wife who had a sharp eye to her own good in this world, and gave alms of what she had no use, for the good of her soul.

One day a hill-man knocked at her door. "Can you lend us a saucepan, good mother?" said he. "There's a wedding in the hill, and all the pots are in use." "Is he to have one?" asked the servant girl who opened the door. "Ay, to be sure," said the house-wife.

But when the maid was taking a saucepan from the shelf, she pinched her arm and whispered sharply, "Not that, you stupid; get the old one out of the cupboard. It leaks, and the hill-men are so neat and such nimble workers that they are sure to mend it before they send it home. So one does a good turn to the good people and saves sixpence from the tinker."

The maid fetched the saucepan, which had been laid by till the tinker's next visit, and gave it to the dwarf, who thanked her and went away.

The saucepan was soon returned neatly mended and ready for use. At supper time the maid filled the pan with milk and set it on the fire for the children's supper, but in a few minutes the milk was so burnt and smoked that no one could touch it, and even the pigs would not drink the wash into which it was thrown.

"A, you good-for-nothing slut!" cried the house-wife, as she this time filled the pan herself. "You would ruin the richest, with your careless ways; there's a whole quart of good milk spoilt at once." "And that's twopence," cried a voice from the chimney, a queer whining voice like some old body who was always grumbling over something.

The house-wife had not left the saucepan for two minutes when the milk boiled over, and it was all burnt and smoked as before. "The pan must be dirty," cried the house-wife in a rage; "and there are two full quarts of milk as good as thrown to the dogs." "*And that's fourpence*," said the voice in the chimney.

After a long scrubbing the saucepan was once more filled and set on the fire, but it was not the least use, the milk was burnt and smoked again, and the house-wife burst into tears at the waste, crying out, "Never before did such a thing happen to me since I kept house! Three quarts of milk burnt for one meal!" "*And that's sixpence*," cried the voice from the chimney. "You didn't save the tinker after all," with which the hill-man himself came tumbling down the chimney, and went off laughing through the door. But from that time the saucepan was as good as any other.

JULIANA HORATIA EWING.

The Giant Walker

OW, all the night around their echoing camp
Was heard continuous from the hills a sound as of the tramp
Of giant footsteps; but, so thick the white mist lay around,
None saw the Walker, save the King. He, starting at the sound,
Called to his foot his fierce red hound; athwart his shoulders cast
A shaggy mantle, grasped his spear, and through the moonlight passed

Alone up dark Ben-Boli's heights, towards which, above the
    woods,
With sound as when at close of eve the noise of falling floods
Is borne to shepherd's ear remote on stilly upland lawn,
The steps along the mountain-side with hollow fall came on.
Fast beat the hero's heart; and close down-crouching by his
    knee
Trembled the hound, while, through the haze, huge as
    through mists at sea,
The week-long sleepless mariner descries some mountain
    cape,
Wreck-infamous, rise on his lee, appeared a monstrous Shape,
Striding impatient, like a man much grieved, who walks
    alone,
Considering of a cruel wrong; down from his shoulders
    thrown
A mantle, skirted stiff with soil splashed from the miry
    ground,
At every stride against his calves struck with as loud rebound
As makes the main-sail of a ship brought up along the blast,
When with the coil of all its ropes it beats the sounding
    mast.
So, striding vast, the giant passed; the King held fast his
    breath—
Motionless, save his throbbing heart; and chill and still as
    death
Stood listening while, a second time, the giant took the round
Of all the camp; but, when at length, for the third time, the
    sound
Came up, and through the parting haze a third time huge
    and dim

Rose out the Shape, the valiant hound sprang forth and
    challenged him.
And forth, disdaining that a dog should put him so to shame,
Sprang Congal, and essayed to speak: "Dread Shadow,
    stand!   Proclaim
What wouldst thou that thou thus all night around my camp
    shouldst keep
Thy troublous vigil banishing the wholesome gift of sleep
From all our eyes, who, though inured to dreadful sounds
    and sights
By land and sea, have never yet, in all our perilous nights,
Lain in the ward of such a guard."
                             The Shape made answer none,
But with stern wafture of its hand went angrier striding on,
Shaking the earth with heavier steps.   Then Congal on his
    track
Sprang fearless.
    "Answer me, thou churl!" he cried, "I bid thee back!"
But while he spoke, the giant's cloak around his shoulders
    grew
Like to a black-bulged thunder-cloud, and sudden, out there
    flew
From all its angry swelling folds, with uproar unconfined,
Direct against the King's pursuit, a mighty blast of wind.
Loud flapped the mantle, tempest-lined, while, fluttering
    down the gale,
As leaves in autumn, man and hound were swept into the
    vale;
And, heard o'er all the huge uproar, through startled Dalaray
The giant went, with stamp and clash, departing south away.
                                  SIR SAMUEL FERGUSON.

The pursuit of the Gilla Dacker

OW, it chanced at one time during the chase, while they were hunting over the plain of Cliach, that Finn went to rest on the hill of Collkilla, which is now called Knockainy; and he had his hunting-tents pitched on a level spot near the summit, and some of his chief heroes tarried with him.

When the King and his companions had taken their places on the hill, the Feni unleashed their gracefully shaped, sweet-voiced hounds through the woods and sloping glens. And it was sweet music to Finn's ear, the cry of the long-snouted dogs, as they routed the deer from their covers and the badgers from their dens; the pleasant, emulating shouts of the youths; the whistling and signalling of the huntsmen; and the encouraging cheers of the mighty heroes, as they spread themselves through the glens and woods, and over the broad green plain of Cliach.

Then did Finn ask who of all his companions would go to the highest point of the hill directly over them to keep watch and ward and to report how the chase went on. For, he said, the Dedannans were ever on the watch to work the Feni mischief by their druidical spells, and more so during the chase than at other times.

Finn Ban Mac Bresal stood forward and offered to go; and, grasping his broad spears, he went to the top, and sat viewing the plain to the four points of the sky. And the King and his companions brought forth the chess-board and chess-men and sat them down to a game.

Finn Ban Mac Bresal had been watching only a little time when he saw on a plain to the east a Fomor of vast size coming towards the hill, leading a horse. As he came nearer Finn Ban observed that he was the ugliest-looking giant his eyes ever lighted on. He had a large, thick body, bloated and swollen out to a great size; clumsy, crooked legs; and broad, flat feet turned inwards. His hands and arms and shoulders were bony and thick and very strong-looking; his neck was long and thin; and while his head was poked forward, his face was turned up, as he stared straight at Finn Mac Bresal. He had thick lips, and long, crooked teeth; and his face was covered all over with bushy hair.

H E was fully armed; but all his weapons were rusty and soiled and slovenly looking. A broad shield of a dirty, sooty colour, rough and battered, hung over his back; he had a long, heavy, straight sword at his left hip; and he held in his left hand two thick-handled, broad-headed spears, old and rusty, and seeming as if they had not been handled for years. In his right hand he held an iron club, which he dragged after him with its end on the ground; and, as it trailed along, it tore up a track as deep as the furrow a farmer ploughs with a team of oxen.

The horse he led was even larger in proportion than the giant himself, and quite as ugly. His great carcass was covered all over with tangled scraggy hair, of a sooty black; you could count his ribs and all the points of his big bones through his hide; his legs were crooked and knotty; his neck was twisted; and as for his jaws, they were so long and heavy that they made his head look twice too large for his body.

The giant held him by a thick halter, and seemed to be dragging him forward by main force, the animal was so lazy and so hard to move. Every now and then, when the beast tried to stand still, the giant would give him a blow on the ribs with his big iron club, which sounded as loud as the thundering of a great billow against the rough-headed rocks of the coast. When he gave him a pull forward by the halter, the wonder was that he did not drag the animal's head away from his body; and, on the other hand, the horse often gave the halter such a tremendous tug backwards that it was equally wonderful how the arm of the giant was not torn away from his shoulder.

WHEN at last he had come up he bowed his head and bended his knee, and saluted the King with great respect.

Finn addressed him; and after having given him leave to speak he asked him who he was, and what was his name, and whether he belonged to one of the noble or ignoble races; also what was his profession or craft, and why he had no servant to attend to his horse.

The big man made answer and said, "King of the Feni, whether I come of a noble or of an ignoble race, that, indeed, I cannot tell, for I know not who my father and mother were. As to where I came from, I am a Fomor of Lochlann in the north; but I have no particular dwelling-place, for I am con-

tinually travelling about from one country to another, serving
the great lords and nobles of the world, and receiving wages
for my service.

"In the course of my wanderings I have often heard of
you, O King, and of your greatness and splendour and royal
bounty; and I have come now to ask you to take me into
your service for one year; and at the end of that time I shall
fix my own wages, according to my custom.

"You ask me also why I have no servant for this great
horse of mine. The reason of that is this: at every meal
I eat my master must give me as much food and drink as
would be enough for a hundred men; and whosoever the lord
or chief may be that takes me into his service, it is quite
enough for him to have to provide for me, without having
also to feed my servant.

"MOREOVER, I am so very heavy and
lazy that I should never be able to keep
up with a company on march if I had
to walk; and this is my reason for
keeping a horse at all.

"My name is the Gilla Dacker, and
it is not without good reason that I am
so called. For there never was a lazier or worse servant
than I am, or one that grumbles more at doing a day's work
for his master. And I am the hardest person in the world
to deal with; for, no matter how good or noble I may think
my master, or how kindly he may treat me, it is hard words
and foul reproaches I am likely to give him for thanks in
the end.

"This, O Finn, is the account I have to give of myself,
and these are my answers to your questions."

"Well," answered Finn, "according to your own account you are not a very pleasant fellow to have anything to do with; and of a truth there is not much to praise in your appearance. But things may not be so bad as you say; and, anyhow, as I have never yet refused any man service and wages, I will not now refuse you."

Whereupon Finn and the Gilla Dacker made covenants, and the Gilla Dacker was taken into service for a year.

"And now," said the Gilla Dacker, "as to this same horse of mine, I find I must attend to him myself, as I see no one here worthy of putting a hand near him. So I will lead him to the nearest stud, as I am wont to do, and let him graze among your horses. I value him greatly, however, and it would grieve me very much if any harm were to befall him; so," continued he, turning to the King, "I put him under your protection, O King, and under the protection of all the Feni that are here present."

T this speech the Feni all burst out laughing to see the Gilla Dacker showing such concern for his miserable, worthless old skeleton of a horse.

Howbeit, the big man, giving not the least heed to their merriment, took the halter off the horse's head and turned him loose among the horses of the Feni.

But now, this same wretched-looking old animal, instead of beginning to graze, as everyone thought he would, ran in among the horses of the Feni, and began straightway to work all sorts of mischief. He cocked his long, hard, switchy tail straight out like a rod, and, throwing up his hind legs, he kicked about on this side and on that, maiming and disabling several of the horses. Sometimes he went tearing through the thickest of the herd, butting at them with his hard, bony forehead; and he opened out his lips with a vicious grin and tore all he could lay hold on with his sharp, crooked teeth, so that none were safe that came in his way either before or behind.

At last he left them, and was making straight across to a small field where Conan Mail's horses were grazing by themselves, intending to play the same tricks among them. But Conan, seeing this, shouted in great alarm to the Gilla Dacker to bring away his horse, and not let him work any more mischief; and threatening, if he did not do so at once, to go himself and knock the brains out of the vicious old brute on the spot.

UT the Gilla Dacker told Conan that he saw no way of preventing his horse from joining the others, except someone put the halter on him. "And," said he to Conan, "there is the halter; and if you are in any fear for your own animals, you may go yourself and bring him away from the field."

Conan was in a mighty rage when he heard this; and as he saw the big horse just about to cross the fence, he snatched up the halter, and, running forward with long strides, he threw it over the animal's head and thought to lead him back. But in a moment the horse stood stock still, and his body and legs became as stiff as if they were made of wood; and though Conan pulled and tugged with might and main, he was not able to stir him an inch from his place.

At last Fergus Finnvel, the poet, spoke to Conan and said,

" I never would have believed, Conan Mail, that you could be brought to do horse-service for any knight or noble in the whole world; but now, indeed, I see that you have made yourself a horse-boy to an ugly foreign giant, so hateful-looking and low-born that not a man of the Feni would have anything to say to him. As you have, however, to mind this old horse in order to save your own, would it not be better for you to mount him and revenge yourself for all the trouble he is giving you, by riding him across the country, over the hill-tops, and down into the deep glens and valleys, and through stones and bogs and all sorts of rough places, till you have broken the heart in his big ugly body ? "

ONAN, stung by the cutting words of the poet and by the jeers of his companions, jumped upon the horse's back, and began to beat him mightily with his heels and with his two big heavy fists to make him go; but the horse seemed not to take the least notice, and never stirred.

" I know the reason he does not go," said Fergus Finnvel; " he has been accustomed to carry a horseman far heavier than you—that is to say, the Gilla Dacker; and he will not move till he has the same weight on his back."

At this Conan Mail called out to his companions, and asked which of them would mount with him and help to avenge the damage done to their horses.

" I will go," said Coil Croda the Battle Victor, son of Criffan; and up he went. But the horse never moved.

Dara Donn Mac Morna next offered to go, and mounted

behind the others; and after him Angus Mac Art Mac Morna. And the end of it was that fourteen men of the Clann Baskin and Clann Morna got up along with Conan; and all began to thrash the horse together with might and main. But they were none the better for it, for he remained standing stiff and immovable as before. They found, moreover, that their seat was not at all an easy one—the animal's back was so sharp and bony.

When the Gilla Dacker saw the Feni beating his horse at such a rate he seemed very angry, and addressed the King in these words:

"KING of the Feni, I now see plainly that all the fine accounts I heard about you and the Feni are false, and I will not stay in your service—no, not another hour. You can see for yourself the ill usage these men are giving my horse without cause; and I leave you to judge whether anyone could put up with it—anyone who had the least regard for his horse. The time is, indeed, short since I entered your service, but I now think it a great deal too long; so pay me my wages and let me go my ways."

But Finn said, "I do not wish you to go; stay on till the end of your year, and then I will pay you all I promised you."

"I swear," answered the Gilla Dacker, "that if this were the very last day of my year, I would not wait till morning for my wages after this insult. So, wages or no wages, I will now seek another master; but from this time forth I shall know what to think of Finn Mac Cumal and his Feni!"

With that the Gilla Dacker stood up as straight as a pillar, and, turning his face towards the south-west, he walked slowly away.

When the horse saw his master leaving the hill he stirred himself at once and walked quietly after him, bringing the fifteen men away on his back. And when the Feni saw this they raised a loud shout of laughter, mocking them.

The Gilla Dacker, after he had walked some little way, looked back, and, seeing that his horse was following, he stood for a moment to tuck up his skirts. Then, all at once changing his pace, he set out with long, active strides; and if you know what the speed of a swallow is flying across a mountain-side, or the dry fairy wind of a March day sweeping over the plains, then you can understand the swiftness of the Gilla Dacker as he ran down the hill-side towards the south-west.

NEITHER was the horse behindhand in the race; for though he carried a heavy load, he galloped like the wind after his master, plunging and bounding forward with as much freedom as if he had nothing at all on his back.

The men now tried to throw themselves off; but this, indeed, they were not able to do, for the good reason that they found themselves fastened firmly, hands and feet and all, to the horse's back.

And now Conan, looking round, raised his big voice and shouted to Finn and the Feni, asking them were they content to let their friends be carried off in that manner by such a horrible, foul-looking old spectre of a horse.

Finn and the others, hearing this, seized their arms and started off in pursuit. Now, the way the Gilla Dacker and

his horse took was first through Fermore, which is at the present day called Hy Conall Gavra; next over the wide, heathy summit of Slieve Lougher; from that to Corca Divna; and they ran along by Slieve Mish till they reached Cloghan Kincat, near the deep green sea.

And so the great horse continued his course without stop or stay, bringing the sixteen Feni with him through the sea. Now, this is how they fared in the sea while the horse was rushing farther and farther to the west: they had always a dry, firm strand under them, for the waters retired before the horse; while behind them was a wild, raging sea, which followed close after and seemed ready every moment to topple over their heads. But, though the billows were tumbling and roaring all round, neither horse nor riders were wetted by as much as a drop of brine or a dash of spray.

Then Finn spoke and asked the chiefs what they thought best to be done; and they told him they would follow whatsoever counsel he and Fergus Finnvel, the poet, gave them. Then Finn told Fergus to speak his mind; and Fergus said:

"My counsel is that we go straightway to Ben Edar, where we shall find a ship ready to sail. For our forefathers, when they wrested the land from the gifted, bright-complexioned Dedannans, bound them by covenant to maintain this ship for ever, fitted with all things needful for a voyage, even to the smallest article, as one of the privileges of Ben Edar; so that if at any time one of the noble sons of Gael Glas wished to sail to distant lands from Erin, he should have a ship lying at hand in the harbour ready to begin his voyage."

THEY agreed to this counsel, and turned their steps without delay northwards towards Ben Edar. They had not gone far when they met two noble-looking youths, fully armed, and wearing over their armour beautiful mantles of scarlet silk, fastened by brooches of gold. The strangers saluted the King with much respect; and the King saluted them in return. Then, having given them leave to converse, he asked them who they were, whither they had come, and who the prince or chief was that they served. And the elder answered:

"My name is Feradach, and my brother's name is Foltlebar; and we are the two sons of the King of Innia. Each of us professes an art; and it has long been a point of dispute between us which art is the better, my brother's or mine.

Hearing that there is not in the world a wiser or more far-seeing man than thou art, O King, we have come to ask thee to take us into thy service among thy household troops for a year, and at the end of that time to give judgment between us in this matter."

Finn asked them what were the two arts they professed.

"My art," answered Feradach, "is this. If at any time a company of warriors need a ship, give me only my joiner's axe and my crann-tavall, and I am able to provide a ship for them without delay. The only think I ask them to do is this—to cover their heads close, and keep them covered, while I give the crann-tavall three blows of my axe. Then I tell them to uncover their heads; and lo, there lies the ship in harbour ready to sail!"

HEN Foltlebar spoke and said, "This, O King, is the art I profess. On land I can track the wild duck over nine ridges and nine glens, and follow her without being once thrown out till I drop upon her in her nest. And I can follow up a track on sea quite as well as on land if I have a good ship and crew."

Finn replied, "You are the very men I want; and I now take you both into my service. At this moment I need a good ship and a skilful pilot more than any two things in the whole world."

Whereupon Finn told them the whole story of the Gilla Dacker's doings from beginning to end. "And we are now," said he, "on our way to Ben Edar to seek a ship that we may follow this giant and his horse and rescue our companions."

Then Feradach said, " I will get you a ship—a ship that will sail as swiftly as a swallow can fly! "

And Foltlebar said, " I will guide your ship in the track of the Gilla Dacker till ye lay hands on him, in whatsoever quarter of the world he may have hidden himself! "

And so they turned back to Cloghan Kincat. And when they had come to the beach Feradach told them to cover their heads, and they did so. Then he struck three blows of his axe on the crann-tavall; after which he made them look. And lo, they saw a ship fully fitted out with oars and sails and with all things needed for a long voyage riding before them in the harbour!

HEN they went on board and launched their ship on the cold, bright sea; and Foltlebar was their pilot and steersman. And they set their sail and plied their slender oars, and the ship moved swiftly westward till they lost sight of the shores of Erin; and they saw nothing all round them but a wide girdle of sea. After some days' sailing a great storm came from the west, and the black waves rose up against them so that they had much ado to keep their vessel from sinking. But through all the roaring of the tempest, through the rain and blinding spray, Foltlebar never stirred from the helm or changed his course, but still kept close on the track of the Gilla Dacker.

At length the storm abated and the sea grew calm. And when the darkness had cleared away they saw to the west, a little way off, a vast rocky cliff towering over their heads to such a height that its head seemed hidden among the clouds. It rose up sheer from the very water, and looked at that distance as smooth as glass, so that at first sight there seemed no way to reach the top.

Foltlebar, after examining to the four points of the sky, found the track of the Gilla Dacker as far as the cliff, but no farther. And he accordingly told the heroes that he thought it was on the top of that rock the giant lived; and that, anyhow, the horse must have made his way up the face of the cliff with their companions.

WHEN the heroes heard this they were greatly cast down and puzzled what to do; for they saw no way of reaching the top of the rock; and they feared they should have to give up the quest and return without their companions. And they sat down and looked up at the cliff with sorrow and vexation in their hearts.

Fergus Finnvel, the poet, then challenged the hero Dermat O'Dyna to climb the rock in pursuit of the Gilla Dacker, and he did so, and on reaching the summit found himself in a beautiful fairy plain. He fared across it and came to a great tree laden with fruit beside a well as clear as crystal. Hard by, on the brink of the well, stood a tall pillar stone, and on its top lay a golden-chased drinking horn. He filled the horn from the well and drank, but had scarcely taken it from his lips when he saw a fully armed wizard champion advancing to meet him with looks and gestures of angry menace. The wizard upbraided him for entering his territory without leave and for drinking out of his well from his drinking horn, and thereupon challenged him to fight. For four days long they fought, the wizard escaping from Dermat every even-fall by leaping into the well and disappearing down through it. But on the fourth evening Dermat closed with the wizard when about to spring into the water, and fell with him into the well.

On reaching the bottom the wizard wrested himself away and started running, and Dermat found himself in a strangely beautiful country with a royal palace hard by, in front of which armed knights were engaged in warlike exercises. Through them the wizard ran, but, when Dermat attempted to follow, his way was barred by their threatening weapons. Nothing daunted, he fell upon them in all his battle fury, and routed them so entirely that they fled and shut themselves up in the castle or took refuge in distant woods.

VERCOME with his battle toil (and smarting all over with wounds) Dermat fell into a dead sleep, from which he was wakened by a friendly blow from the flat of a sword held by a young, golden-haired hero, who proved to be the brother of the Knight of Valour, King of that country of Tir-fa-tonn, whom in the guise of the Knight of the Fountain, Dermat had fought and chased away.

A part of the kingdom belonging to him had been seized by his wizard brother, and he now seeks and obtains Dermat's aid to win it back for him.

When Dermat at last meets Finn and the other Feni who had gone in pursuit of him into the Kingdom of Sorca, at the summit of the great rock, he is able to relate how he headed the men of the Knight of Valour against the Wizard King, and slew him and defeated his army.

"And now," continued he, bringing forth the Knight of Valour from among the strange host, "this is he who was formerly called the Knight of Valour, but who is now the King of Tir-fa-tonn. Moreover, this King has told me, having himself found it out by his druidical art, that it was Avarta the Dedannan (the son of Illahan of the Many-coloured Raiment) who took the form of the Gilla Dacker, and who brought the sixteen Feni away to the Land of Promise, where he now holds them in bondage."

Then Foltlebar at once found the tracks of the Gilla Dacker and his horse. He traced them from the very edge of the rock across the plain to the sea at the other side; and they brought round their ship and began their voyage. But this time Foltlebar found it very hard to keep on the track; for the Gilla Dacker, knowing that there were not in the world men more skilled in following up a quest than the Feni, took great pains to hide all traces of the flight of himself and his horse; so that Foltlebar was often thrown out; but he always recovered the track after a little time.

ND so they sailed from island to island and from bay to bay, over many seas and by many shores, ever following the track, till at length they arrived at the Land of Promise. And when they had made the land, and knew for a certainty that this was indeed the Land of Promise, they rejoiced greatly; for in this land Dermat O'Dyna had been nurtured by Mannanan Mac Lir of the Yellow Hair.

Then they held council as to what was best to be done; and Finn's advice was that they should burn and spoil the country in revenge of the outrage that had been done to his people. Dermat, however, would not hear of this. And he said:

" Not so, O King. The people of this land are of all men the most skilled in druidic art; and it is not well that they should be at feud with us. Let us rather send to Avarta a trusty herald to demand that he should set our companions at liberty. If he does so, then we shall be at peace; if he refuse, then shall we proclaim war against him and his people, and waste this land with fire and sword till he be forced, even by his own people, to give us back our friends."

This advice was approved by all. And then Finn said:

" But how shall heralds reach the dwelling of this enchanter; for the ways are not open and straight, as in other lands, but crooked and made for concealment, and the valleys and plains are dim and shadowy and hard to be traversed?"

B UT Foltlebar, nothing daunted by the dangers and the obscurity of the way, offered to go with a single trusty companion; and they took up the track and followed it without being once thrown out, till they reached the mansion of Avarta. There they found their friends amusing themselves on the green outside the palace walls; for, though kept captive in the island, yet were they in no wise restrained, but were treated by Avarta with much kindness. When they saw the heralds coming towards them their joy knew no bounds; they crowded round to embrace them, and asked them many questions regarding their home and their friends.

At last Avarta himself came forth and asked who these strangers were; and Foltlebar replied:

" We are of the people of Finn Mac Cumal, who has sent us as heralds to thee. He and his heroes have landed on this island guided hither by me; and he bade us tell thee that he has come to wage war and to waste this land with fire and sword as a punishment for that thou hast brought away his people by foul spells, and even now keepest them in bondage."

When Avarta heard this he made no reply, but called a council of his chief men to consider whether they should send back to Finn an answer of war or of peace. And they, having much fear of the Feni, were minded to restore Finn's people and to give him his own award in satisfaction for the injury done to him; and to invite Finn himself and those who had come with him to a feast of joy and friendship in the house of Avarta.

VARTA himself went with Foltlebar to give this message. And after he and Finn had exchanged friendly greetings, he told them what the council had resolved; and Finn and Dermat and the others were glad at heart. And Finn and Avarta put hand in hand and made a league of friendship.

So they went with Avarta to his house, where they found their lost friends; and, being full of gladness, they saluted and embraced each other. Then a feast was prepared; and they were feasted for three days, and they ate and drank and made merry.

On the fourth day a meeting was called on the green to hear the award. Now, it was resolved to make amends on the one hand to Finn, as King of the Feni, and on the other to those who had been brought away by the Gilla Dacker. And when all were gathered together Finn was first asked to name his award; and this is what he said:

" I shall not name an award, O Avarta; neither shall I accept an eric from thee. But the wages I promised thee when we made our covenant at Knockainy, that I will give thee. For I am thankful for the welcome thou hast given us here; and I wish that there should be peace and friendship between us for ever."

But Conan, on his part, was not so easily satisfied; and he said to Finn:

ITTLE hast thou endured, O Finn, in this matter; and thou mayst well waive thy award. But hadst thou, like us, suffered from the sharp bones and the rough carcass of the Gilla Dacker's monstrous horse in a long journey from Erin to the Land of Promise, across wide seas, through tangled woods, and over rough-headed rocks, thou wouldst then, methinks, name an award."

At this, Avarta and the others who had seen Conan and his companions carried off on the back of the big horse could scarce keep from laughing; and Avarta said to Conan:

" Name thy award, and I will fulfil it every jot; for I have heard of thee, Conan, and I dread to bring the gibes and taunts of thy foul tongue on myself and my people."

" Well, then," said Conan, " my award is this: that you choose fifteen of the best and noblest men in the Land of Promise, among whom are to be your own best beloved friends; and that you cause them to mount on the back of the big horse, and that you yourself take hold of his tail. In this manner you shall fare to Erin, back again by the self-same track the horse took when he brought us hither— through the same surging seas, through the same thick thorny woods, and over the same islands and rough rocks and dark glens. And this, Avarta, is my award," said Conan.

Now, Finn and his people were rejoiced exceedingly when they heard Conan's award—that he asked from Avarta nothing more than like for like. For they feared much that he might claim treasure of gold and silver, and thus bring reproach on the Feni.

Avarta promised that everything required by Conan should be done, binding himself in solemn pledges. Then the heroes took their leave; and having launched their ship on the broad, green sea, they sailed back by the same course to Erin. And they marched to their camping-place at Knockainy, where they rested in their tents.

VARTA then chose his men. And he placed them on the horse's back, and he himself caught hold of the tail; and it is not told how they fared till they made harbour and landing-place at Cloghan Kincat. They delayed not, but straightway journeyed over the self-same track as before till they reached Knockainy.

Finn and his people saw them afar off coming towards the hill with great speed; the Gilla Dacker, quite as large and as ugly as ever, running before the horse; for he had let go the tail at Cloghan Kincat. And the Feni could not help laughing heartily when they saw the plight of the fifteen chiefs on the great horse's back; and they said with one voice that Conan had made a good award that time.

When the horse reached the spot from which he had at first set out the men began to dismount. Then the Gilla Dacker, suddenly stepping forward, held up his arm and pointed earnestly over the heads of the Feni towards the field where the horses were standing; so that the heroes were startled, and turned round every man to look. But nothing was to be seen except the horses grazing quietly inside the fence.

Finn and the others now turned round again with intent to speak to the Gilla Dacker and bring him and his people into the tents; but much did they marvel to find them all gone. The Gilla Dacker and his great horse and fifteen nobles of the Land of Promise had disappeared in an instant; and neither Finn himself nor any of his chiefs ever saw them afterwards.

PATRICK WESTON JOYCE.

Jamie Freel and the Young Lady

(*Ulster Irish.*)

OWN in Fannet, in times gone by, lived Jamie Freel and his mother. Jamie was the widow's sole support; his strong arm worked for her untiringly, and as each Saturday night came round he poured his wages into her lap, thanking her dutifully for the halfpence which she returned him for tobacco.

He was extolled by his neighbours as the best son ever known or heard of. But he had neighbours of whose opinions he was ignorant—neighbours who lived pretty close to him, whom he had never seen, who are, indeed, rarely seen by mortals, except on May Eves or Halloweens.

An old ruined castle, about a quarter of a mile from his cabin, was said to be the abode of the "wee folk." Every Halloween were the ancient windows lighted up, and passersby saw little figures flitting to and fro inside the building, while they heard the music of flutes and pipes.

It was well known that fairy revels took place; but nobody had the courage to intrude on them.

Jamie had often watched the little figures from a distance, and listened to the charming music, wondering what the inside of the castle was like; but one Halloween he got up, and took his cap, saying to his mother, " I'm awa to the castle to seek my fortune."

" What! " cried she. " Would you venture there—you that's the widow's only son? Dinna be sae venturesome and foolitch, Jamie! They'll kill you, an' then what'll come o' me? "

" Never fear, mother; nae harm'll happen me, but I maun gae."

E set out, and, as he crossed the potato field, came in sight of the castle, whose windows were ablaze with light that seemed to turn the russet leaves, still clinging to the crab-tree branches, into gold.

Halting in the grove at one side of the ruin, he listened to the elfin revelry, and the laughter and singing made him all the more determined to proceed.

Numbers of little people, the largest about the size of a child of five years old, were dancing to the music of flutes and fiddles, while others drank and feasted.

" Welcome, Jamie Freel! Welcome, welcome, Jamie! " cried the company, perceiving their visitor. The word " Welcome " was caught up and repeated by every voice in the castle.

Time flew, and Jamie was enjoying himself very much, when his hosts said, " We're going to ride to Dublin to-night to steal a young lady. Will you come, too, Jamie Freel? "

" Ay, that I will," cried the rash youth, thirsting for adventure.

A troop of horses stood at the door. Jamie mounted, and his steed rose with him into the air. He was presently flying over his mother's cottage, surrounded by the elfin troop, and on and on they went, over bold mountains, over little hills, over the deep Lough Swilley, over towns and cottages, where people were burning nuts and eating apples and keeping merry Halloween. It seemed to Jamie that they flew all round Ireland before they got to Dublin.

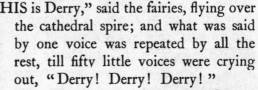

"THIS is Derry," said the fairies, flying over the cathedral spire; and what was said by one voice was repeated by all the rest, till fifty little voices were crying out, " Derry! Derry! Derry! "

In like manner was Jamie informed as they passed over each town on the route, and at length he heard the silvery voices cry, " Dublin! Dublin! "

It was no mean dwelling that was to be honoured by the fairy visit, but one of the finest houses in Stephen's Green.

The troop dismounted near a window, and Jamie saw a beautiful face on a pillow in a splendid bed. He saw the young lady lifted and carried away, while the stick which was dropped in her place on the bed took her exact form.

The lady was placed before one rider and carried a short way, then given another, and the names of the towns were cried as before.

They were approaching home. Jamie heard "Rathmullan," "Milford," "Tamney," and then he knew they were near his own house.

"You've all had your turn at carrying the young lady," said he. "Why wouldn't I get her for a wee piece?"

"Ay, Jamie," replied they pleasantly, "you may take your turn at carrying her, to be sure."

Holding his prize very tightly he dropped down near his mother's door.

"Jamie Freel! Jamie Freel! is that the way you treat us?" cried they, and they, too, dropped down near the door.

Jamie held fast, though he knew not what he was holding, for the little folk turned the lady into all sorts of strange shapes. At one moment she was a black dog, barking and trying to bite; at another a glowing bar of iron, which yet had no heat; then again a sack of wool.

UT still Jamie held her, and the baffled elves were turning away when a tiny woman, the smallest of the party, exclaimed, "Jamie Freel has her awa frae us, but he sall nae hae gude of her, for I'll mak' her deaf and dumb," and she threw something over the young girl.

While they rode off, disappointed, Jamie Freel lifted the latch and went in.

"Jamie man!" cried his mother, "you've been awa all night. What have they done on you?"

"Naething bad, mother; I hae the very best o' gude luck. Here's a beautiful young lady I hae brought you for company."

"Bless us and save us!" exclaimed his mother; and for some minutes she was so astonished she could not think of anything else to say.

Jamie told the story of the night's adventure, ending by saying, "Surely you wouldna have allowed me to let her gang with them to be lost for ever?"

"But a *lady*, Jamie! How can a lady eat we'er (our) poor diet and live in we'er poor way? I ax you that, you foolitch fellow!"

"Well, mother, sure it's better for her to be over here nor yonder," and he pointed in the direction of the castle.

Meanwhile the deaf and dumb girl shivered in her light clothing, stepping close to the humble turf fire.

"Poor crathur, she's quare and handsome! Nae wonder they set their hearts on her," said the old woman, gazing at their guest with pity and admiration. "We maun dress her first; but what in the name o' fortune hae I fit for the likes of her to wear?"

HE went to her press in "the room" and took out her Sunday gown of brown drugget. She then opened a drawer and drew forth a pair of white stockings, a long snowy garment of fine linen, and a cap, her "dead dress," as she called it.

These articles of attire had long been ready for a certain triste ceremony, in which she would some day fill the chief part, and only saw the light occasionally when they were hung out to air; but she was willing to give even these to the fair trembling visitor, who was turning in dumb sorrow and wonder from her to Jamie, and from Jamie back to her.

The poor girl suffered herself to be dressed, and then sat down on a "creepie" in the chimney corner and buried her face in her hands.

"What'll we do to keep up a lady like thou?" cried the old woman.

"I'll work for you both, mother," replied the son.

"An' how could a lady live on we'er poor diet?" she repeated.

"I'll work for her," was all Jamie's answer.

He kept his word. The young lady was very sad for a long time, and tears stole down her cheeks many an evening, while the old woman span by the fire and Jamie made salmon nets, an accomplishment acquired by him in hopes of adding to the comfort of their guest.

BUT she was always gentle, and tried to smile when she perceived them looking at her; and by degrees she adapted herself to their ways and mode of life. It was not very long before she began to feed the pig, mash potatoes and meal for the fowls, and knit blue worsted socks.

So a year passed and Halloween came round again. "Mother," said Jamie, taking down his cap, "I'm off to the ould castle to seek my fortune."

"Are you mad, Jamie?" cried his mother in terror; "sure they'll kill you this time for what you done on them last year."

Jamie made light of her fears and went his way.

As he reached the crab-tree grove he saw bright lights in the castle windows as before, and heard loud talking. Creeping under the window he heard the wee folk say, "That was a poor trick Jamie Freel played us this night last year, when he stole the young lady from us."

"Ay," said the tiny woman, "an' I punished him for it, for there she sits a dumb image by the hearth, but he does na' know that three drops out o' this glass that I hold in my hand wad gie her her hearing and speech back again."

Jamie's heart beat fast as he entered the hall. Again he was greeted by a chorus of welcomes from the company—"Here comes Jamie Freel! Welcome, welcome, Jamie!"

As soon as the tumult subsided the little woman said, "You be to drink our health, Jamie, out o' this glass in my hand."

Jamie snatched the glass from her and darted to the door. He never knew how he reached his cabin, but he arrived there breathless and sank on a stove by the fire.

"YOU'RE kilt, surely, this time, my poor boy," said his mother.

"No, indeed, better luck than ever this time!" and he gave the lady three drops of the liquid that still remained at the bottom of the glass, notwithstanding his mad race over the potato field.

The lady began to speak, and her first words were words of thanks to Jamie.

The three inmates of the cabin had so much to say to one another that, long after cock-crow, when the fairy music had quite ceased, they were talking round the fire.

"Jamie," said the lady, "be pleased to get me paper and

pen and ink that I may write to my father and tell him what has become of me."

She wrote, but weeks passed and she received no answer. Again and again she wrote, and still no answer.

At length she said, "You must come with me to Dublin, Jamie, to find my father."

"I hae no money to hire a car for you," he answered; "an' how can you travel to Dublin on your foot?"

But she implored him so much that he consented to set out with her and walk all the way from Fannet to Dublin. It was not as easy as the fairy journey; but at last they rang the bell at the door of the house in Stephen's Green.

"Tell my father that his daughter is here," said she to the servant who opened the door.

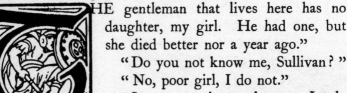

"HE gentleman that lives here has no daughter, my girl. He had one, but she died better nor a year ago."

"Do you not know me, Sullivan?"

"No, poor girl, I do not."

"Let me see the gentleman. I only ask to see him."

"Well, that's not much to ax. We'll see what can be done."

In a few moments the lady's father came to the door.

"How dare you call me your father?" cried the old gentleman angrily. "You are an impostor. I have no daughter."

"Look in my face, father, and surely you'll remember me."

"My daughter is dead and buried. She died a long, long time ago." The old gentleman's voice changed from anger to sorrow. "You can go," he concluded.

"Stop, dear father, till you look at this ring on my finger. Look at your name and mine engraved on it."

"It certainly is my daughter's ring, but I do not know how you came by it. I fear in no honest way."

"Call my mother—*she* will be sure to know me," said the poor girl, who by this time was weeping bitterly.

"My poor wife is beginning to forget her sorrow. She seldom speaks of her daughter now. Why should I renew her grief by reminding her of her loss?"

But the young lady persevered till at last the mother was sent for.

"Mother," she began, when the old lady came to the door, "don't *you* know your daughter?"

"I have no daughter. My daughter died, and was buried a long, long time ago."

"Only look in my face and surely you'll know me."

The old lady shook her head.

"YOU have all forgotten me; but look at this mole on my neck. Surely, mother, you know me now?"

"Yes, yes," said her mother, "my Gracie had a mole on her neck like that; but then I saw her in the coffin, and saw the lid shut down upon her."

It became Jamie's turn to speak, and he gave the history of the fairy journey, of the theft of the young lady, of the figure he had seen laid in its place, of her life with his mother in Fannet, of last Halloween, and of the three drops that had released her from her enchantments.

She took up the story when he paused and told how kind the mother and son had been to her.

The parents could not make enough of Jamie. They treated him with every distinction, and when he expressed his wish to return to Fannet, said they did not know what to do to express their gratitude.

But an awkward complication arose. The daughter would not let him go without her. "If Jamie goes, I'll go, too," she said. "He saved me from the fairies, and has worked for me ever since. If it had not been for him, dear father and mother, you would never have seen me again. If he goes, I'll go, too."

This being her resolution, the old gentleman said that Jamie should become his son-in-law. The mother was brought from Fannet in a coach-and-four, and there was a splendid wedding.

They all lived together in the grand Dublin house, and Jamie was heir to untold wealth at his father-in-law's death.

LETITIA MACLINTOCK.

A Legend of Knockmany

IT so happened that Finn and his gigantic relatives were all working at the Giant's Causeway in order to make a bridge, or, what was still better, a good stout pad-road across to Scotland, when Finn, who was very fond of his wife, Oonagh, took it into his head that he would go home and see how the poor woman got on in his absence. So accordingly he pulled up a fir-tree, and after lopping off the roots and branches, made a walking-stick of it and set out on his way to Oonagh.

Finn lived at this time on Knockmany Hill, which faces Cullamore, that rises up, half hill, half mountain, on the opposite side.

The truth is that honest Finn's affection for his wife was by no manner of means the whole cause of his journey home. There was at that time another giant, named Far Rua—some say he was Irish and some say he was Scotch—but whether Scotch or Irish, sorrow doubt of it but he was a *targer*. No other giant of the day could stand before him;

and such was his strength that, when well vexed, he could
give a stamp that shook the country about him. The fame
and name of him went far and near, and nothing in the shape
of a man, it was said, had any chance with him in a fight.
Whether the story is true or not I cannot say, but the report
went that by one blow of his fist he flattened a thunderbolt,
and kept it in his pocket in the shape of a pancake to show
to all his enemies when they were about to fight him.
Undoubtedly he had given every giant in Ireland a considerable beating, barring Finn M'Coul himself; and he swore
that he would never rest night or day, winter or summer,
till he could serve Finn with the same sauce, if he could
catch him. Finn, however, had a strong disinclination to
meet a giant who could make a young earthquake or flatten
a thunderbolt when he was angry, so accordingly he kept
dodging about from place to place—not much to his credit
as a Trojan, to be sure—whenever he happened to get the
hard word that Far Rua was on the scent of him. And the
long and the short of it was that he heard Far Rua was
coming to the Causeway to have a trial of strength with him;
and he was, naturally enough, seized in consequence with
a very warm and sudden fit of affection for his wife, who
was delicate in her health, poor woman, and leading, besides,
a very lonely, uncomfortable life of it in his absence.

"God save all here," said Finn good-humouredly, putting
his honest face into his own door.

"Musha, Finn, avick, an' you're welcome to your own
Oonagh, you darlin' bully." Here followed a smack that
it is said to have made the waters of the lake curl, as it were,
with kindness and sympathy.

"Faith," said Finn, "beautiful; and how are you, Oonagh

—and how did you sport your figure during my absence, my bilberry?"

"Never a merrier—as bouncing a grass widow as ever there was in sweet 'Tyrone among the bushes.'"

Finn gave a short, good-humoured cough, and laughed most heartily to show her how much he was delighted that she made herself happy in his absence.

"An' what brought you home so soon, Finn?" said she.

WHY, avourneen," said Finn, putting in his answer in the proper way, "never the thing but the purest of love and affection for yourself. Sure, you know that's truth, anyhow, Oonagh."

Finn spent two or three happy days with Oonagh, and felt himself very comfortable considering the dread he had of Far Rua. This, however, grew upon him so much that his wife could not but perceive something lay on his mind which he kept altogether to himself. Let a woman alone in the meantime for ferreting or wheedling a secret out of her good man when she wishes. Finn was a proof of this.

"It's this Far Rua," said he, "that's troublin' me. When the fellow gets angry and begins to stamp he'll shake you a whole townland, and it's well known that he can stop a thunderbolt, for he always carries one about with him in the shape of a pancake to show to anyone that might misdoubt it."

As he spoke he clapped his thumb in his mouth, as he always did when he wanted to prophesy or to know anything.

"He's coming," said Finn; "I see him below at Dungannon."

"An' who is it, avick?"

"Far Rua," replied Finn, "and how to manage I don't know. If I run away I am disgraced, and I know that sooner or later I must meet him, for my thumb tells me so."

"When will he be here?" says she.

"To-morrow, about two o'clock," replied Finn with a groan.

"Don't be cast down," said Oonagh; "depend on me, and, maybe, I'll bring you out of this scrape better than ever you could bring yourself."

THIS quieted Finn's heart very much, for he knew that Oonagh was hand-and-glove with the fairies; and, indeed, to tell the truth, she was supposed to be a fairy herself. If she was, however, she must have been a kind-hearted one, for by all accounts she never did anything but good in the neighbourhood.

Now, it so happened that Oonagh had a sister named Granua living opposite to them, on the very top of Cullamore, which I have mentioned already, and this Granua was quite as powerful as herself. The beautiful valley that lies between the Granlisses is not more than three or four miles broad, so that of a summer evening Granua and Oonagh were able to hold many an agreeable conversation across it, from one hill-top to the other. Upon this occasion Oonagh resolved to consult her sister as to what was best to be done in the difficulty that surrounded them.

"Granua," said she, "are you at home?"

"No," said the other, "I'm picking bilberries at Althadhawan" (the Devil's Glen).

"Well," said Oonagh, "go up to the top of Cullamore, look about you, and then tell us what you see."

"Very well," replied Granua, after a few minutes; "I am there now."

"What do you see?" asked the other.

"Goodness be about us!" exclaimed Granua, "I see the biggest giant that ever was known coming up from Dungannon."

"Ay," said Oonagh, "there's our difficulty. That's Far Rua, and he's comin' up now to leather Finn. What's to be done?"

'LL call to him," she replied, "to come up to Cullamore and refresh himself, and maybe that will give you and Finn time to think of some plan to get yourselves out of the scrape. But," she proceeded, "I'm short of butter, having in the house only half a dozen firkins, and as I'm to have a few giants and giantesses to spend the evenin' with me I'd feel thankful, Oonagh, if you'd throw me up fifteen or sixteen tubs, or the largest miscaun you've got, and you'll oblige me very much."

"I'll do that with a heart and a half," replied Oonagh; "and, indeed, Granua, I feel myself under great obligations to you for your kindness in keeping him off us till we see what can be done; for what would become of us all if anything happened Finn, poor man!"

She accordingly got the largest miscaun of butter she had—which might be about the weight of a couple of dozen millstones, so that you can easily judge of its size—and calling up her sister, "Granua," says she, "are you ready?

I'm going to throw you up a miscaun, so be prepared to catch it."

" I will," said the other. " A good throw, now, and take care it does not fall short."

Oonagh threw it, but in consequence of her anxiety about Finn and Far Rua she forgot to say the charm that was to send it up, so that instead of reaching Cullamore, as she expected, it fell about half-way between the two hills at the edge of the Broad Bog, near Augher.

"MY curse upon you! " she exclaimed, "you've disgraced me. I now change you into a grey stone. Lie there as a testimony of what has happened, and may evil betide the first living man that will ever attempt to move or injure you! "

And, sure enough, there it lies to this day, with the mark of the four fingers and thumb imprinted on it, exactly as it came out of her hand.

" Never mind," said Granua, " I must only do the best I can with Far Rua. If all fail, I'll give him a cast of heather broth, or a panada of oak bark. But, above all things, think of some plan to get Finn out of the scrape he's in, or he's a lost man. You know you used to be sharp and ready-witted; and my own opinion is, Oonagh, that it will go hard with you, or you'll outdo Far Rua yet."

She then made a high smoke on the top of the hill, after which she put her finger in her mouth and gave three whistles, and by that Far Rua knew that he was invited to the top of Cullamore—for this was the way that the Irish long ago gave a sign to all strangers and travellers to let them know they are welcome to come and take share of whatever was going.

In the meantime Finn was very melancholy, and did not know what to do, or how to act at all. Far Rua was an ugly customer, no doubt, to meet with; and, moreover, the idea of the confounded "cake" aforesaid flattened the very heart within him. What chance could he have, strong and brave as he was, with a man who could, when put in a passion, walk the country into earthquakes and knock thunderbolts into pancakes? The thing was impossible, and Finn knew not on what hand to turn him. Right or left, backward or forward, where to go he could form no guess whatever.

ONAGH," said he, " can you do anything for me? Where's all your invention? Am I to be skivered like a rabbit before your eyes and to have my name disgraced for ever in the sight of all my tribe, and me the best man among them? How am I to fight this man-mountain —this huge cross between an earthquake and a thunderbolt— with a pancake in his pocket that was once——?"

"Be aisy, Finn," replied Oonagh. "Troth, I'm ashamed of you. Keep your toe in your pump, will you? Talking of pancakes, maybe we'll give him as good as any he brings with him—thunderbolts or otherwise. If I don't treat him to as smart feeding as he's got this many a day, don't trust Oonagh again. Leave him to me, and do just as I bid you."

This relieved Finn very much, for, after all, he had great confidence in his wife, knowing, as he did, that she had got him out of many a quandary before. The present, however, was the greatest of all; but, still, he began to get courage and to eat his victuals as usual. Oonagh then drew the nine woollen threads of different colours, which she always did to find out the best way of succeeding in anything of importance she went about. She then plaited them into three plaits, with three colours in each, putting one on her right arm, one round her heart, and the third round her right ankle, for then she knew that nothing could fail her that she undertook.

HAVING everything now prepared, she sent round to the neighbours and borrowed one-and-twenty iron griddles, which she took and kneaded into the hearts of one-and-twenty cakes of bread, and these she baked on the fire in the usual way, setting them aside in the cupboard according as they were done. She then put down a large pot of new milk, which she made into curds and whey, and gave Finn due instructions how to use the curds when Far Rua should come. Having done all this, she sat down quite contented waiting for his arrival on the next day about two o'clock, that being the hour at which he was expected—for Finn knew as much by the sucking of his thumb. Now, this was a curious property that Finn's thumb had; but notwithstanding all the wisdom and logic he used to suck out of it, it could never have stood to him here were it not for the wit of his wife. In this very thing, moreover, he was very much resembled by his great foe, Far Rua; for it was well known that the huge strength that he possessed all lay in the middle finger of his right hand, and that if he happened by any chance to lose it, he was no more, notwithstanding his bulk, than a common man.

At length the next day he was seen coming across the valley, and Oonagh knew that it was time to commence operations. She immediately made the cradle, and desired Finn to lie down in it and cover himself up with the clothes.

"You must pass for your own child," said she, "so just lie there snug and say nothing, but be guided by me." This, to be sure, was wormwood to Finn—I mean going into the cradle in such a cowardly manner—but he knew Oonagh very well; and finding that he had nothing else for it, with a very rueful face he gathered himself into it and lay snug, as she had desired him.

ABOUT two o'clock, as he had been expected, Far Rua came in. "God save all here!" said he. "Is this where the great Finn M'Coul lives?"

"Indeed it is, honest man," replied Oonagh. "God save you kindly— won't you be sitting?"

"Thank you, ma'am," says he, sitting down. "You're Mrs. M'Coul, I suppose?"

"I am," says she, "and I have no reason, I hope, to be ashamed of my husband."

"No," said the other; "he has the name of being the strongest and bravest man in Ireland. But, for all that, there's a man not far from you that's very anxious of taking a shake with him. Is he at home?"

"Why, no, then," she replied; "and if ever a man left in a fury he did. It appears that someone told him of a big bosthoon of a giant called Far Rua being down at the Causeway to look for him, and so he set out there to try if he could catch him. Troth, I hope, for the poor giant's sake, he won't meet with him, for if he does Finn will make paste of him at once."

"Well," said the other, "I am Far Rua, and I have been seeking him these twelve minths, but he always kept clear of me; and I will never rest day or night till I lay my hands on him."

At this Oonagh set up a loud laugh of great contempt, by the way, and looked at him as if he were only a mere handful of a man.

"Did you ever see Finn?" said she, changing her manner all at once.

"How could I?" said he. "He always took care to keep his distance."

"I THOUGHT so," she replied. "I judged as much; and if you take my advice, you poor-looking creature, you'll pray night and day that you may never see him, for I tell you it will be a black day for you when you do. But, in the meantime, you perceive that the wind's on the door, and as Finn himself is far from home, maybe you'd be civil enough to turn the house, for it's always what Finn does when he's here."

This was a startler, even to Far Rua; but he got up, however, and after pulling the middle finger of his right hand until it cracked three times, he went outside, and getting his arms about the house, completely turned it as she had wished. When Finn saw this he felt a certain description of moisture, which shall be nameless, oozing out through every pore of his skin; but Oonagh, depending upon her woman's wit, felt not a whit daunted.

"Arrah, then," said she, "as you're so civil, maybe you'd do another obliging turn for us, as Finn's not here to do it himself. You see, after this long stretch of dry weather that we've had, we feel very badly off for want of water. Now, Finn says there's a fine spring well somewhere under the rocks behind the hill there below, and it was his intention to pull them asunder; but having heard of you he left the place in such a fury that he never thought of it. Now, if you try to find it, troth, I'd feel it a kindness."

HE then brought Far Rua down to see the place, which was then all one solid rock; and after looking at it for some time, he cracked his right middle finger nine times, and, stooping down, tore a cleft about four hundred feet deep and a quarter of a mile in length, which has since been christened by the name of Lumford's Glen. This feat nearly threw Oonagh herself off her guard; but what won't a woman's sagacity and presence of mind accomplish?

"You'll now come in," said she, "and eat a bit of such humble fare as we can give. Finn, even though you and he were enemies, would scorn not to treat you kindly in his own house; and, indeed, if I didn't do it even in his absence, he would not be pleased with me."

She accordingly brought him in, and placing half a dozen of the cakes we spoke of before him, together with a can or two of butter, a side of boiled bacon, and a stack of cabbage, she desired him to help himself—for this, be it known, was long before the invention of potatoes. Far Rua, who, by the way, was a glutton as well as a hero, put one of the cakes

in his mouth to take a huge whack out of it, when both Finn
and Oonagh were stunned with a noise that resembled something between a growl and a yell. "Blood and fury!" he
shouted out. "How is this? Here are two of my teeth
out! What kind of bread is this you gave me?"

"What's the matter?" said Oonagh coolly.

"Matter!" shouted the other. "Why, here are two of
the best teeth in my head gone."

"Why," said she, "that's Finn's bread—the only bread
he ever eats when at home; but, indeed, I forgot to tell you
that nobody can eat it but himself and that child in the cradle
there. I thought, however, that as you were reported to be
rather a stout little fellow of your size you might be able to
manage it, and I did not wish to affront a man that thinks
himself able to fight Finn. Here's another cake—maybe
it's not so hard as that."

AR RUA, at the moment, was not only
hungry, but ravenous, so he accordingly
made a fresh set at the second cake, and
immediately another yell was heard
twice as loud as the first. "Thunder
and giblets!" he roared, "take your
bread out of this, or I will not have a
tooth in my head; there's another pair
of them gone."

"Well, honest man," replied Oonagh, "if you're not able
to eat the bread say so quietly, and don't be awakening the
child in the cradle there. There, now, he's awake upon me!"

Finn now gave a skirl that frightened the giant, as coming
from such a youngster as he was represented to be.
"Mother," said he, "I'm hungry—get me something to eat."

Oonagh went over, and putting into his hand a cake *that had no griddle in it*—Finn, whose appetite in the meantime was sharpened by what he saw going forward, soon made it disappear. Far Rua was thunderstruck, and secretly thanked his stars that he had the good fortune to miss meeting Finn, for, as he said to himself, I'd have no chance with a man who could eat such bread as that, which even his son that's in the cradle can munch before my eyes.

" I'd like to take a glimpse at the lad in the cradle," said he to Oonagh, " for I can tell you that the infant who can manage that nutriment is no joke to look at or to feed of a scarce summer."

" With all the veins of my heart," replied Oonagh.   " Get up, acushla, and show this decent little man something that won't be unworthy of your father, Finn M'Coul."

FINN, who was dressed for the occasion as much like a boy as possible, got up, and bringing Far Rua out, " Are you strong ? " said he.

" Thunder and ounze ! " exclaimed the other, " what a voice in so small a chap ! "

" Are you strong? " said Finn again. " Are you able to squeeze water out of that white stone? " he asked, putting one into Far Rua's hand. The latter squeezed and squeezed the stone, but to no purpose; he might pull the rocks of Lumford's Glen asunder, and flatten a thunderbolt, but to squeeze water out of a white stone was beyond his strength. Finn eyed him with great contempt as he kept straining and squeezing and squeezing and straining till he got black in the face with the efforts.

"Ah, you're a poor creature," said Finn. "You a giant! Give me the stone here, and when I'll show what Finn's little son can do you may then judge of what my daddy himself is."

Finn then took the stone, and then, slyly exchanging it for the curds, he squeezed the latter until the whey, as clear as water, oozed out in a little shower from his hand.

"I'll now go in," said he, "to my cradle; for I scorn to lose my time with anyone that's not able to eat my daddy's bread, or squeeze water out of a stone. Bedad, you had better be off out of this before he comes back, for if he catches you, it's in flummery he'd have you in two minutes."

AR RUA, seeing what he had seen, was of the same opinion himself; his knees knocked together with the terror of Finn's return, and he accordingly hastened in to bid Oonagh farewell, and to assure her that, from that day out, he never wished to hear of, much less to see, her husband. "I admit fairly that I'm not a match for him," said he, "strong as I am. Tell him I will avoid him as I would the plague, and that I will make myself scarce in this part of the country while I live."

Finn, in the meantime, had gone into the cradle, where he lay very quietly, his heart in his mouth with delight that Far Rua was about to take his departure without discovering the tricks that been played off on him.

"It's well for you," said Oonagh, "that he doesn't happen to be here, for it's nothing but hawk's meat he'd make of you."

"I know that," said Far Rua, "divel a thing else he'd make of me; but, before I go, will you let me feel what kind of teeth they are that can eat griddle-cakes like *that*?" and he pointed to it as he spoke.

"With all the pleasure in life," says she; "only as they're far back in his head you must put your finger a good way in.'

Far Rua was surprised to find so powerful a set of grinders in one so young; but he was still much more so on finding, when he took his hand from Finn's mouth, that he had left the very finger upon which his whole strength depended behind him. He gave one loud groan and fell down at once with terror and weakness. This was all Finn wanted, who now knew that his most powerful and bitterest enemy was completely at his mercy. He instantly started out of the cradle, and in a few minutes the great Far Rua, that was for such a length of time the terror of him and all his followers, was no more.

WILLIAM CARLETON.

The Ninepenny Fidil

Y father and mother
were Irish
And I am Irish
too;
I bought a wee fidil
for ninepence
And that is Irish
too;

I'm up in the morning early
To meet the break of day,
And to the lintwhite's piping
The many's the tunes I play!

One pleasant eve in June-time
I met a lochrie man,
His face and hands were weazen,
His height was not a span.
He boor'd me for my fidil—
"You know," says he, "like you,
"My father and mother were Irish,
"And I am Irish too!"

He took my wee red fidil,
And such a tune he turned,
The Glaisé in it whispered
The Lionan in it m'urned;

149

Says he, "My lad, you're lucky,
  "I wisht I was like you,
"You're lucky in your birth-star,
  "And in your fidil too!"

He gave me back my fidil,
  My fidil-stick also,
And stepping like a May-boy,
  He jumped the Lear-gaidh-knowe.
I never saw him after,
  Nor met his gentle kind,
But whiles I think I hear him,
  A-wheening in the wind!

JOSEPH CAMPBELL.

The festivities at the house of Conan of Ceann Sleibhe

"WIN victory and blessings, O Fionn," said Conan, "and tell me who was the man that, having only one leg, one arm, and one eye, escaped from you in consequence of his swiftness, and outstripped the Fenians of Eire, and why is this proverb used, 'As Roc came to the house of Fionn'?"

"I will tell you that," said Fionn. "One day the chief of the Fenians and I went to Teamhair Luachra, and we took nothing in the chase that same day but one fawn. When it had been cooked it was fetched to me for the purpose of dividing it. I gave a portion of it to each of the Fenian chiefs, and there remained none for my own share but a haunch bone. Gobha Gaoithe, son of Ronan, presented

himself, and requested me to give him the haunch. I accordingly gave it to him. He then declared that I gave him that
portion on account of his swiftness of foot : and he went
out on the plain, but he had only gone a short distance when
Caoilte, son of Ronan, his own brother, overtook him, and
brought the haunch back again to me, and we had no further
dispute about the matter. We had not been long so when
we saw a huge, obnoxious, massy-boned, black, detestable
giant, having only one eye, one arm, and one leg, hop forward
towards us. He saluted us. I returned the salutation, and
asked him whence he came. 'I am come by the powers of
the agility of my arm and leg,' responded he, 'having heard
there is not one man in the world more liberal in bestowing
gifts than you, O Fionn; therefore, I am come to solicit wealth
and valuable gifts from you.' I replied that were all the
wealth of the world mine I would give him neither little
nor much. He then declared 'they were all liars who
asserted that I never gave a refusal to any person.' I replied
that if he were a man I would not give him a refusal. 'Well,
then,' said the giant, 'let me have that haunch you have in
your hand, and I will say good-bye to the Fenians, provided
that you allow me the length of the haunch as a distance, and
that I am not seized upon until I make my first hop.' Upon
hearing this I gave the haunch into the giant's hand, and
he hopped over the lofty stockades of the town; he then
made use of the utmost swiftness of his one leg to outstrip
all the rest of the Fenians. When the Fenian chiefs saw
that, they started in pursuit of the giant, while I and the
band of minstrels of the town went to the top of the dun to
watch their proceedings. When I saw that the giant had
outstripped them a considerable distance, I put on my run-

ning habiliments, and, taking no weapon but Mac an Loin
in my hand, I started after the others. I overtook the hind-
most division on Sliabh an Righ, the middle (next) division
at Limerick, and the chiefs of the Fenians at Ath Bo, which
is called Ath-Luain (Athlone), and those first in the pursuit
at Rinn-an-Ruaigh, to the right-hand side of Cruachan of
Connacht, where he (the giant) was distant less than a
javelin's cast from me. The giant passed on before me and
crossed Eas Roe (now Ballyshannon), of the son of Mod-
huirn, without wetting his foot. I leaped over it after him.
He then directed his course towards the estuary of Binn-
Edair, keeping the circuit of Eire to his right hand. The
giant leaped over the estuary, and it was a leap similar to
flight over the sea. I sprang after him, and having caught
him by the small of the back, laid him prostrate on the earth.
'You have dealt unjustly by me, O Fionn,' cried the giant;
'for it was not with you I arranged the combat, but with
the Fenians.' I replied that the Fenians were not perfect,
except I myself were with them. We had not remained long
thus when Liagan Luaimneach, from Luachar Deaghaidh,
came to us. He was followed by Caoilte Mac Ronan,
together with the swiftest of the Fenians. Each of them
couched his javelin, intending to drive it through the giant
and kill him in my arms, but I protected him from their
attacks. Soon after this the main body of the Fenians
arrived; they enquired what was the cause of the delay that
the giant had not been slain. 'That is bad counsel,' said
the giant, 'for a better man than I am would be slain in
my eric.' We bound the giant strongly on that occasion;
and soon after Bran Beag O'Buadhchan came to invite me
to a feast, and all the Fenians of Eire, who had been present,

accompanied him to his house. The banqueting hall had
been prepared for our reception at that time, and the giant
was dragged into the middle of the house, and was there
placed in the sight of all present. They asked him who
he was. 'Roc, son of Diocan, is my name,' replied he, 'that
is, I am son to the Legislator of Aengus of the Brugh in
the south. My betrothed poured a current of surprising
affection and a torrent of deep love upon Sgiath Breac, son
of Dathcaoin yonder, who is your foster son, O Fionn; it
hurt my feelings severely to hear her boast of the swiftness
and bravery of her lover in particular, and of the Fenians
in general, and I declared that I would challenge him and
all the Fenians of Eire to run a race with me; but she sneered
at me. I then went to my beloved friend, Aengus of the
Brugh, to bemoan my fate; and he metamorphosed me thus,
and bestowed on me the swiftness of a druidical wind, as
you have seen. This is my history for you; and you ought
to be well satisfied with all the hurt and injury you have
inflicted upon me already.'

HEN I repented me of the indignity put
upon the giant, and I released him from
his bonds and I bade Liagan Luaimneach companion him to the presence
of his betrothed one and testify to her
on my behalf of his prowess in the race,
wherein he had outstripped all the
Fenians of Eire, save only myself. So the two went forth
together in friendly amity, and Roc, for the champion feat
reported of him by Liagan Luaimneach, recovered the affection of his betrothed, and straightway took her to wife.
From that adventure, indeed, arose the proverb, 'As Roc

came to the House of Fionn,' and so that is the answer to your question, O Conan," said Fionn.

"Win victory and blessings, O Fenian King," said Conan; "it is with clear memory and sweet words you relate these things. Tell me now the meaning of the byword, 'The hospitality of Fionn in the house of Cuanna.'"

"I will tell you the truth concerning that, O Conan," said Fionn. "Oisin, Caoilte, Mac Lughaidh, Diarmuid O'Duibhne, and myself happened one day, above all other days, to be on the summit of Cairn Feargall. We were accompanied by our five hounds, namely, Bran, Sceoluing, Sear Dubh, Luath Luachar, and Anuaill. We had not long been there when we perceived a rough, tall, huge giant approaching us. He carried an iron fork upon his back, and a grunting hog was placed between the prongs of the fork; a young girl of mature age followed and forced the giant on his way before her. 'Let someone go forward and accost those people,' said I. Diarmuid O'Duibhne followed, but did not overtake them. The other three and I started up, and followed Diarmuid and the giant. We overtook Diarmuid, but did not come up with the giant or the girl; for a dark, gloomy, druidical mist showered down between us and them, so that we could not discern what road they took. When the mist cleared away we looked around us, and discovered a light-roofed, comfortable-looking house at the edge of the ford near at hand. We proceeded to the house, before which spread a lawn upon which were two fountains. At the brink of one fountain lay a rude iron vessel, and a vessel of bronze at the brink of the other. Those we met in the house were an aged, hoary-headed man standing by the door jamb to the right hand, and a beautiful maid sitting before him; a rough, rude, huge giant before the fire busily cooking a hog; and an old man at the other side of the fire, having an iron-grey head of hair and twelve eyes in his head, while the twelve sons (germs) of discord beamed in each eye. There was also in the house a ram with a white belly, a jet-black head, dark-green horns, and green feet; and there was in the end of the house a hag covered with a dark ash-coloured garment. There were no persons in the house except these. The man at the door-post welcomed us; and we five, having our five hounds with us, sat on the floor of the bruighean. 'Let submissive homage be done to Fionn Mac Cumhaill and his people,' said the man at the door-post. 'My case is that of a man begging a request, but obtaining neither the smaller nor the greater part of it,' said the giant. Nevertheless, he rose up and did respectful homage to us. After a while I became suddenly thirsty, and no person present perceived it but Caoilte, who began to complain bitterly on that account. 'You have no cause to complain, Caoilte,' said the man of the door-post, 'but only to step outside and fetch a drink for Fionn from whichever of the fountains you please.' Caoilte did so, and fetched the bronze vessel brimful to me and gave me to drink. I took a drink from it, and the water tasted like honey while I was drinking, but bitter as gall when I put the vessel from my lips; so that darting pains and symptoms of death seized me and agonising pangs from the poisonous draught. I could be but with difficulty recognised; and the lamentation of Caoilte on account of my being in that condition was greater than that he had before given vent to on account of my thirst. The man at the door-post desired Caoilte to go out and bring me a drink from the other fountain. Caoilte obeyed, and

brought me the iron vessel brimful. I never underwent so
much hardship in battle or conflict as I then suffered while
drinking, in consequence of the bitterness of the draught;
but as soon as I put the vessel from my lips I recovered
my own colour and appearance, and that gave joy and happiness to my people.

"The man then asked if the hog which was in the boiler
was yet cooked. 'It is cooked,' replied the giant, 'and allow
me to divide it.' 'How will you divide it?' said the man
of the house. 'I will give one hindquarter to Fionn and
his hounds; the other hindquarter to Fionn's four men; the
forepart to myself; the chine and rump to the old man who
sits at the opposite side of the fire and to the hag in yonder
corner; and the giblets to you and the young woman who
is opposite to you.' 'I pledge my word,' said the man of
the house, 'you have divided it very fairly.' 'I pledge my
word,' exclaimed the ram, 'that the division is very unfair
so far as I am concerned, for I have been altogether forgotten.'
And so saying, he immediately snatched the quarter that lay
before my four men, and carried it away into a corner, where
he began to devour it. The four men instantly attacked
the ram all at once with their swords, but though they laid
on violently, it did not affect him in the least, and the blows
fell away as from a stone or rock, so that they were forced
to resume their seats. 'Upon my veracity, he is doomed
for evil who owns as companions such four fellows as you
are, who tamely suffer one single sheep to carry away your
food and devour it before your faces,' exclaimed the man
with the twelve eyes; and at the same time going up to the
ram, he caught him by the feet and gave him a violent pitch
out of the door, so that he fell on his back on the ground;

and from that time we saw him no more. Soon after this the hag started up, and having thrown her ashy-grey coverlet over my four men, metamorphosed them into four withered, drooping-headed old men. When I saw that I was seized with great fear and alarm; and when the man at the door-post perceived this, he desired me to come over to him, place my head on his bosom, and sleep. I did so; and the hag got up and took her coverlet off my four men; and when I awoke I found them restored to their own shape, and that was a great happiness to me. 'O Fionn,' asked the man of the door-post, 'do you feel surprised at the appearance and arrangements of this house?' I assured him that I never saw anything which surprised me more. 'Well, then, I will explain the meaning of all these things to you,' said the man. 'The giant carrying the grunting hog between the prongs of the iron fork, whom you first saw, is he who is yonder, and his name is SLOTH. She who is close to me is the young woman who had been forcing him along, that is ENERGY; and ENERGY compels SLOTH forward with her; for ENERGY moves, in the twinkling of the eye, a greater distance than the foot can travel in a year. The old man of the bright eyes yonder signifies the WORLD; and he is more powerful than anyone, which has been proved by his rendering the ram powerless. That ram which you saw signifies the CRIMES of the man. That hag there beyond is withering OLD AGE, and her clothing has withered your four men. The two wells from which you drank the two draughts mean FALSEHOOD and TRUTH; for while telling a lie one finds it sweet, but it becomes bitter at the last. Cuanna from Innistuil is my own name. I do not reside here, but having conceived a wonderful love for you, O Fionn, on account of your superiority in wisdom and general celebrity, I therefore put those things into the way before you in order that I might see you. And this story shall be called, to the end of the world, the Hospitality of Cuanna's House to Fionn. Let you and your men come together, and do ye five sleep until morning.' Accordingly we did so, and when we awoke in the morning we found ourselves on the summit of Cairn Feargaill, with our hounds and arms by us. So there is the meaning of the byword, 'The hospitality of Fionn in the house of Cuanna,' O Conan," said Fionn.

(Translated from the Irish by Nicholas O'Kearney.)

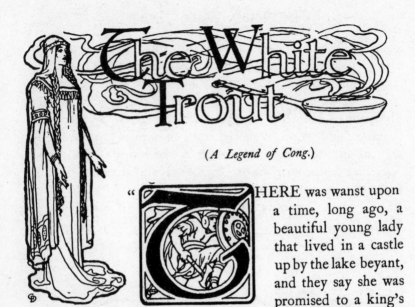

The White Trout

(A Legend of Cong.)

"THERE was wanst upon a time, long ago, a beautiful young lady that lived in a castle up by the lake beyant, and they say she was promised to a king's son, and they wor to be married, when, all of a suddent, he was murthered, the crathur (Lord help us!) and threwn in the lake abou, and so, of coorse, he couldn't keep his promise to the fair lady—and more's the pity.

"Well, the story goes that she went out iv her mind, bekase of loosin' the king's son—for she was tindher-hearted, God help her! like the rest iv us—and pined away after him, until at last no one about seen her, good or bad; and the story wint that the fairies took her away.

"Well, sir, in coorse o' time the white throut, God bless it! was seen in the sthrame beyant; and sure the people didn't know what to think of the crathur, seein' as how a *white* brown throut was never heerd av afore nor sence; and years upon years the throut was there, just where you seen it this blessed minit, longer nor I can tell—aye, throth, and beyant the memory o' th' ouldest in the village.

160

"At last the people began to think it must be a fairy; for what else could it be?—and no hurt nor harm was iver put an the throut, until some wicked sinners of sojers kem to these parts, and laughed at all the people, and gibed and jeered them for thinkin' o' the likes; and one o' them in partic'lar (bad luck to him—God forgi' me for sayin' it!) swore he'd catch the throut and ate it for his dinner—the blackguard!

"WELL, what would you think o' the villiany of the sojer?—sure enough he cotch the throut, and away wid him home, and puts an the fryin' pan, and into it he pitches the purty little thing. The throut squeeled all as one as a Christian crathur, and, my dear, you'd think the sojer id split his sides laughin'—for he was a harden'd villian; and when he thought one side was done, he turns it over to fry the other; and what would you think? but the divil a taste of a burn was an it at all at all; and sure the sojer thought it was a *quare* throut that couldn't be briled; 'but,' says he, 'I'll give it another turn by and by'—little thinkin' what was in store for him, the haythen!

"Well, when he thought that side was done he turns it again—and lo and behould you, the divil a taste more done that side was nor the other. 'Bad luck to me,' says the sojer, 'but that bates the world,' says he; 'but I'll thry you agin, my darlint,' says he, 'as cunnin' as you think yourself'— and so with that he turns it over and over, but not a sign av the fire was an the purty throut. 'Well,' says the desperate villian—(for sure, sir, only he was a desperate villian *entirely*; he might know he was doin' a wrong thing, seein' that all his endayvours was no good)—'well,' says he, 'my jolly little throut, maybe you're fried enough, though you don't seem over well dress'd; but you may be better than you look, like a singed cat, and a tit-bit, afther all,' says he; and with that he ups with his knife and fork to taste a piece o' the throut—but, my jew'l, the minit he puts his knife into the fish there was a murtherin' screech, that you'd think the life id lave you if you heerd it, and away jumps the throut out av the fryin' pan into the middle o' the flure; and an the spot where it fell up riz a lovely lady—the beautifullest young crathur that eyes ever seen, dressed in white, and a band o' goold in her hair, and a sthrame o' blood runnin' down her arm.

" ' OOK where you cut me, you villian,' says she, and she held out her arm to him—and, my dear, he thought the sight id lave his eyes.

" ' Couldn't you lave me cool and comfortable in the river where you snared me, and not disturb me in my duty? ' says she.

" Well, he thrimbled like a dog in a wet sack, and at last he stammered out somethin', and begged for his life, and ax'd her ladyship's pardin, and said he didn't know she was an duty, or he was too good a sojer not to know betther nor to meddle with her.

" ' I *was* on duty then,' says the lady; 'I was watchin' for my thrue love that is comin' by wather to me,' says she; ' an' if he comes while I am away, an' that I miss iv him, I'll turn you into a pinkeen, and I'll hunt you up and down for evermore, while grass grows or wather runs.'

"Well, the sojer thought the life id lave him at the thoughts iv his bein' turned into a pinkeen, and begged for marcy; and, with that, says the lady:

"'Renounce your evil coorses,' says she, 'you villian, or you'll repint it too late. Be a good man for the futhur, and go to your duty reg'lar. And now,' says she, 'take me back and put me into the river agin, where you found me.'

"'Oh, my lady,' says the sojer, 'how could I have the heart to drownd a beautiful lady like you?'

"BUT before he could say another word the lady was vanished, and there he saw the little throut an the ground. Well, he put it in a clane plate, and away he run for the bare life, for fear her lover would come while she was away; and he run, and he run, ever till he came to the cave agin, and threw the throut into the river. The minit he did, the wather was as red as blood until the sthrame washed the stain away; and to this day there's a little red mark an the throut's side where it was cut.

"Well, sir, from that day out the sojer was an althered man, and reformed his ways, and wint to his duty reg'lar, and fasted three times a week—though it was never fish he tuk an fastin' days; for afther the fright he got fish id never rest an his stomach—savin' your presence. But, anyhow, he was an althered man, as I said before; and in coorse o' time he left the army, and turned hermit at last; and they say he *used to pray evermore for the sowl of the White Throut.*"

SAMUEL LOVER.

The wonderful Cake

 MOUSE, a rat, and a little red hen once lived together in the same cottage, and one day the little red hen said, "Let us bake a cake and have a feast." "Let us," says the mouse, and "let us," says the rat. "Who'll go and get the wheat ground?" says the hen. "I won't," says the mouse; "I won't," says the rat. "I will myself," says the little red hen.

"Who'll make the cake?" "I won't," says the mouse; "I will," says the rat. "Indeed, you shall not," says the little red hen.

Well, while the hen was stretching her hand out for it—"Hey Presto!" out rolled the cake from the cottage, and

164

after it ran the mouse, the rat, and the little red hen.

When it was running away it went by a barn full of threshers, and they asked it where it was running. "Oh," says it, " I'm running away from the mouse, the rat, and the little red hen, and from you, too, if I can." So they rushed away after it with their flails, and it ran, and it ran till it came to a ditch full of ditchers, and they asked it where it was running.

H, I am running away from the mouse, the rat, and the little red hen, and from a barn full of threshers, and from you, too, if I can."

Well, they all ran after it along with the rest, till it came to a well full of washers, and they asked the same question, and it returned the same answer, and after it they went.

At last it came to a ford where it met with a fox, and he asked where it was running. " Oh, I'm running away from the mouse, the rat, and the little red hen, from a barn full of threshers, a ditch full of ditchers, a well full of washers, and from you, too, if I can."

" But you can't cross the ford," says the fox. " And can't you carry me over?" says the cake. " What'll you give me?" says the fox. " A kiss at Christmas and an egg at Easter," says the cake.

" Very well," says the fox—"up with you." So he sat on his haunches with his nose in the air, and the cake got up by his tail till it sat on his crupper.

" Now, over with you," says the cake. " You're not high enough," says the fox. Then it scrambled up on his shoulder. " Up higher still," says he; "you wouldn't be safe there." "Am I right now?" says he. "You'll be safer on the ridge pole of my nose."

"Well," says the cake, "I think I can go no further. "Oh, yes," says he, and he shot it up in the air, caught it in his mouth, and sent it down the Red Lane. And that was the end of the cake.

The legend of the little Weaver of Duleek Gate

(*A Tale of Chivalry.*)

YOU see, there was a waiver lived wanst upon a time in Duleek here, hard by the gate, and a very honest, industherous man he was by all accounts. Well, it was one mornin' that his housekeeper called to him, and he sitting very busy throwin' the shuttle; and says she, "Your brekquest is ready!" "Lave me alone," says he; "I'm busy with a patthern here that is brakin' my heart, and until I complate and masther it intirely I won't quit."

"Oh, think o' the iligant stirabout that'll be spylte intirely."

"To the divil with the stirabout!" says he.

"God forgive you," says she, "for cursin' your good brekquest."

Well, he left the loom at last and wint over to the stirabout, and what would you think, but whin he looked at it, it was as black as a crow; for, you see, it was in the hoighth o' summer, and the flies lit upon it to that degree that the stirabout was fairly covered with them.

WHY, thin, bad luck to your impidence," says the waiver; "would no place sarve you but that? And is it spyling my brekquest yiz are, you dirty bastes?" And with that, bein' altogether cruked tempered at the time, he lifted his hand, and he made one great slam at the dish o' stirabout and killed no less than three score and tin flies at the one blow. It was three score and tin exactly, for he counted the carcasses one by one, and laid them out on a clane plate for to view them.

Well, he felt a powerful sperit risin' in him when he seen the slaughter he done at one blow, and with that he got as consaited as the very dickens, and not a sthroke more work he'd do that day, but out he wint, and was fractious and impident to everyone he met, and was squarein' up into their faces and sayin', "Look at that fist! That's the fist that killed three score and tin at one blow. Whoo! It is throwin' away my time I have been all my life," says he, "stuck to my loom, nothin' but a poor waiver, when it is Saint George or the Dhraggin I ought to be, which is two of the sivin champions o' Christendom. I'm determined on it, and I'll set off immediately and be a knight arriant."

Well, sure enough, he wint about among his neighbours the

next day, and he got an owld kittle from one and a saucepan from another, and he took them to the tailor, and he sewed him up a shuit o' tin clothes like any knight arriant, and he borrowed a pot lid, and *that* he was very partic'lar about, bekase it was his shield, and he wint to a friend o' his, a painther and glaizier, and made him paint an his shield in big letthers:

> "I'M THE MAN OF ALL MIN,
> THAT KILL'D THREE SCORE AND TIN
> AT A BLOW."

"When the people sees that," says the waiver to himself, "the sorra one will dar for to come near me."

AND with that he towld the housekeeper to scour out the small iron pot for him, "for," says he, "it will make an iligant helmet." And when it was done he put it an his head, and says she, "Is it puttin' a great heavy iron pot an your head you are by way iv a hat?"

"Sartinly," says he, "for a knight arriant should always have a woight an his brain."

"But," says she, "there's a hole in it, and it can't keep out the weather."

"It will be the cooler," says he, puttin' it an him; "besides, if I don't like it, it is aisy to stop it with a wisp o' sthraw, or the like o' that."

"The three legs of it looks mighty quare stickin' up," says she.

"Every helmet has a spike stickin' out o' the top of it," says the waiver, "and if mine has three, it's only the grandher it is."

"Well," says the housekeeper, getting bitther at last, "all I can say is, it isn't the first sheep's head was dhress'd in it."

"Your sarvint, ma'am," says he; and off he set.

Well, he was in want of a horse, and so he wint to a field hard by where the miller's horse was grazin' that used to carry the ground corn round the counthry.

"This is the idintical horse for me," says the waiver. "He is used to carryin' flour and male; and what am I but the flower o' shovelry in a coat o' mail; so that the horse won't be put out iv his way in the laste."

BUT as he was ridin' him out o' the field, who should see him but the miller. "Is it stalin' my horse you are, honest man?" says the miller.

"No," says the waiver; "I'm only goin' to axercise him," says he, "in the cool o' the evenin'; it will be good for his health."

"Thank you kindly," says the miller, "but lave him where he is, and you'll obleege me."

"I can't afford it," says the waiver, runnin' the horse at the ditch.

"Bad luck to your impidence," says the miller; "you've as much tin about you as a thravellin' tinker, but you've more brass. Come back here, you vagabone," says he.

But he was too late—away galloped the waiver, and took the road to Dublin, for he thought the best thing he could do was to go to the King o' Dublin (for Dublin was a grate place thin, and had a king iv its own), and he thought maybe the King o' Dublin would give him work. Well, he was four days goin' to Dublin, for the baste was not the best,

and the roads worse, not all as one as now; but there was
no turnpikes then, glory be to God! Whin he got to Dublin
he wint sthrait to the palace, and whin he got into the coort-
yard he let his horse go and graze about the place, for the
grass was growin' out betune the stones; everything was
flourishin' thin in Dublin, you see. Well, the King was
lookin' out of his dhrawin'-room windy for divarshin, whin
the waiver kem in; but the waiver pretended not to see him,
and he wint over to a stone sate undher the windy—for, you
see, there was stone sates all around about the place for the
accommodation o' the people—for the King was a dacent,
obleegin' man. Well, as I said, the waiver wint over and
lay down an one o' the sates, just undher the King's windy,
and purtended to go asleep; but he took care to turn out
the front of his shield that had the letthers an it. Well,
my dear, with that the King calls out to one of the lords
of his coort that was standin' behind him howldin' up the
skirt of his coat, according to rayson, and says he, "Look
here," says he, "what do you think of a vagabone like that
comin' undher my very nose to go sleep? It is thrue I'm
a good King," says he, "and I 'commodate the people by
havin' sates for them to sit down and enjoy the raycreation and
contimplation of seein' me here lookin' out o' my dhrawin'-
room windy for divarshin; but that is no rayson they are
to make a hotel o' the place and come and sleep here. Who
is it at all?" says the King.

"Not a one o' me knows, plaze your majesty."

"I think he must be a furriner," says the King, "bekase
his dhress is outlandish."

"And doesn't know manners, more betoken," says the
lord.

"I'll go down and circumspect him myself," says the King.
"Folly me," says he to the lord, wavin' his hand at the same
time in the most dignacious manner.

Down he wint accordingly, followed by the lord; and whin
he wint over to where the waiver was lying, sure, the first
thing he seen was his shield with the big letthers an it, and
with that, says he to the lord, "By dad," says he, "this is
the very man I want."

"For what, plaze your majesty?" says the lord.

"O kill that vagabone dhraggin, to be
sure," says the King.

"Sure, do you think he could kill
him," says the lord, "whin all the
stoutest knights in the land wasn't
aiquil to it, but never kem back, and
was ate up alive by the cruel desaiver."

"Sure, don't you see there," says the King, pointin' at
the shield, "that he killed three score and tin at one blow;
and the man that done that, I think, is a match for anything."

So, with that, he wint over to the waiver and shuck him
by the shouldher for to wake him, and the waiver rubbed
his eyes as if just wakened, and the King says to him, "God
save you!" said he.

"God save you kindly!" says the waiver, purtendin' he
was quite onknowst who he was spakin' to.

"Do you know who I am," says the King, "that you
make so free, good man?"

"No, indeed," says the waiver; "you have the advantage
o' me."

"To be sure I have," says the King, moighty high; "sure,
ain't I the King o' Dublin?" says he.

The Legend of the little
Weaver of Duleek Gate

The waiver dhropped down on his two knees forninst the King, and says he, "I beg God's pardon and yours for the liberty I tuk; plaze your holiness, I hope you'll excuse it."

"No offince," says the King; "get up, good man. And what brings you here?" says he.

"I'm in want o' work, plaze your riverence," says the waiver.

"Well, suppose I give you work?" says the King.

"I'll be proud to sarve you, my lord," says the waiver.

"Very well," says the King. "You killed three score and tin at one blow, I understan'," says the King.

"Yis," says the waiver; "that was the last thrifle o' work I done, and I'm afeared my hand 'ill go out o' practice if I don't get some job to do at wanst."

"YOU shall have a job immediantly," says the King. "It is not three score and tin, or any fine thing like that; it is only a blaguard dhraggin that is disturbin' the counthry and ruinatin' my tinanthry wid aitin' their powlthry, and I'm lost for want of eggs," says the King.

"Throth, thin, plaze your worship," says the waiver, "you look as yellow as if you swallowed twelve yolks this minit."

"Well, I want this dhraggin to be killed," says the King. "It will be no throuble in life to you; and I'm only sorry that it isn't betther worth your while, for he isn't worth fearin' at all; only I must tell you that he lives in the county Galway, in the middle of a bog, and he has an advantage in that."

"Oh, I don't value it in the laste," says the waiver; "for

the last three score and tin I killed was in a soft place."

"When will you undhertake the job then?" says the King.

"Let me at him at wanst," says the waiver.

"That's what I like," says the King; "you're the very man for my money," says he.

"Talkin' of money," says the waiver, "by the same token, I'll want a thrifle o' change from you for my thravellin' charges."

"AS much as you plaze," says the King; and with the word he brought him into his closet, where there was an owld stockin' in an oak chest burstin' wid goolden guineas.

"Take as many as you plaze," says the King; and sure enough, my dear, the little waiver stuffed his tin clothes as full as they could howld with them.

"Now, I'm ready for the road," says the waiver.

"Very well," says the King; "but you must have a fresh horse," says he.

"With all my heart," says the waiver, who thought he might as well exchange the miller's owld garron for a betther.

And, maybe, it's wondherin' you are that the waiver would think of goin' to fight the dhraggin afther what he heerd about him when he was purtendin' to be asleep. But he had no sitch notion: all he intended was—to fob the goold and ride back again to Duleek with his gains and a good horse. But, you see, cute as the waiver was, the King was cuter still; for these high quolity, you see, is great desaivers; and so the horse the waiver was put an was learned an

purpose; and, sure, the minit he was mounted away pow-
dhered the horse, and the divil a toe he'd go but right down
to Galway. Well, for four days he was goin' evermore,
until at last the waiver seen a crowd o' people runnin' as
if Owld Nick was at their heels, and they shoutin' a thousand
murdhers and cryin', "The dhraggin, the dragghin!" and
he couldn't stop the horse nor make him turn back, but
away he pelted right forinst the terrible baste that was comin'
up to him, and there was the most nefarious smell o' sulphur,
savin' your presence, enough to knock you down; and, faith,
the waiver seen he had no time to lose, and so he threwn
himself off the horse and made to a three that was growin'
nigh hand, and away he clambered up into it as nimble as
a cat; and not a minit had he to spare, for the dhraggin kem
up in a powerful rage, and he devoured the horse, body and
bones, in less than no time; and then he began to sniffle and
scent about for the waiver, and at last he clapt his eye an
him where he was up in the three, and says he, "In throth,
you might as well come down out o' that," says he, "for I'll
have you as sure as eggs is mate."

"Divil a fut I'll go down," says the waiver.

"Sorra care I care," says the dhraggin, "for you're as
good as ready money in my pocket this minit, for I'll lie
undher this three," says he, and sooner or later you must
fall to my share"; and, sure enough, he sot down and began
to pick his teeth with his tail afther the heavy brekquest
he made that mornin' (for he ate a whole village, let alone
the horse), and he got dhrowsy at last and fell asleep; but
before he wint to sleep he wound himself all round the three,
all as one as a lady windin' ribbon round her finger, so that
the waiver could not escape.

Well, as soon as the waiver knew he was dead asleep by the snorin' of him—and every snore he let out of him was like a clap o' thunder——

The minit, the waiver began to creep down the three as cautious as a fox; and he was very nigh hand the bottom when, bad cess to it, a thievin' branch he was dipindin' an bruk, and down he fell right atop o' the dhraggin. But if he did, good luck was an his side, for where should he fall but with his two legs right acrass the dhraggin's neck, and, my jew'l, he laid howlt o' the baste's ears, and there he kept his grip, for the dhraggin wakened and endayvoured for to bite him; but, you see, by rayson the waiver was behind his ears he could not come at him, and, with that, he endayvoured for to shake him off; but the divil of a stir could he stir the waiver; and though he shuk all the scales an his body he could not turn the scale again the waiver.

"BY the hokey, this is too bad intirely," says the dhraggin; "but if you won't let go," says he, "by the powers o' wildfire, I'll give you a ride that 'ill astonish your siven small sinses, my boy"; and with that away he flew like mad; and where do you think he did fly? By dad, he flew sthraight for Dublin—divil a less. But the waiver bein' an his neck was a great disthress to him, and he would rather have made him an inside *passenger*; but, anyway, he flew and he flew till he kem slap up agin the palace o' the King; for, bein' blind with the rage, he never seen it, and he knocked his brains out—that is, the small thrifle he had, and down he fell spacheless. An', you see, good luck would have it that the King o' Dublin was

lookin' out iv his dhrawin'-room windy for divarshin that
day also, and whin he seen the waiver ridin' and the fiery
dhraggin (for he was blazin' like a tar barrel), he called out
to his coortyers to come and see the show. "By the
powdhers o' war, here comes the knight arriant," says the
King, "ridin' the dhraggin that's all afire, and if he gets
into the palace, yiz must be ready wid the fire ingines," says
he, "for to put him out." But when they seen the dhraggin
fall outside they all run downstairs and scampered into the
palace yard for to circumspect the curiosity; and by the time
they got down the waiver had got off o' the dhraggin's neck,
and runnin' up to the King, says he, "Plaze your holiness,"
says he, "I did not think myself worthy of killin' this
facetious baste, so I brought him to yourself for to do him
the honour of decripitation by your own royal five fingers.
But I tamed him first before I allowed him the liberty for
to dar' to appear in your royal prisince, and you'll oblige
me if you just make your mark with your own hand upon
the onruly baste's neck." And with that the King, sure
enough, dhrew out his sword and took the head aff the
dirty brute as clane as a new pin. Well, there was great
rejoicin' in the coort that the dhraggin was killed; and says
the King to the little waiver, says he, "You are a knight
arriant as it is, and so it would be no use for to knight you
over agin; but I will make you a lord," says he.

"Oh, Lord!" says the waiver, thunderstruck like at his
own good luck.

"I will," says the King; "and as you are the first man
I ever heerd tell of that rode a dhraggin, you shall be called
Lord Mount Dhraggin," says he.

"But that is not all I'll do for you," says the King; "I'll

give you my daughter, too, in marriage," says he. Now, you see, that was nothing more than what he promised the waiver in his first promise; for by all accounts the King's daughter was the greatest dhraggin ever was seen, and had the divil's own tongue, and a beard a yard long, which she purtended was put an her, by way of a penance, by Father Mulcahy, her confissor; but it was well known it was in the family for ages, and no wondher it was so long by rayson of that same.

SAMUEL LOVER.

Mor of Cloyne

Mor of Cloyne, a Munster Princess, is singing at the door of a Fairy Rath to her sister, a captive within it, the magic tune by which she once escaped from a like captivity.

LITTLE Sister, whom the Fay
    Hides away within his doon,
Deep below yon seeding fern,
    Oh, list and learn my magic tune.

Long ago, when snared like thee
    By the Shee, my harp and I
O'er them wove the slumber spell,
    Warbling well its lullaby.

Till with dreamy smiles they sank,
    Rank on rank, before the strain;
And I rose from out the rath,
    And found my path to earth again.

Little Sister, to my woe
    Hid below among the Shee,
List and learn the magic tune,
    That it full soon may succour thee.
        ALFRED PERCEVAL GRAVES.

Lawn Dyarrig and the Knight of Terrible Valley

(*As told by an Irish Peasant.*)

HERE was a King in his own time in Erin, and he went hunting one day. The King met a man whose head was out through his cap, whose elbows and knees were out through his clothing, and whose toes were out through his shoes.

The man went up to the King, gave him a blow on the face, and drove three teeth from his mouth. The same blow put the King's head in the dirt. When he rose from the earth, the King went back to his castle, and lay down sick and sorrowful.

The King had three sons, and their names were Ur, Arthur, and Lawn Dyarrig. The three were at school that day, and came home in the evening. The father sighed when the sons were coming in.

"What is wrong with our father?" asked the eldest.

"Your father is sick on his bed," said the mother.

The three sons went to their father and asked what was on him.

"A strong man that I met to-day gave me a blow in the face, put my head in the dirt, and knocked three teeth from my mouth. What would you do to him if you met him?" asked the father of the eldest son.

"If I met that man," replied Ur, "I would make four parts of him between four horses."

"OU are my son," said the King. "What would you do if you met him?" asked he then as he turned to the second son.

"If I had a grip on that man I would burn him between four fires."

"You, too, are my son. What would you do?" asked the King of Lawn Dyarrig.

"If I met that man, I would do my best against him, and he might not stand long before me."

"You are not my son. I would not lose lands or property on you," said the father. "You must go from me, and leave this to-morrow."

On the following morning the three brothers rose with the dawn; the order was given Lawn Dyarrig to leave the castle and make his own way for himself. The other two brothers were going to travel the world to know could they find the man who had injured their father. Lawn Dyarrig lingered outside till he saw the two, and they going off by themselves.

"It is a strange thing," said he, "for two men of high degree to go travelling without a servant."

"We need no one," said Ur.

"Company wouldn't harm us," said Arthur.

The two let Lawn Dyarrig go with them as a serving-boy, and set out to find the man who had struck down their father. They spent all that day walking, and came late to a house where one woman was living. She shook hands with Ur and Arthur, and greeted them. Lawn Dyarrig she kissed and welcomed; called him son of the King of Erin.

"IT is a strange thing to shake hands with the elder, and kiss the younger," said Ur.

"This is a story to tell," said the woman, "the same as if your death were in it."

They made three parts of that night. The first part they spent in conversation, the second in telling tales, the third in eating and drinking, with sound sleep and sweet slumber. As early as the day dawned next morning the old woman was up, and had food for the young men. When the three had eaten, she spoke to Ur, and this is what she asked of him: "What was it that drove you from home, and what brought you to this place?"

"A champion met my father, and took three teeth from him and put his head in the dirt. I am looking for that man, to find him alive or dead."

"That was the Green Knight from Terrible Valley. He is the man who took the three teeth from your father. I am three hundred years living in this place, and there is not a year of the three hundred in which three hundred heroes, fresh, young, and noble, have not passed on the way to Terrible Valley, and never have I seen one coming back, and each of them had the look of a man better than you. And now where are you going, Arthur?"

"I am on the same journey with my brother."

"Where are you going, Lawn Dyarrig?"

"I am going with these as a servant," said Lawn Dyarrig.

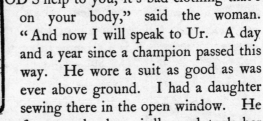

"G OD'S help to you, it's bad clothing that's on your body," said the woman. "And now I will speak to Ur. A day and a year since a champion passed this way. He wore a suit as good as was ever above ground. I had a daughter sewing there in the open window. He came outside, put a finger under her girdle, and took her with him. Her father followed straightway to save her, but I have never seen daughter nor father from that day to this. That man was the Green Knight of Terrible Valley. He is better than all the men that could stand on a field a mile in length and a mile in breadth. If you take my advice you'll turn back and go home to your father."

'Tis how she vexed Ur with this talk, and he made a vow to himself to go on. When Ur did not agree to turn home, the woman said to Lawn Dyarrig, "Go back to my chamber; you'll find in it the apparel of a hero."

He went back, and there was not a bit of the apparel he did not go into with a spring.

"You may be able to do something now," said the woman, when Lawn Dyarrig came to the front. "Go back to my chamber and search through all the old swords. You will find one at the bottom. Take that."

He found the old sword, and at the first shake that he gave he knocked seven barrels of rust out of it; after the second shake it was as bright as when made.

"You may be able to do well with that," said the woman. "Go out, now, to that stable abroad, and take the slim white steed that is in it. That one will never stop nor halt in any place till he brings you to the Eastern World. If you like, take these two men behind you; if not, let them walk. But I think it is useless for you to have them at all with you."

Lawn Dyarrig went out to the stable, took the slim white steed, mounted, rode to the front, and catching the two brothers, planted them on the horse behind him.

"NOW, Lawn Dyarrig," said the woman, "this horse will never stop till he stands on the little white meadow in the Eastern World. When he stops, you'll come down, and cut the turf under his beautiful right front foot."

The horse started from the door, and at every leap he crossed seven hills and valleys, seven castles with villages, acres, roods, and odd perches. He could overtake the whirlwind before him seven hundred times before the whirlwind behind him could overtake him once. Early in the afternoon of the next day he was in the Eastern World. When he dismounted, Lawn Dyarrig cut the sod from under the foot of the slim white steed, in the name of the Father, Son, and Holy Ghost, and Terrible Valley was down under him there What he did next was to tighten the reins on the neck of the steed and let him go home.

"Now," said Lawn Dyarrig to his brothers, "which would you rather be doing—making a basket or twisting gads (withes)?"

"We would rather be making a basket; our help is among ourselves," answered they.

Ur and Arthur went at the basket and Lawn Dyarrig at twisting the gads. When Lawn Dyarrig came to the opening with the gads all twisted and made into one, they hadn't the ribs of the basket in the ground yet.

"Oh, then, haven't ye anything done but that?"

"Stop your mouth," said Ur, "or we'll make a mortar of your head on the next stone."

"To be kind to one another is the best for us," said Lawn Dyarrig. "I'll make the basket."

WHILE they'd be putting one rod in the basket he had the basket finished.

"Oh, brother," said they, "you are a quick workman."

They had not called him brother since they left home till that moment.

"Who will go in the basket now?" said Lawn Dyarrig when it was finished and the gad tied to it.

"Who but me?" said Ur. "I am sure, brothers, if I see anything to frighten me you'll draw me up."

"We will," said the other two.

He went in, but had not gone far when he cried to pull him up again.

"By my father, and the tooth of my father, and by all that is in Erin, dead or alive, I would not give one other sight on Terrible Valley!" he cried, when he stepped out of the basket.

"Who will go now?" said Lawn Dyarrig.

"Who will go but me?" answered Arthur.

Whatever length Ur went, Arthur didn't go the half of it.

" By my father, and the tooth of my father, I wouldn't give another look at Terrible Valley for all that's in Erin, dead or alive! "

" I will go now," said Lawn Dyarrig, "and as I put no foul play on you, I hope ye'll not put foul play on me."

" We will not, indeed," said they.

WHATEVER length the other two went, Lawn Dyarrig didn't go the half of it, till he stepped out of the basket and went down on his own feet. It was not far he had travelled in Terrible Valley when he met seven hundred heroes guarding the country.

" In what place here has the Green King his castle? " asked he of the seven hundred.

" What sort of a sprisawn goat or sheep from Erin are you? " asked they.

" If we had a hold of you, the two arms of me, that's a question you would not put a second time; but if we haven't you, we'll not be so long."

They faced Lawn Dyarrig then and attacked him; but he went through them like a hawk or a raven through small birds. He made a heap of their feet, a heap of their heads, and a castle of their arms.

After that he went his way walking, and had not gone far when he came to a spring. " I'll have a drink before I go further," thought he. With that he stooped down and took a drink of the water. When he had drunk he lay on the ground and fell asleep.

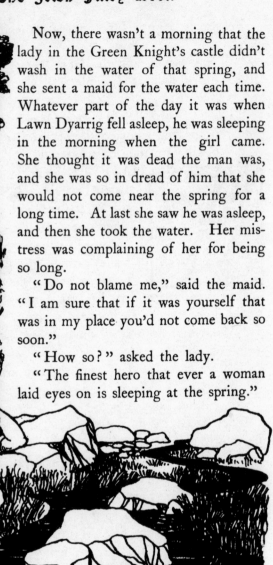

Now, there wasn't a morning that the lady in the Green Knight's castle didn't wash in the water of that spring, and she sent a maid for the water each time. Whatever part of the day it was when Lawn Dyarrig fell asleep, he was sleeping in the morning when the girl came. She thought it was dead the man was, and she was so in dread of him that she would not come near the spring for a long time. At last she saw he was asleep, and then she took the water. Her mistress was complaining of her for being so long.

"Do not blame me," said the maid. "I am sure that if it was yourself that was in my place you'd not come back so soon."

"How so?" asked the lady.

"The finest hero that ever a woman laid eyes on is sleeping at the spring."

" That's a thing that cannot be till Lawn Dyarrig comes to the age of a hero. When that time comes he'll be sleeping at the spring."

" He is in it now," said the girl.

The lady did not stop to get any drop of the water on herself, but ran quickly from the castle. When she came to the spring she roused Lawn Dyarrig. If she found him lying, she left him standing. She smothered him with kisses, drowned him with tears, dried him with garments of fine silk and with her own hair. Herself and himself locked arms and walked into the castle of the Green Knight. After that they were inviting each other with the best food and entertainment till the middle of the following day. Then the lady said :

" WHEN the Green Knight bore me away from my father and mother he brought me straight to this castle, but I put him under bonds not to marry me for seven years and a day, and he cannot; still, I must serve him. When he goes fowling he spends three days away and the next three days at home. This is the day for him to come back, and for me to prepare his dinner. There is no stir that you or I have made here to-day but that brass head beyond there will tell of it."

" It is equal to you what it tells," said Lawn Dyarrig, " only make ready a clean long chamber for me."

She did so, and he went back into it. Herself rose up then to prepare dinner for the Green Knight. When he came, she welcomed him as every day. She left down his food before him, and he sat to take his dinner. He was sitting with knife and fork in hand when the brass head spoke. "I thought when I saw you taking food and drink with your wife that you had the blood of a man in you. If you could see that sprisawn of a goat or sheep out of Erin taking meat and drink with her all day, what would you do?"

"Oh, my suffering and sorrow!" cried the knight. "I'll never take another bite or sup till I eat some of his liver and heart. Let three hundred heroes, fresh and young, go back and bring his heart to me, with the liver and lights, till I eat them."

THE three hundred heroes went, and hardly were they behind in the chamber when Lawn Dyarrig had them all dead in one heap.

"He must have some exercise to delay my men, they are so long away," said the knight. "Let three hundred more heroes go for his heart, with the liver and lights, and bring them here to me."

The second three hundred went, and as they were entering the chamber Lawn Dyarrig was making a heap of them, till the last one was inside, where there were two heaps.

"He has some way of coaxing my men to delay," said the knight. "Do you go now, three hundred of my savage hirelings, and bring him." The three hundred savage hirelings went, and Lawn Dyarrig let every man of them enter before he raised a hand, then he caught the bulkiest of them all by the two ankles, and began to wallop the others with him, and he walloped them till he drove the life out of the two hundred and ninety-nine. The bulkiest one was worn to the shin-bones that Lawn Dyarrig held in his two hands. The Green Knight, who thought Lawn Dyarrig was coaxing the men, called out then, "Come down, my men, and take dinner."

"I'll be with you," said Lawn Dyarrig, "and have the best food in the house, and I'll have the best bed in the house. God not be good to you for it, either."

E went down to the Green Knight, and took the food from before him and put it before himself. Then he took the lady, set her on his own knee, and he and she went on eating. After dinner he put his finger under her girdle, took her to the best chamber in the castle, and stood on guard upon it till morning. Before dawn the lady said to Lawn Dyarrig:

"If the Green Knight strikes the pole of combat first, he'll win the day; if you strike first, you'll win if you do what I tell you. The Green Knight has so much enchantment that if he sees it is going against him the battle is, he'll rise like a fog in the air, come down in the same form, strike you, and make a green stone of you. When yourself and himself are going out to fight in the morning, cut a sod a perch long, in the name of the Father, Son, and Holy Ghost; you'll leave the sod on the next little hillock you meet. When the Green Knight is coming down and is ready to strike, give him a blow with the sod. You'll make a green stone of him."

As early as the dawn Lawn Dyarrig rose and struck the pole of combat. The blow that he gave did not leave calf, foal, lamb, kid, or child waiting for birth, without turning them five times to the left and five times to the right.

"What do you want?" asked the knight.

"All that's in your kingdom to be against me the first quarter of the day, and yourself the second quarter.

"You have not left in the kingdom now but myself, and it is early enough for you that I'll be at you."

The knight faced him, and they went at each other, and fought till late in the day. The battle was strong against Lawn Dyarrig, when the lady stood in the door of the castle. "INCREASE on your blows and increase on your courage," cried she. "There is no woman here but myself to wail over you, or to stretch you before burial."

When the knight heard the voice he rose in the air like a lump of fog. As he was coming down Lawn Dyarrig struck him with the sod on the right side of his breast, and made a green stone of him.

The lady rushed out then, and whatever welcome she had for Lawn Dyarrig the first time, she had twice as much now. Herself and himself went into the castle, and spent that night very comfortably. In the morning they rose early, and collected all the gold, utensils, and treasures. Lawn Dyarrig found the three teeth of his father in a pocket of the Green Knight, and took them. He and the lady brought all the riches to where the basket was. "If I send up this beautiful lady," thought Lawn Dyarrig, "she may be taken from me by my brothers; if I remain below with her, she may be taken from me by people here." He put her in the basket, and she gave him a ring so that they might know each other if they met. He shook the gad, and she rose in the basket.

When Ur saw the basket, he thought, "What's above let it be above, and what's below let it stay where it is."

"I'll have you as wife for ever for myself," said he to the lady.

"I put you under bonds," says she, "not to lay a hand on me for a day and three years."

"That itself would not be long even if twice the time," said Ur.

The two brothers started home with the lady; on the way Ur found the head of an old horse with teeth in it, and took them, saying, "These will be my father's three teeth."

THEY travelled on, and reached home at last. Ur would not have left a tooth in his father's mouth, trying to put in the three that he had brought; but the father stopped him.

Lawn Dyarrig, left in Terrible Valley, began to walk around for himself. He had been walking but one day when whom should he meet but the lad Short-clothes, and he saluted him. "By what way can I leave Terrible Valley?" asked Lawn Dyarrig.

"If I had a grip on you that's what you wouldn't ask me a second time," said Short-clothes.

"If you haven't touched me, you will before you are much older."

"If you do, you will not treat me as you did all my people and my master."

"I'll do worse to you than I did to them," said Lawn Dyarrig.

They caught each other then, one grip under the arm and one on the shoulder. 'Tis not long they were wrestling when Lawn Dyarrig had Short-clothes on the earth, and he gave him the five thin tyings dear and tight.

"You are the best hero I have ever met," said Short-clothes; "give me quarter for my soul—spare me. When I did not tell you of my own will, I must tell in spite of myself."

"It is as easy for me to loosen you as to tie you," said Lawn Dyarrig, and he freed him.

"Since you are not dead now," said Short-clothes, "there is no death allotted to you. I'll find a way for you to leave Terrible Valley. Go and take that old bridle hanging there beyond and shake it; whatever beast comes and puts its head into the bridle will carry you."

LAWN DYARRIG shook the bridle, and a dirty, shaggy little foal came and put its head in the bridle. Lawn Dyarrig mounted, dropped the reins on the foal's neck, and let him take his own choice of roads. The foal brought Lawn Dyarrig out by another way to the upper world, and took him to Erin. Lawn Dyarrig stopped some distance from his father's castle, and knocked at the house of an old weaver.

"Who are you?" asked the old man.

"I am a weaver," said Lawn Dyarrig.

"What can you do?"

"I can spin for twelve and twist for twelve."

"This is a very good man," said the old weaver to his sons, "let us try him."

The work they had been doing for a year he had done in one hour. When dinner was over the old man began to wash and shave, and his two sons began to do the same.

"Why is this?" asked Lawn Dyarrig.

"Haven't you heard that Ur, son of the King, is to marry to-night the woman that he took from the Green Knight of Terrible Valley?"

"I have not," said Lawn Dyarrig; "as all are going to the wedding, I suppose I may go without offence?"

"Oh, you may," said the weaver; "there will be a hundred thousand welcomes before you."

"Are there any linen sheets within?"

"There are," said the weaver.

"It is well to have bags ready for yourself and two sons."

THE weaver made bags for the three very quickly. They went to the wedding. Lawn Dyarrig put what dinner was on the first table into the weaver's bag, and sent the old man home with it. The food of the second table he put in the eldest son's bag, filled the second son's bag from the third table, and sent the two home.

The complaint went to Ur that an impudent stranger was taking all the food.

"It is not right to turn any man away," said the bridegroom, "but if that stranger does not mind he will be thrown out of the castle."

"Let me look at the face of the disturber," said the bride.

"Go and bring the fellow who is troubling the guests," said Ur to the servants.

Lawn Dyarrig was brought right away, and stood before the bride, who filled a glass with wine and gave it to him. Lawn Dyarrig drank half the wine, and dropped in the ring which the lady had given him in Terrible Valley.

When the bride took the glass again the ring went of itself with one leap on to her finger. She knew then who was standing before her.

"This is the man who conquered the Green Knight and saved me from Terrible Valley," said she to the King of Erin; "this is Lawn Dyarrig, your son."

Lawn Dyarrig took out the three teeth and put them in his father's mouth. They fitted there perfectly, and grew into their old place. The King was satisfied, and as the lady would marry no man but Lawn Dyarrig, he was the bridegroom.

"I MUST give you a present," said the bride to the Queen. "Here is a beautiful scarf which you are to wear as a girdle this evening."

The Queen put the scarf round her waist.

"Tell me now," said the bride to the Queen, "who was Ur's father."

"What father could he have but his own father, the King of Erin?"

"Tighten, scarf," said the bride.

That moment the Queen thought that her head was in the sky and the lower half of her body down deep in the earth.

"Oh, my grief and my woe!" cried the Queen.

"Answer my question in truth, and the scarf will stop squeezing you. Who was Ur's father?"

"The gardener," said the Queen.

"Whose son is Arthur?"

"The King's son."

"Tighten, scarf," said the bride.

If the Queen suffered before, she suffered twice as much this time, and screamed for help.

"Answer me truly, and you'll be without pain; if not, death will be on you this minute. Whose son is Arthur?"

"The swineherd's."

"Who is the King's son?"

"The King has no son but Lawn Dyarrig."

"Tighten, scarf."

The scarf did not tighten, and if the Queen had been commanding it a day and a year it would not have tightened, for the Queen told the truth that time. When the wedding was over, the King gave Lawn Dyarrig half his kingdom, and made Ur and Arthur his servants.

JEREMIAH CURTIN.

The Horned Women

RICH woman sat up late one night carding and preparing wool while all the family and servants were asleep. Suddenly a knock was given at the door, and a voice called out, "Open! Open!"

"Who is there?" said the woman of the house.

"I am the Witch of the One Horn," was answered.

The mistress, supposing that one of her neighbours had called and required assistance, opened the door, and a woman entered, having in her hand a pair of wool carders, and bearing a horn on her forehead, as if growing there. She sat down by the fire in silence, and began to card the wool with violent haste. Suddenly she paused, and said aloud, "Where are the women; they delay too long?"

Then a second knock came to the door, and a voice called as before, "Open! Open!"

The mistress felt herself constrained to rise and open to the call, and immediately a second witch entered, having two horns on her forehead, and in her hand a wheel for spinning wool.

"Give me place," she said; "I am the Witch of the Two Horns"; and she began to spin as quick as lightning.

And so the knocks went on, and the call was heard and the witches entered, until at last twelve women sat round the fire—the first with one horn, the last with twelve horns.

And they carded the thread and turned their spinning-wheels, and wound and wove.

ALL singing together an ancient rhyme, but no word did they speak to the mistress of the house. Strange to hear and frightful to look upon were these twelve women, with their horns and their wheels; and the mistress felt near to death, and she tried to rise that she might call for help, but she could not move, nor could she utter a word or a cry, for the spell of the witches was upon her.

Then one of them called to her in Irish, and said, "Rise, woman, and make us a cake" Then the mistress searched for a vessel to bring water from the well that she might mix the meal and make the cake, but she could find none.

And they said to her, "Take a sieve, and bring water in it." And she took the sieve, and went to the well; but the water poured from it, and she could fetch none for the cake, and she sat down by the well and wept.

Then came a voice by her, and said, "Take yellow clay

and moss and bind them together, and plaster the sieve so that it will hold."

This she did, and the sieve held the water for the cake; and the voice said again:

"Return, and when thou comest to the north angle of the house cry aloud three times, and say, 'The mountain of the Fenian women and the sky over it is all on fire.'"

And she did so.

When the witches inside heard the call, a great and terrible cry broke from their lips, and they rushed forth with wild lamentations and shrieks, and fled away to Slievenamon, where was their chief abode. But the Spirit of the Well bade the mistress of the house to enter and prepare her home against the enchantments of the witches, if they returned again.

AND first, to break their spells, she sprinkled the water in which she had washed her child's feet (the feet-water) outside the door on the threshold; secondly, she took the cake which the witches had made in her absence, of meal mixed with the blood drawn from the sleeping family, and she broke the cake in bits, and placed a bit in the mouth of each sleeper, and they were restored; and she took the cloth they had woven, and placed it half in and half out of the chest with the padlock; and, lastly, she secured the door with a great crossbeam fastened in the jambs, so that they could not enter, and having done these things she waited.

Not long were the witches in coming, and they raged and called for vengeance.

"Open! Open!" they screamed. "Open, feet-water!"

"I cannot," said the feet-water; "I am scattered on the ground, and my path is down to the Lough."

"Open, open, wood and trees and beam!" they cried to the door.

"I cannot," said the door, "for the beam is fixed in the jambs, and I have no power to move."

"Open, open, cake that we have made and mingled with blood!" they cried again.

"I cannot," said the cake, "for I am broken and bruised, and my blood is on the lips of the sleeping children."

Then the witches rushed through the air with great cries, and fled back to Slievenamon, uttering strange curses on the Spirit of the Well, who had wished their ruin. But the woman and the house were left in peace, and a mantle dropped by one of the witches was kept hung up by the mistress as a sign of the night's awful contest; and this mantle was in possession of the same family from generation to generation for five hundred years after.

LADY WILDE.

The Quare Gander

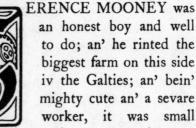

"ERENCE MOONEY was an honest boy and well to do; an' he rinted the biggest farm on this side iv the Galties; an' bein' mighty cute an' a sevare worker, it was small wonder he turned a good penny every harvest. But, unluckily, he was blessed with an ilegant large family iv daughters, an' iv coorse, his heart was allamost bruck, striving to make up fortunes for the whole of them. An' there wasn't a conthrivance iv any soart or description for makin' money out iv the farm but he was up to.

"Well, among the other ways he had iv gettin' up in the world he always kep a power iv turkeys, and all soarts iv poultrey; an' he was out iv all rason partial to geese—an' small blame to him for that same—for twice't a year you can pluck them as bare as my hand—an' get a fine price for the feathers, an' plenty of rale sizable eggs—an' when they are too ould

202

to lay any more, you can kill them, an' sell them to the gintlemen for goslings, d'ye see, let alone that a goose is the most manly bird that is out.

"Well, it happened in the coorse iv time that one ould gandher tuck a wondherful likin' to Terence, an' divil a place he could go serenadin' about the farm, or lookin' afther the men, but the gandher id be at his heels, an' rubbin' himself agin his legs, an' lookin' up in his face jist like any other Christian id do; an', begorra, the likes iv it was never seen—Terence Mooney an' the gandher wor so great.

N' at last the bird was so engagin' that Terence would not allow it to be plucked any more, an' kep it from that time out for love an' affection—just all as one like one iv his childer.

"But happiness in perfection never lasts long, an' the neighbours begin'd to suspect the nathur an' intentions iv the gandher, an' some iv them said it was the divil, an' more iv them that it was a fairy.

"Well, Terence could not but hear something of what was sayin', an' you may be sure he was not altogether asy in his mind about it, an' from one day to another he was gettin' more ancomfortable in himself, until he detarmined to sind for Jer Garvan, the fairy docthor, in Garryowen, an' it's he was the illigant hand at the business, an' divil a sperit id say a crass word to him, no more nor a priest. An', moreover, he was very great wid ould Terence Mooney—this man's father that was.

"So without more about it he was sint for, an', sure enough, the divil a long he was about it, for he kem back that very evenin' along wid the boy that was sint for him, an' as soon as he was there, an' tuck his supper, an' was done talkin' for a while, he begin'd, of coorse, to look into the gandher.

"Well, he turned it this away an' that away, to the right an' to the left, an' straight-ways an' upside-down, an' when he was tired handlin' it, says he to Terence Mooney:

"'Terence,' says he, 'you must remove the bird into the next room,' says he, 'an' put a petticoat,' says he, 'or anny other convaynience round his head,' says he.

"'An' why so?' says Terence.

"'Becase,' says Jer, says he.

"'Becase what?' says Terence.

"'ECASE,' says Jer, 'if it isn't done you'll never be asy agin,' says he, 'or pusillanimous in your mind,' says he; 'so ax no more questions, but do my biddin',' says he.

"'Well,' says Terence, 'have your own way,' says he.

"An' wid that he tuck the ould gandher an' giv' it to one iv the gossoons.

"'An' take care,' says he, 'don't smother the crathur,' says he.

"Well, as soon as the bird was gone, says Jer Garvan, says he:

"'Do you know what that old gandher *is*, Terence Mooney?'

"'Divil a taste,' says Terence.

"'Well, then,' says Jer, 'the gandher is your own father,' says he.

"'It's jokin' you are,' says Terence, turnin' mighty pale; 'how can an ould gandher be my father?' says he.

"'I'm not funnin' you at all,' says Jer; 'it's thrue what I tell you, it's your fathei's wandhrin' sowl,' says he, 'that's naturally tuck pissession iv the ould gandher's body,' says he. 'I know him many ways, and I wondher,' says he, 'you do not know the cock iv his eye yourself,' says he.

"'Oh, blur an' ages!' says Terence, 'what the divil will I ever do at all at all,' says he; 'it's all over wid me, for I plucked him twelve times at the laste,' says he.

"'That can't be helped now,' says Jer; 'it was a sevare act, surely,' says he, 'but it's too late to lamint for it now,' says he; 'the only way to prevint what's past,' says he, 'is to put a stop to it before it happens,' says he.

"'HRUE for you,' says Terence, 'but how the divil did you come to the knowledge iv my father's sowl,' says he, 'bein' in the ould gandher,' says he.

"'If I tould you,' says Jer, 'you would not undherstand me,' says he, 'without book-larnin' an' gasthronomy,' says he; 'so ax me no questions,' says he, 'an' I'll tell you no lies. But b'lieve me in this much,' says he, 'it's your father that's in it,' says he; 'an' if I don't make him spake to-morrow mornin',' says he, 'I'll give you lave to call me a fool,' says he.

"'Say no more,' says Terence; 'that settles the business,' says he; 'an' oh, blur and ages! is it not a quare thing,' says he, 'for a dacent, respictable man,' says he, 'to be walkin' about the counthry in the shape iv an ould gandher,' says he;

'and oh, murdher, murdher! is not it often I plucked him,' says he, 'an' tundher and ouns! might not I have ate him?' says he; and wid that he fell into a could parspiration, savin' your prisince, an' on the pint iv faintin' wid the bare notions iv it.

"Well, whin he was come to himself agin, says Jerry to him, quite an' asy:

"'Terence,' says he, 'don't be aggravatin' yourself,' says he; 'for I have a plan composed that 'ill make him spake out,' says he, 'an' tell what it is in the world he's wantin',' says he; 'an' mind an' don't be comin' in wid your gosther, an' to say agin anything I tell you,' says he, 'but jist purtind, as soon as the bird is brought back,' says he, 'how that we're goin' to sind him to-morrow mornin' to market,' says he. 'An' if he don't spake to-night,' says he, 'or gother himself out iv the place,' says he, 'put him into the hamper airly, and sind him in the cart,' says he, 'straight to Tipperary, to be sould for atin',' says he, 'along wid the two gossoons,' says he, 'an' my name isn't Jer Garvan,' says he, 'if he doesn't spake out before he's half-way,' says he. 'An' mind,' says he, 'as soon as iver he says the first word,' says he, 'that very minute bring him aff to Father Crotty,' says he; 'an' if his raverince doesn't make him ratire,' says he, 'like the rest iv his parishioners, glory be to God,' says he, 'into the siclusion iv the flames iv purgathory,' says he, 'there's no vartue in my charums,' says he.

"Well, wid that the ould gandher was let into the room agin, an' they all begin'd to talk iv sindin' him the nixt mornin' to be sould for roastin' in Tipperary, jist as if it was a thing andoubtingly settled. But divil a notice the gandher tuck, no more nor if they wor spaking iv the Lord-

Liftinar t; an' Terence desired the boys to get ready the kish for the poulthry, an' to 'settle it out wid hay soft an' shnug,' says he, 'for it's the last jauntin' the poor ould gandher 'ill get in this world,' says he.

"Well, as the night was gettin' late, Terence was growin' mighty sorrowful an' down-hearted in himself entirely wid the notions iv what was goin' to happen. An' as soon as the wife an' the crathurs wor fairly in bed, he brought out some illigint potteen, an' himself an' Jer Garvan sot down to it; an', begorra, the more anasy Terence got, the more he dhrank, and himself and Jer Garvan finished a quart betune them. It wasn't an imparial, though, an' more's the pity, for them wasn't anvinted antil short since; but divil a much matther it signifies any longer if a pint could hould two quarts, let alone what it does, sinst Father Mathew —the Lord purloin his raverince—begin'd to give the pledge, an' wid the blessin' iv timperance to deginerate Ireland.

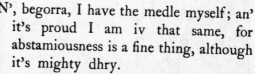

"A N', begorra, I have the medle myself; an' it's proud I am iv that same, for abstamiousness is a fine thing, although it's mighty dhry.

"Well, whin Terence finished his pint, he thought he might as well stop; 'for enough is as good as a faste,' says he; 'an' I pity the vagabond,' says he, 'that is not able to conthroul his licquor,' says he, 'an' to keep constantly inside iv a pint measure,' says he; an' wid that he wished Jer Garvan a good night an' walked out iv the room.

"But he wint out the wrong door, bein' a thrifle hearty in himself an' not rightly knowin' whether he was standin' on his head or his heels, or both iv them at the same time, an' in place iv gettin' into bed, where did he thrun himself but into the poulthry hamper that the boys had settled out ready for the gandher in the mornin'. An', sure enough, he sunk down soft an' complate through the hay to the bottom; an' wid the turnin' and roulin' about in the night, the divil a bit iv him but was covered up as shnug as a lumper in a pittaty furrow before mornin'.

"So wid the first light, up gets the two boys that wor to take the sperit, as they consaved, to Tipperary; an' they cotched the ould gandher an' put him in the hamper, an' clapped a good wisp iv hay an the top iv him, an' tied it down sthrong wid a bit iv a coard, an' med the sign iv the crass over him, in dhread iv any harum, an' put the hamper up an the car, wontherin' all the while what in the world was makin' the ould bird so surprisin' heavy.

ELL, they wint along quite anasy towards Tipperary, wishin' every minute that some iv the neighbours bound the same way id happen to fall in with them, for they didn't half like the notions iv havin' no company but the bewitched gandher, an' small blame to them for that same.

"But although they wor shaking in their skhins in dhread iv the ould bird beginnin' to converse them every minute, they did not let an to one another, but kep singin' an' whistlin' like mad to keep the dread out iv their hearts.

"Well, afther they wor on the road betther nor half an hour, they kem to the bad bit close by Father Crotty's, an' there was one divil of a rut three feet deep at the laste; an' the car got sich a wondherful chuck goin' through it that it wakened Terence widin in the basket.

"'Bad luck to ye,' says he, 'my bones is bruck wid yer thricks; what the divil are ye doin' wid me?'

"'Did ye hear anything quare, Thady?' says the boy that was next to the car, turnin' as white as the top iv a mushroom; 'did ye hear anything quare soundin' out iv the hamper?' says he.

"'No, nor you,' says Thady, turnin' as pale as himself. 'It's the ould gandher that's gruntin' wid the shakin' he's gettin',' says he.

"'Where the divil have ye put me into?' says Terence inside. 'Bad luck to your sowls,' says he; 'let me out, or I'll be smothered this minute,' says he.

"'HERE'S no use in purtending,' says the boy; 'the gandher's spakin', glory be to God,' says he.

"'Let me out, you murdherers,' says Terence.

"'In the name iv the blessed Vargin,' says Thady, 'an' iv all the holy saints, hould yer tongue, you unnatheral gandher,' says he.

"'Who's that, that dar to call me nicknames?' says Terence inside, roaring wid the fair passion. 'Let me out, you blasphamious infiddles,' says he, 'or by this crass I'll stretch ye,' says he.

"'In the name iv all the blessed saints in heaven,' says Thady, 'who the divil are ye?'

"'Who the divil would I be, but Terence Mooney,' says he. 'It's myself that's in it, you unmerciful bliggards,' says he. 'Let me out, or, by the holy, I'll get out in spite iv yes,' says he, 'an', by jaburs, 'I'll wallop yes in arnest,' says he.

"'It's ould Terence, sure enough,' says Thady. 'Isn't it cute the fairy docthor found him out?' says he.

"'I'm an the pint of snuffication,' says Terence. 'Let me out, I tell you, an' wait till I get at ye,' says he, 'for, begorra, the divil a bone in your body but I'll powdher,' says he.

"An' wid that he beginned kickin' and flingin' inside in the hamper, and dhrivin' his legs agin the sides iv it, that it was a wonder he did not knock it to pieces.

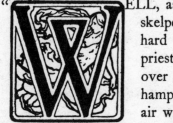

"ELL, as soon as the boys seen that they skelped the ould horse into a gallop as hard as he could peg towards the priest's house, through the ruts, an' over the stones; an' you'd see the hamper fairly flyin' three feet up in the air with the joultin'; glory be to God.

"So it was small wondher, by the time they got to his raverince's door, the breath was fairly knocked out of poor Terence, so that he was lyin' speechless in the bottom iv the hamper.

"Well, whin his raverince kem down, they up an' they tould him all that happened, an' how they put the gandher in the hamper, an' how he beginned to spake, an' how he confissed that he was ould Terence Mooney; an' they axed his honour to advise them how to get rid iv the sperit for good an' all.

"So says his raverince, says he:

"'I'll take my booke,' says he, 'an' I'll read some rale

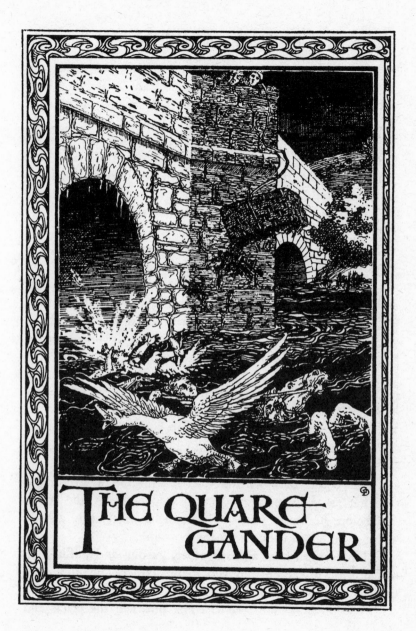

THE QUARE GANDER

sthrong holy bits out iv it,' says he, 'an' do you get a rope and put it round the hamper,' says he, 'an' let it swing over the runnin' wather at the bridge,' says he, 'an' it's no matther if I don't make the sperit come out iv it,' says he.

"Well, wid that the priest got his horse, and tuck his booke in undher his arm, an' the boys follied his raverince, ladin' the horse down to the bridge, an' divil a word out iv Terence all the way, for he seen it was no use spakin', an' he was afeard if he med any noise they might thrait him to another gallop an' finish him intirely.

"Well, as soon as they wor all come to the bridge, the boys tuck the rope they had wid them an' med it fast to the top iv the hamper, an' swung it fairly over the bridge, lettin' it hang in the air about twelve feet out iv the wather.

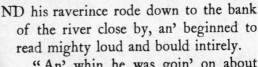 ND his raverince rode down to the bank of the river close by, an' beginned to read mighty loud and bould intirely.

"An' whin he was goin' on about five minutes, all at onst the bottom iv the hamper kem out, an' down wint Terence, falling splash into the wather, an' the ould gandher a-top iv him. Down they both wint to the bottom, wid a souse you'd hear half a mile off.

"An' before they had time to rise agin, his raverince, wid the fair astonishment, giv his horse one dig iv the spurs, an' before he knew where he was, in he wint, horse an' all, a-top iv them, an' down to the bottom.

"Up they all kem agin together, gaspin' and puffin', an' off down wid the current wid them, like shot in under the arch iv the bridge till they kem to the shallow wather.

"The ould gandher was the first out, and the priest and

Terence kem next, pantin' an' blowin' an' more than half dhrounded, an' his raverince was so freckened wid the dhroundin' he got and wid the sight iv the sperit, as he consaved, that he wasn't the better of it for a month.

"An' as soon as Terence could spake he swore he'd have the life of the two gossoons; but Father Crotty would not give him his will. An' as soon as he was got quiter they all endivoured to explain it; but Terence consaved he went raly to bed the night before, an' his wife said the same to shilter him from the suspision for havin' th' dhrop taken. An' his raverince said it was a mysthery, an' swore if he cotched anyone laughin' at the accident he'd lay the horse-whip across their shoulders.

"An' Terence grew fonder an' fonder iv the gandher every day, until at last he died in a wondherful old age, lavin' the gandher afther him an' a large family iv childher.

"An' to this day the farm is rinted by one iv Terence Mooney's lenial and legitimate postariors."

JOSEPH SHERIDAN LE FANN.

The Fairies' Passage

AP, tap, rap, rap! "Get up, gaffer
    Ferryman."
"Eh! Who is there?" The clock
    strikes three.
"Get up, do, gaffer! You are the
    very man
We have been long, long, longing to
    see."
The ferryman rises, growling and grumbling,
And goes fum-fumbling, and stumbling, and tumbling
Over the wares on his way to the door.
But he sees no more
Than he saw before,
Till a voice is heard: "O Ferryman, dear!
Here we are waiting, all of us, here.
We are a wee, wee colony, we;
Some two hundred in all, or three.
Ferry us over the River Lee

Ere dawn of day,
And we will pay
The most we may
In our own wee way!"

"Who are you? Whence came you?
What place are you going to?"
"Oh, we have dwelt over-long in this land:
The people get cross, and are growing so knowing, too!
Nothing at all but they now understand.
We are daily vanishing under the thunder
Of some huge engine or iron wonder;
That iron—ah! it has entered our souls."
"Your souls? O gholes!
You queer little drolls,
Do you mean——?" "Good gaffer, do aid us with speed,
For our time, like our stature, is short indeed!
And a very long way we have to go:
Eight or ten thousand miles or so,
Hither and thither, and to and fro,
With our pots and pans
And little gold cans;
But our light caravans
Run swifter than man's."

"Well, well, you may come," said the ferryman affably;
"Patrick, turn out, and get ready the barge."
Then again to the little folk: "Tho' you seem laughably
Small, I don't mind, if your coppers be large."
Oh, dear! what a rushing, what pushing, what crushing
(The watermen making vain efforts at hushing

The hubbub the while), there followed these words!
What clapping of boards,
What strapping of cords,
What stowing away of children and wives,
And platters, and mugs, and spoons, and knives!
Till all had safely got into the boat,
And the ferryman, clad in his tip-top coat,
And his wee little fairies were safely afloat;
Then ding, ding, ding,
And kling, kling, kling,
How the coppers did ring
In the tin pitcherling!

Off, then, went the boat, at first very pleasantly,
Smoothly, and so forth; but after a while
It swayed and it swagged this and that way, and presently
Chest after chest, and pile after pile
Of the little folk's goods began tossing and rolling,
And pitching like fun, beyond fairy controlling.
O Mab! if the hubbub were great before,
It was now some two or three million times more.
Crash! went the wee crocks and the clocks; and the locks
Of each little wee box were stove in by hard knocks;
And then there were oaths, and prayers, and cries:
"Take care!"—"See there!"—"Oh, dear, my eyes!"—
"I am killed!"—"I am drowned!"—with groans and sighs,
Till to land they drew.
"Yeo-ho! Pull to!
Tiller-rope, thro' and thro'!"
And all's right anew.
"Now jump upon shore, ye queer little oddities.

(Eh, what is this? . . . Where are they, at all?
Where are they, and where are their tiny commodities?
Well, as I live!" . . .) He looks blank as a wall,
Poor ferryman! Round him and round him he gazes,
But only gets deeplier lost in the mazes
Of utter bewilderment. All, all are gone,
And he stands alone,
Like a statue of stone,
In a doldrum of wonder. He turns to steer,
And a tinkling laugh salutes his ear,
With other odd sounds: "Ha, ha, ha, ha!
Fol lol! zidzizzle! quee, quee! bah, bah!
Fizzigigiggidy! pshee! sha, sha!"
"O ye thieves, ye thieves, ye rascally thieves!"
The good man cries. He turns to his pitcher,
And there, alas, to his horror perceives
That the little folk's mode of making him richer
Has been to pay him with withered leaves!

JAMES CLARENCE MANGAN.

The King of the Black Desert

This story was told by one Laurence O'Flynn from near Swinford, in the County Mayo, to my friend, the late F. O'Conor, of Athlone, from whom I got it in Irish. It is the eleventh story in the "Sgeuluidhe Gaodhalach," and is here for the first time literally translated into English.

AN CHRAOIBHIN AOIBHINN.

WHEN O'Conor was King over Ireland he was living in Rathcroghan, of Connacht. He had one son, but he, when he grew up, was wild, and the King could not control him, because he would have his own will in everything. One morning he went out—

His hound at his foot,
And his hawk on his hand,
And his fine black horse to bear him—

and he went forward, singing a verse of a song to himself, until he came as far as a big bush that was growing on the brink of a glen. There was a grey old man sitting at the foot of the bush, and he said, "King's son, if you are able to play as well as you are able to sing songs, I would like to play a game with you." The King's son thought that it was a silly old man that was in it, and he alighted, threw bridle over branch, and sat down by the side of the grey old man.

The old man drew out a pack of cards and asked, " Can you play these? "

" I can," said the King's son.

" What shall we play for? " said the grey old man.

" Anything you wish," says the King's son.

" All right; if I win you must do for me anything I shall ask of you, and if you win I must do for you anything you ask of me," says the grey old man.

" I'm satisfied," says the King's son.

THEY played the game, and the King's son beat the grey old man. Then he said, " What would you like me to do for you, King's son? "

" I won't ask you to do anything for me," says the King's son. " I think that you are not able to do much."

" Don't mind that," said the old man. " You must ask me to do something. I never lost a bet yet that I wasn't able to pay it."

As I said, the King's son thought that it was a silly old man that was in it, and to satisfy him he said to him, " Take the head off my stepmother and put a goat's head on her for a week."

" I'll do that for you," said the grey old man.

The King's son went a-riding on his horse—

His hound at his foot,
His hawk on his hand—

219

and he faced for another place, and never thought more about the grey old man until he came home.

He found a cry and great grief in the castle. The servants told him that an enchanter had come into the room where the Queen was, and had put a goat's head on her in place of her own head.

"By my hand, but that's a wonderful thing," says the King's son. "If I had been at home I'd have whipt the head off him with my sword."

There was great grief on the King, and he sent for a wise councillor, and asked him did he know how the thing happened to the Queen.

"Indeed, I cannot tell you that," said he; "it's a work of enchantment.

The King's son did not let on that he had any knowledge of the matter, but on the morrow morning he went out—

> His hound at his foot,
> His hawk on his hand,
> And his fine black horse to bear him—

and he never drew rein until he came as far as the big bush on the brink of the glen. The grey old man was sitting there under the bush, and said, "King's son, will you have a game to-day?" The King's son got down and said, "I will." With that he threw bridle over branch and sat down by the side of the old man. He drew out the cards and asked the King's son did he get the thing he had won yesterday.

"That's all right," said the King's son.

"We'll play for the same bet to-day," says the grey old man.

"I'm satisfied," said the King's son.

They played—the King's son won. "What would you like me to do for you this time?" says the grey old man. The King's son thought and said to himself, "I'll give him a hard job this time." Then he said, "There's a field of seven acres at the back of my father's castle; let it be filled to-morrow morning with cows, and no two of them to be of one colour, or one height, or one age."

"That shall be done," says the grey old man.

The King's son went riding on his horse—

> His hound at his foot,
> His hawk on his hand—

and faced for home. The King was sorrowful about the Queen; there were doctors out of every place in Ireland, but they could not do her any good.

N the morning of the next day the King's herd went out early, and he saw the field at the back of the castle filled with cows, and no two of them of the same colour, the same age, or the same height. He went in and told the King the wonderful news. "Go and drive them out," says the King. The herd got men, and went with them driving out the cows, but no sooner would he put them out on one side than they would come in on the other. The herd went to the King again, and told him that all the men that were in Ireland would not be able to put out these cows that were in the field. "They're enchanted cows," said the King.

When the King's son saw the cows, he said to himself,

"I'll have another game with the grey old man to-day!"
That morning he went out—

His hound at his foot,
His hawk on his hand,
And his fine black horse to bear him—

and he never drew rein till he came as far as the big bush
on the brink of the glen. The grey old man was there
before him, and asked him would he have a game of cards.

"I will," says the King's son; "but you know well that
I can beat you playing cards."

"We'll have another game, then," says the grey old man.
"Did you ever play ball?"

"I did, indeed," said the King's son; "but I think that
you are too old to play ball, and, besides that, we have no
place here to play it."

"If you're contented to play, I'll find a place," says the
grey old man.

"I'm contented," says the King's son.

"Follow me," says the grey old man.

THE King's son followed him through the
glen until he came to a fine green hill.
There he drew out a little enchanted
rod, spoke some words which the
King's son did not understand, and
after a moment the hill opened and
the two went in, and they passed
through a number of splendid halls until they came out
into a garden. There was everything finer than another in
that garden, and at the bottom of the garden there was a
place for playing ball. They threw up a piece of silver to
see who would have hand-in, and the grey old man got it.

They began then, and the grey old man never stopped until he won out the game. The King's son did not know what he would do. At last he asked the old man what would he desire him to do for him.

"I am King over the Black Desert, and you must find out myself and my dwelling-place within a year and a day, or I shall find you out and you shall lose your head."

Then he brought the King's son out the same way by which he went in. The green hill closed behind them, and the grey old man disappeared out of sight.

The King's son went home, riding on his horse—

> His hound at his foot,
> His hawk on his hand—

and he sorrowful enough.

THAT evening the King observed that there was grief and great trouble on his young son, and when he went to sleep the King and every person that was in the castle heard heavy sighings and ravings from him. The King was in grief—a goat's head to be on the Queen—but he was seven times worse when they told him the (whole) story how it happened from beginning to end.

He sent for a wise councillor, and asked him did he know where the King of the Black Desert was living.

"I do not, indeed," said he; "but as sure as there's a tail on the cat, unless the young heir finds out that enchanter he will lose his head."

There was great grief that day in the castle of the King. There was a goat's head on the Queen, and the King's son was going searching for an enchanter, without knowing whether he would ever come back.

After a week the goat's head was taken off the Queen, and her own head was put upon her. When she heard of how the goat's head was put upon her, a great hate came upon her against the King's son, and she said " that he may never come back, alive or dead."

Of a Monday morning he left his blessing with his father and his kindred; his travelling bag was bound upon his shoulder, and he went—

> His hound at his foot,
> His hawk on his hand,
> And his fine black horse to bear him.

He walked that day until the sun was gone beneath the shadow of the hills and till the darkness of the night was coming, without knowing where he could get lodgings. He noticed a large wood on his left-hand side, and he drew towards it as quickly as he could, hoping to spend the night under the shelter of the trees. He sat down at the foot of a large oak tree, and opened his travelling bag to take some food and drink, when he saw a great eagle coming towards him.

"Do not be afraid of me, King's son; I know you—you are the son of O'Conor, King of Ireland. I am a friend, and if you give me your horse to give to eat to four hungry birds that I have, I shall bear you farther than your horse would bear you, and, perhaps, I would put you on the track of him you are looking for."

"You can have the horse, and welcome," says the King's son, "although I'm sorrowful at parting from him."

"All right, I shall be here to-morrow at sunrise." With that she opened her great gob, caught hold of the horse, struck in his two sides against one another, took wing, and disappeared out of sight.

The King's son ate and drank his enough, put his travelling bag under his head, and it was not long till he was asleep, and he never awoke till the eagle came and said, "It is time for us to be going; there is a long journey before us. Take hold of your bag and leap up upon my back."

"But to my grief," says he, "I must part from my hound and my hawk."

"Do not be grieved," says she; "they will be here before you when you come back."

Then he leaped up on her back. She took wing, and off

and away with her through the air. She brought him across hills and hollows, over a great sea, and over woods, till he thought that he was at the end of the world. When the sun was going under the shadow of the hills, she came to earth in the midst of a great desert, and said to him, "Follow the path on your right-hand side, and it will bring you to the house of a friend. I must return again to provide for my birds."

He followed the path, and it was not long till he came to the house, and he went in. There was a grey old man sitting in the corner. He rose and said, "A hundred thousand welcomes to you, King's son, from Rathcroghan of Connacht."

"I have no knowledge of you," said the King's son.

"I was acquainted with your grandfather," said the grey old man. "Sit down; no doubt there is hunger and thirst on you."

"I'm not free from them," said the King's son.

The old man then smote his two palms against one another, and two servants came and laid a board with beef, mutton, pork, and plenty of bread before the King's son, and the old man said to him:

"EAT and drink your enough. Perhaps it may be a long time before you get the like again."

He ate and drank as much as he desired, and thanked him for it.

Then the old man said, "You are going seeking for the King of the Black Desert. Go to sleep now, and I will go through my books to see if I can find out the dwelling-place of that King." Then he smote his palms together, and a servant came, and he told him, "Take the King's son to his chamber." He took him to a fine chamber, and it was not long till he fell asleep.

On the morning of the next day the old man came and said:

" Rise up, there is a long journey before you. You must do five hundred miles before midday."

" I could not do it," said the King's son.

" If you are a good rider I will give you a horse that will bring you over the journey."

" I will do as you say," said the King's son.

The old man gave him plenty to eat and to drink, and, when he was satisfied, he gave him a little white garron, and said, " Give the garron his head, and when he stops look up into the air, and you will see three swans as white as snow. Those are the three daughters of the King of the Black Desert. There will be a green napkin in the mouth of one of them: that is the youngest daughter, and there is not anyone alive except her who could bring you to the house of the King of the Black Desert. When the garron stops you will be near a lake. The three swans will come to land on the brink of that lake, and they will make three young women of themselves, and they will go into the lake swimming and dancing. Keep you eye on the green napkin, and when you get the young women in the lake, go and get the napkin, and do not part with it. Go into hiding under a tree, and when the young women will come out, two of them will make swans of themselves, and will go away in the air. Then the youngest daughter will say, " I will do anything for him who will give me my napkin." Come forward then and give her the napkin, and say there is nothing you want but to bring you to her father's house, and tell her you are a king's son from a powerful country."

The King's son did everything as the old man desired him, and when he gave the napkin to the daughter of the King of the Black Desert, he said, " I am the son of O'Conor,

King of Connaught. Bring me to your father. Long am I seeking him."

" Would not it be better for me to do something else for you?" said she.

"I do not want anything else," said he.

"If I show you the house will you not be satisfied?" said she.

"I will be satisfied," said he.

"Now," said she, upon your life do not tell my father that it was I who brought you to his house, and I shall be a good friend to you; but let on," said she, "that you have great powers of enchantment."

"I will do as you say," says he.

Then she made a swan of herself, and said, "Leap up on my back and put you hands under my neck, and keep a hard hold."

E did so, and she shook her wings, and off and away with her over hills and over glens, over sea and over mountains, until she came to earth as the sun was going under. Then she said to him, "Do you see that great house yonder? That is my father's house. Farewell. Any time that you are in danger I shall be at your side." Then she went from him.

The King's son went to the house and went in, and who should he see sitting in a golden chair but the grey old man who had played the cards and the ball with him.

"King's son," said he, "I see that you have found me out before the day and the year. How long since you left home?"

"This morning, when I was rising out of my bed, I saw a rainbow. I gave a leap, spread my two legs on it, and slid as far as this."

"By my hand, it was a great feat you performed," said the old King.

"I could do a more wonderful thing than that if I chose," said the King's son.

"I have three things for you to do," says the old King, "and if you are able to do them, you shall have the choice of my three daughters for wife, and unless you are able to do them, you shall lose your head, as a good many other young men have lost it before you."

"Then," he said, "there be's neither eating nor drinking in my house except once in the week, and we had it this morning."

"It's all one to me," said the King's son. "I could fast for a month if I were on a pinch."

"No doubt you can go without sleep also," says the old King.

 "I CAN, without doubt," said the King's son.

"You shall have a hard bed to-night, then," says the old King. "Come with me till I show it to you." He brought him out then and showed him a great tree with a fork in it, and said, "Get up there and sleep in the fork, and be ready with the rise of the sun."

He went up into the fork, but as soon as the old King was asleep the young daughter came and brought him into a fine room, and kept him there until the old King was about to rise. Then she put him out again into the fork of the tree.

With the rise of the sun the old King came to him, and said, "Come down now and come with me until I show you the thing that you have to do to-day."

He brought the King's son to the brink of a lake and showed him an old castle, and said to him, "Throw every stone in that castle out into the loch, and let you have it done before the sun goes down in the evening." He went away from him then.

The King's son began working, but the stones were stuck to one another so fast that he was not able to raise one of them, and if he were to be working until this day, there would not be one stone out of the castle. He sat down then, thinking what he ought to do, and it was not long until the daughter of the old King came to him and said, "What is the cause of your grief?" He told her the work which he had to do. "Let that put no grief on you; I will do it," said she. Then she gave him bread, meat, and wine, pulled out a little enchanted rod, struck a blow on the old castle, and in a moment every stone of it was at the bottom of the lake. "Now," said she, "do not tell my father that it was I who did the work for you."

When the sun was going down in the evening, the old King came and said, "I see that you have your day's work done."

"I have," said the King's son; "I can do any work at all."

The old King thought now that the King's son had great powers of enchantment, and he said to him, "Your day's work for to-morrow is to lift the stones out of the loch, and to set up the castle again as it was before."

THE KING OF THE BLACK DESERT

He brought the King's son home, and said to him, "Go to sleep in the place where you were last night."

When the old King went to sleep the young daughter came and brought him into the fine chamber, and kept him there till the old King was about to rise in the morning. Then she put him out again in the fork of the tree.

At sunrise the old King came and said, "It's time for you to get to work."

"There's no hurry on me at all," says the King's son, "because I know I can readily do my day's work."

E then went to the brink of the lake, but he was not able to see a stone, the water was that black. He sat down on a rock, and it was not long until Finnuala —that was the name of the old King's daughter—came to him and said, "What have you to do to-day?" He told her, and she said, "Let there be no grief on you. I can do that work for you." Then she gave him bread, beef, mutton, and wine. After that she drew out the little enchanted rod, smote the water of the lake with it, and in a moment the old castle was set up as it had been the day before. Then she said to him, "On your life, don't tell my father that I did this work for you, or that you have any knowledge of me at all."

On the evening of that day the old King came and said, "I see that you have the day's work done."

"I have," said the King's son; "that was an easy-done job."

Then the old King thought that the King's son had more power of enchantment than he had himself, and he said,

"You have only one other thing to do." He brought him home then, and put him to sleep in the fork of the tree, but Finnula came and put him into the fine chamber, and in the morning she sent him out again into the tree. At sunrise the old King came to him, and said, "Come with me till I show you your day's work."

He brought the King's son to a great glen, and showed him a well, and said, "My grandmother lost a ring in that well, and do you get it for me before the sun goes under this morning."

Now, this well was one hundred feet deep and twenty feet round about, and it was filled with water, and there was an army out of hell watching the ring.

WHEN the old King went away Finnuala came and asked, "What have you to do to-day?" He told her, and she said, "That is a difficult task, but I shall do my best to save your life. Then she gave him beef, bread, and wine. Then she made a diver of herself, and went down into the well. It was not long till he saw smoke and lightning coming up out of the well, and he heard a sound like thunder, and anyone who would be listening to that noise, he would think that the army of hell was fighting.

At the end of a while the smoke went away, the lightning and thunder ceased, and Finnuala came up with the ring. She handed the ring to the King's son, and said, "I won the battle, and your life is saved." But, look, the little finger of my right hand is broken. But perhaps it's a lucky thing that it was broken. When my father comes do not give him the ring, but threaten him stoutly. He will bring you, then, to choose your wife, and this is how you shall make your choice. I and my sisters will be in a room; there will be a hole in the door, and we shall all put our hands out in a cluster. You will put your hand through the hole, and the hand that you will keep hold of when my father will open the door, that is the hand of her you shall have for wife. You can know me by my broken little finger."

"I can; and the love of my heart you are, Finnuala," says the King's son.

On the evening of that day the old King came and asked, "Did you get my grandmother's ring?"

"I did, indeed," says the King's son. "There was an army out of hell guarding it, but I beat them; and I would beat seven times as many. Don't you know I'm a Connachtman?"

"GIVE me the ring," says the old King. "Indeed, I won't give it," says he. "I fought hard for it. But do you give me my wife; I want to be going." The old King brought him in, and said, "My three daughters are in that room before you. The hand of each of them is stretched out, and she on whom you will keep your hold until I open the door, that one is your wife."

The King's son thrust his hand through the hole that was in the door, and caught hold of the hand with the broken little finger, and kept a tight hold of it until the old King opened the door of the room.

"This is my wife," said the King's son. "Give me now your daughter's fortune."

" She has no fortune to get, but the brown slender steed to bring you home, and that ye may never come back, alive or dead! "

The King's son and Finnuala went riding on the brown slender steed, and it was not long till they came to the wood where the King's son left his hound and his hawk. They were there before him, together with his fine black horse. He sent the brown slender steed back then. He set Finnuala riding on his horse, and leaped up himself—

> His hound at his heel,
> His hawk on his hand—

and he never stopped till he came to Rathcroghan.

There was great welcome before him there, and it was not long till himself and Finnuala were married. They spent a long, prosperous life. But it is scarcely that even the track of this old castle is to be found to-day in Rathcroghan of Connacht.

DOUGLAS HYDE.

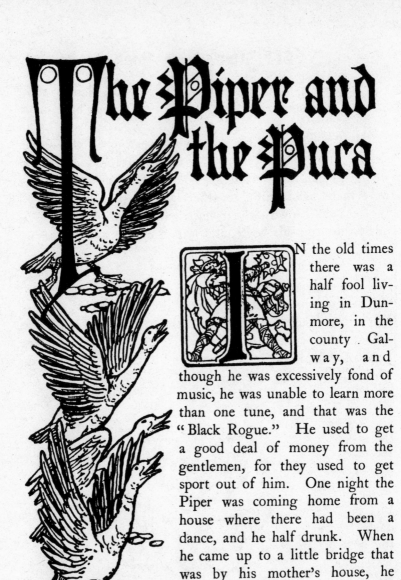

The Piper and the Puca

IN the old times there was a half fool living in Dunmore, in the county . Galway, and though he was excessively fond of music, he was unable to learn more than one tune, and that was the "Black Rogue." He used to get a good deal of money from the gentlemen, for they used to get sport out of him. One night the Piper was coming home from a house where there had been a dance, and he half drunk. When he came up to a little bridge that was by his mother's house, he squeezed the pipes on, and began playing the "Black Rogue." The Púca came behind him, and flung him on his own back.   There were long horns on the Púca, and the Piper got a good grip of them, and then he said :

"Destruction on you, you nasty beast; let me home.   I have a tenpenny-piece in my pocket for my mother, and she wants snuff."

"Never mind your mother," said the Púca, "but keep your hold.   If you fall, you will break your neck and your pipes."   Then the Púca said to him, "Play up for me the 'Shan Van Vocht.'"

"I don't know it," said the Piper.

"NEVER mind whether you do or you don't," said the Púca.   "Play up, and I'll make you know."

The Piper put wind in his bag, and he played such music as made himself wonder.

"Upon my word, you're a fine music-master," says the Piper, then; "but tell me where you're for bringing me."

"There's a great feast in the house of the Banshee, on the top of Croagh Patric, to-night," says the Púca, "and I'm for bringing you there to play music, and, take my word, you'll get the price of your trouble."

"By my word, you'll save me a journey, then," says the Piper, "for Father William put a journey to Croagh Patric on me because I stole the white gander from him last Martinmas."

The Púca rushed him across hills and bogs and rough places, till he brought him to the top of Croagh Patric.

Then the Púca struck three blows with his foot, and a great door opened, and they passed in together into a fine room.

The Piper and
the Púca

The Piper saw a golden table in the middle of the room, and hundreds of old women sitting round about it.

The old women rose up, and said, "A hundred thousand welcomes to you, you Púca of November. Who is this you have with you?"

"The best Piper in Ireland," says the Púca.

One of the old women struck a blow on the ground, and a door opened in the side of the wall, and what should the Piper see coming out but the white gander which he had stolen from Father William.

"Y my conscience, then," says the Piper, "myself and my mother ate every taste of that gander, only one wing, and I gave that to Red Mary, and it's she told the priest I stole his gander."

The gander cleaned the table, and carried it away, and the Púca said, "Play up music for these ladies."

The Piper played up, and the old women began dancing, and they were dancing till they were tired. Then the Púca said to pay the Piper, and every old woman drew out a gold piece and gave it to him.

"By the tooth of Patric," says he, "I'm as rich as the son of a lord."

"Come with me," says the Púca, "and I'll bring you home."

They went out then, and just as he was going to ride on the Púca, the gander came up to him and gave him a new set of pipes.

The Púca was not long until he brought him to Dunmore, and he threw the Piper off at the little bridge, and then he told him to go home, and says to him, " You have two things now that you never had before—you have sense and music." The Piper went home, and he knocked at his mother's door, saying, " Let me in, I'm as rich as a lord, and I'm the best Piper in Ireland."

" You're drunk," says the mother.

" No, indeed," says the Piper, " I haven't drunk a drop."

The mother let him in, and he gave her the gold pieces, and, " Wait now," says he, " till you hear the music I'll play."

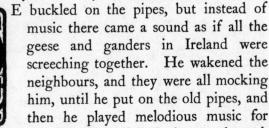

E buckled on the pipes, but instead of music there came a sound as if all the geese and ganders in Ireland were screeching together. He wakened the neighbours, and they were all mocking him, until he put on the old pipes, and then he played melodious music for them; and after that he told them all he had gone through that night.

The next morning, when his mother went to look at the gold pieces, there was nothing there but the leaves of a plant.

The piper went to the priest and told him his story, but the priest would not believe a word from him, until he put the pipes on him, and then the screeching of the ganders and the geese began.

" Leave my sight, you thief," says the priest.

But nothing would do the Piper till he put the old pipes on him to show the priest that his story was true.

He buckled on the old pipes, and he played melodious music, and from that day till the day of his death there was never a Piper in the county Galway was as good as he was.

DOUGLAS HYDE.

240

The Fairy Changeling

ERMOD O'BYRNE of Omah town
In his garden strode up and down;
He pulled his beard, and he beat his
    breast;
And this is his trouble and woe con-
    fessed:

"The good-folk came in the night, and they
Have stolen my bonny wean away;
Have put in his place a changeling,
A weashy, weakly, wizen thing!

"From the speckled hen nine eggs I stole,
And lighting a fire of a glowing coal,
I fried the shells, and I spilt the yolk;
But never a word the stranger spoke.

241

"A bar of metal I heated red
To frighten the fairy from its bed,
To put in the place of this fretting wean
My own bright beautiful boy again.

"But my wife had hidden it in her arms,
And cried, 'For shame!' on my fairy charms;
She sobs, with the strange child on her breast,
'I love the weak, wee babe the best!'"

To Dermod O'Byrne's, the tale to hear,
The neighbours came from far and near;
Outside his gate, in the long boreen,
They crossed themselves, and said between

Their muttered prayers, "He has no luck!
For sure the woman is fairy-struck,
To leave her child a fairy guest,
And love the weak, wee wean the best!"

DORA SIGERSON.

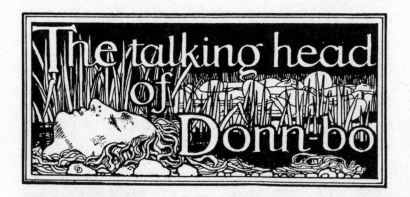

The talking head of Donn-bo

HERE is an old tale told in Erin of a lovable and bright and handsome youth named Donn-bo, who was the best singer of "Songs of Idleness" and the best teller of "King Stories" in the world. He could tell a tale of each king who reigned in Erin, from the "Tale of the Destruction of Dind Righ," when Cova Coelbre was killed, down to the kings who reigned in his own time.

On a night before a battle, the warriors said, "Make minstrelsy to-night for us, Donn-bo." But Donn-bo answered, "No word at all will come on my lips to-night; therefore, for this night let the King-buffoon of Ireland amuse you. But to-morrow, at this hour, in whatsoever place they and I shall be, I will make minstrelsy for the fighting men." For the warriors had said that unless Donn-bo would go with them on that hosting, not one of them would go.

The battle was past, and on the evening of the morrow

at that same hour Donn-bo lay dead, his fair young body
stretched across the body of the King of Ireland, for he had
died in defending his chief. But his head had rolled away
among a wisp of growing rushes by the waterside.

At the feasting of the army on that night a warrior said,
"Where is Donn-bo, that he may make minstrelsy for us,
as he promised us at this hour yesternight, and that he may
tell us the 'King Stories of Erin'?"

A valiant champion of the men of Munster answered, "I
will go over the battle-field and seek for him." He enquired
among the living for Donn-bo, but he found him not, and
then he searched hither and thither among the dead.

AT last he came where the body of the
King of Erin lay, and a young, fair
corpse beside it. In all the air about
there was the sound of minstrelsy, low
and very sweet; dead bards and poets
reciting in faint whispers old tales and
poems to dead chiefs.

The wild, clear note of the battle-march, the *dord fiansa*,
played by the drooping hands of slain warriors upon the
points of broken spears, low like the echo of an echo, sounded
in the clump of rushes hard by; and, above them all, a voice,
faint and very still, that sang a song that was sweeter than
the tunes of the whole world beside.

The voice that sang was the voice of the head of Donn-bo.
The warrior stooped to pick up the head.

"Do not touch me," said the head, "for we are com-
manded by the King of the Plains of Heaven to make music
to-night for our lord, the King of Erin, the shining one
who lies dead beside us; and though all of us are lying dead

likewise, no faintness or feebleness shall prevent us from obeying that command. Disturb me not."

" The hosts of Leinster are asking thee to make minstrelsy for them, as thou didst promise yesternight," said the messenger.

" When my minstrelsy here is done, I will go with thee," saith the head; "but only if Christ, the Son of God, in whose presence I now am, go with me, and if thou takest me to my body again." "That shall be done, indeed," saith the messenger, and when it had ceased chanting for the King of Erin he carried away the head.

When the messenger came again amongst the warriors they stopped their feasting and gathered round him. " Hast thou brought anything from the battle-field?" they cried.

" I have brought the head of Donn-bo," said the man.

"Set it upon a pillar that we may see and hear it," cried they all; and they said, " It is no luck for thee to be like that, Donn-bo, and thou the most beautiful minstrel and the best in Erin. Make music, for the love of Jesus Christ, the Son of God. Amuse the Leinster men to-night as thou didst amuse thy lord a while ago."

Then Donn-bo turned his face to the wall, that the darkness might be around him, and he raised his melody in the quiet night; and the sound of that minstrelsy was so piteous and sad that the hosts sat weeping at the sound of it. Then was the head taken to his body, and the neck joined itself to the shoulders again, and Donn-bo was at rest.

This is the story of the " Talking Head of Donn-bo."

ELEANOR HULL.

THE BRACKET BULL

I wrote this story carefully down, word for word, from the telling of two men — the first, Shawn Cunningham, of Ballinphuil, and the second, Martin Brennan of Ballinlocha, in the barony of Frenchpark. They each told the same story, but Martin Brennan repeated the end of it at greater length than the other. The first half is written down word for word from the mouth of Cunningham, the second half from that of Brennan.

AN CHRAOIBHIN AOIBHINN.

HERE was a man in it long ago, and long ago it was, and if he was in it then he would not be in it now. He was married, and his wife was lost (i.e., died), and he had only one son by the first wife. Then he married the second wife. This second wife had not much regard for the son, and he was obliged to go out on the mountain, far from the house, to take care of the cattle.

There was a bracket (speckled) bull amongst the cows out on the mountain, and of a day that there was great hunger on the lad, the bracket bull heard him complaining and wringing his two hands, and he moved over to him and

246

said to him, "You are hungry, but take the horn off me and lay it on the ground; put your hand into the place where the horn was and you will find food."

When he heard that he went over to the bull, took hold of the horn, twisted it, and it came away with him in his hand. He laid it on the ground, put in his hand, and drew out food and drink and a table-cloth. He spread the table-cloth on the ground, set the food and drink on it, and then he ate and drank his enough. When he had his enough eaten and drunk, he put the table-cloth back again, and left the horn back in the place where it was before.

WHEN he came home that evening he did did not eat a bit of his supper, and his stepmother said to herself that he (must have) got something to eat out on the mountain since he was not eating any of his supper.

When he went out with his cattle the next day his stepmother sent her own daughter out after him, and told her to be watching him till she should see where he was getting the food. The daughter went and put herself in hiding, and she was watching him until the heat of the day came: but when the middle of the day was come she heard every music more excellent than another, and she was put to sleep by that truly melodious music. The bull came then, and the lad twisted the horn off him and drew out the table-cloth, the food, and the drink, and ate and drunk his enough. He put back the horn again then. The music was stopped and the daughter woke up, and was watching him until the evening came, and he drove the cows home then. The mother asked her did she see anything in the field, and she said that she did not. The lad did not eat two bites of his supper, and there was wonder on the stepmother.

The next day when he drove out the cows the stepmother told the second daughter to follow him, and to be watching him till she would see where he was getting things to eat. The daughter followed him and put herself in hiding, but when the heat of the day came the music began and she fell asleep. The lad took the horn off the bull, drew out the table-cloth, the food, and drink, ate and drank his enough, and put back the horn again. The girl woke then, and was watching him until the evening. When the evening came he drove the cows home, and he was not able to eat his supper any more than the two evenings before. The stepmother asked the daughter did she see anything, and she said she did not. There was wonder on the stepmother.

The next day, when the lad went out herding the cows, the stepmother sent the third daughter out after him, and threatened her not to fall asleep, but to have a good watch. The daughter followed the lad, and went into hiding. This daughter had three eyes, for she had an eye in the back of her head. When the bracket bull began playing every music more excellent than another, he put the other eyes to sleep, but he was not able to put the third eye to sleep. When the heat of the day came she saw the bracket bull coming to the boy, and the boy taking the horn off him and eating.

She ran home then, and said to her mother that there wasn't such a dinner in the world as was being set before the boy out of the horn of the bracket bull.

Then the mother let on that she was sick, and she killed a cock, and she let down its blood into her bed, and she put up a sup of the blood into her mouth, and she sent for her husband, saying that she was finding death (dying). Her husband came in, and he saw the blood, and he said, "Anything that is in the world that would save her that she must get it." She said that there wasn't a thing in the world that would save her but a piece of the bracket bull that was on the mountain.

"You must get that," said he.

The bracket bull used to be the first one of the cattle that used to come in every night, and the stepmother sent for two butchers, and she set them on each side of the gate to kill the bracket bull when he would come.

THE bracket bull said to the boy, "I'll be swept (done for) to-night, unless another cow goes before me." He put another cow out before him, and the two butchers were standing on each side of the gate to kill the first one that would come in. The bull sent the cow out before him, going through the gate, and they killed her : and then the stepmother got a piece of her to eat, and she thought that it was the bracket bull that she was eating, and she got better then.

The next night, when the lad came home with the cattle, he ate no more of his supper than any other night, and there was wonder on the stepmother. She heard after this that the bracket bull was in it (i.e., alive) all through, and that he was not killed at that time.

When she heard that she killed a cock, and she let down some of its blood into her bed, and she put a sup of the blood into her mouth, and she played the same trick over again, and said that there was nothing at all to cure her but a piece of the bracket bull.

The butchers were sent for, and they were ready to kill the bracket bull as soon as he came in. The bracket bull sent another one of the cattle in before himself, and the butchers killed it. The woman got part of its flesh, and she thought it was part of the bracket bull she was eating, and she got better.

She found out afterwards that it was not the bracket bull that was dead, and she said, "Never mind; I'll kill the bracket bull yet!"

HE next day, when the lad was herding the cows on the mountain, the bracket bull came and said to him, "Take the horn off me and eat your enough now. That's the last time for you. They are waiting to kill me to-night, but don't you be afraid. It is not they who shall kill me, but another bull shall kill me. Get up on my back now."

The lad got up on his back then and they went home. The two butchers were on each side of the gate waiting for him. The bracket bull struck a horn on each side of him, and he killed the two butchers. Out with him then, and the lad on his back.

He went into a wild wood, and he himself and the lad spent the night in that wood. He was to fight with the other bull on the next day.

When the day came, the bracket bull said, "Take the horn off me and eat your enough—that's the last luck you have. I am to fight with the other bull immediately, and I shall escape from him to-day, but he will have me dead to-morrow by twelve o'clock."

Himself and the other bull fought that day, and the bracket bull came back in the evening, and he himself and the lad passed that night in the wood.

When the next day came, the bracket bull said to him, "Twist the horn off me and eat your enough—that's the last luck you'll have. Listen now to the thing that I'm telling you. When you'll see me dead, go and cut a strip of skin of the back and a strip of the stomach off me, and make a belt of it, and at any time at all there will be any hard pinch on you, you shall have my power."

HE bracket bull went then to fight with the other bull, and the other bull killed him. The other bull went away then. The lad came to the bracket bull where he was lying on the ground, and he was not dead, out-and-out. When he saw the boy coming he said, "Oh," said he, "make haste as well as you can in the world, and take out your knife and cut that strip off me, or you will be killed as well as myself."

There was a trembling in the poor creature's hand, and he was not able to cut a piece at all off the bull, after his feeding him for so long, and after the kindness he had got from him.

The bracket bull spoke again, and told him to cut the strip off him on the instant, and that it would assist him as long as he would be alive. He cut a strip off the back then, and another strip off the belly, and he went away.

There was plenty of trouble and of grief on him, going

of him, and he ought to have that on him too, and he departing without any knowledge of where he was making for, or where he would go.

A gentleman met him on the road, and asked him where he was going. The lad said that he did not himself know where he was going, but that he was going looking for work.

" What are you able to do? " says the gentleman.

" I'm as good a herd as ever you saw, but I'll not tell you a lie—I can do nothing but herding; but, indeed, I'll do that as well as any man that ever you saw."

"T'S you I want," says the gentleman. "There are three giants up by my land, on the one mearing with me, and anything that will go in on their land they will keep it, and I cannot take it off them again. That's all they're asking—my cattle to go in across the mearing to them."

" Never mind them. I'll go bail that I'll take good heed of them, and that I'll not let anything in to them."

The gentleman brought him home then, and he went herding for him. When the grass was getting scarce, he was driving the cows further out. There was a big stone wall between the land of the giants and his master's land. There was fine grass on the other side of the wall. When he saw that, he threw down a gap in the wall and let in the pigs and the cows. He went up into a tree then, and was throwing down apples and all sorts (of fruit) to the pigs.

A giant came out, and when he saw the lad up on the tree throwing down the apples to the pigs, the head rose on him (i.e., he got furious). He came to the tree. " Get down out of that," says he. "I think you big for one bite and small for two bites; come down till I draw you under my long cold teeth."

"Arrah, take yourself easy," says the boy; "perhaps it's too quick I'd come down to you."

"I won't be talking to you any longer," says the giant. He got a leverage on the tree and drew it up out of the roots.

"O down, black thong, and squeeze that fellow," says the lad, for he remembered the advice of the bracket bull. On the instant the black thong leaped out of his hand, and squeezed the giant so hard that the two eyes were going out on his head, for stronger was the power of the bull than the power of the giant. The giant was not able to put a stir out of himself, and he promised anything at all—only to save his life for him. "Anything at all you want," says he to the lad, "you must get it from me."

"I'm not asking anything at all except the loan of the sword that's under your bed," says he.

"I give it to you, and welcome," says the giant. He went in, and brought out the sword with him.

"Try it on the three biggest trees that are in the wood, and you won't feel it in your hand going through them," says the giant.

"I don't see any tree in the wood bigger or uglier than yourself," says he, drawing the sword and whipping the head off him, so that he sent it seven furrows and seven ridges with that stroke.

"If I were to get on the body again," said the head, and

it talking, "and the men of the world wouldn't get me off the trunk again."

"I'll take good care myself of that," says the lad.

When he drove the cows home in the evening, they had that much milk that they had not half enough of vessels, and two coopers were obliged to make new vessels to hold the quantity of milk they had.

"You're the best lad that ever I met," says the gentleman, and he was thankful to him.

The giants used to put—each man of them—a shout of him every evening. The people only heard two shouts that evening. "There's some change in the caher* to-night," said the gentleman, when he heard the two shouts.

"H," says the lad, "I saw one of them going away by himself to-day, and he did not come home yet."

On the next day the lad drove out his cattle until he came to the big stone wall, and he threw a gap in it, and let the cattle into the same place. He went up into a tree and began throwing down the apples. The second giant came running, and said, "What's the meaning of throwing my wall and letting in your cattle on my estate? Get down out of that at once. You killed my brother yesterday."

"Go down, black thong, and bind that one," says the lad. The thong squeezed him so that he was not able to put a stir out of himself, and he promised the lad anything at all—only to spare his life.

---

* Stone fort or rampart or castle.

"I am asking nothing of you but the loan of the old sword that is under your bed."

"I'll give you that, and welcome." He went in, and brought out the sword with him. Each man of them had a sword, and every sword better than another.

"Try that sword on the six biggest trees that are in the wood, and it will go through them without turning the edge."

"I don't see any tree in the wood bigger or uglier than yourself," says he, drawing the sword and whipping the head off him, so that he sent it seven furrows and seven ridges from the body.

"Oh," said the head, "if I were to get going on the body again, and the men of the world wouldn't get me off it again."

"OH, I'll take care of that myself," says the boy.

When he drove the cows home that night there was wonder on the people when they saw the quantity of milk they had. The gentleman said that there was another change in the caher that day again, as he did not hear but only one shout, but the lad said that he saw another one going away that day, and that it was likely that he did not come back yet.

On the next day he went out, and drove the pigs and the cows up to the hall door, and was throwing down the apples to them. The third giant came out—the eldest man of them—and he was full mad after his two brothers being dead, and the teeth that were in his head were making a handstick for him. He told the boy to come down; that he did not know what he would do to him after his having killed his two brothers. "Come down," says he, "till I draw you under my long, cold teeth"; and it was on him the long, cold teeth were, and no lie.

"Go down, black thong, and bind that one till the eyes will be going out on his head with the power of the squeezing that you'll give him."

The black thong leaped from him, and it bound the giant until the two eyes were going out on his head with the squeezing and with the tightening it gave him, and the giant promised to give him anything at all; "but spare my life," says he.

"I'm only asking the loan of the old sword that's under your bed," said the lad.

"HAVE it, and welcome," says the giant. He went in, and brought out the sword with him. "Now," says the giant, "strike the two ugliest stumps in the wood, and the sword will cut them without getting a bentedge."

"Musha, then, by Mary," says the boy, "I don't see any stump in the wood uglier than yourself," and he struck him so that he sent his head seven furrows and seven ridges from the body.

"Ochone for ever!" says the head. "If I were to get going on the body again, the men of the world—they wouldn't get me off the body again."

"I'll take care of that myself," says the boy.

When he came home that night the coopers were not able to make enough of vessels for them to hold the quantity of milk that the cows had, and the pigs were not able to eat with the quantity of apples that they had eaten before that.

He was a while in that way herding the cows and everything that was in the castle, he had it. There was no one at all going near the castle, for there was fear on them.

There was a fiery dragon in that country, and he used to come every seven years, and unless there would be a young woman ready bound before him he would drive the sea through the land, and he would destroy the people. The day came when the dragon was to come, and the lad asked his master to let him go to the place where the dragon was coming. "What's the business you have there?" says the master. "There will be horsemen and coaches and great people there, and the crowds will be gathered together in it out of every place. The horses would rise up on top of you, and you would be crushed under their feet; and it's better for you to stop at home."

"I'LL stop," said the lad. But when he got them all gone he went to the castle of the three giants, and he put a saddle on the best steed they had, and a fine suit on himself, and he took the first giant's sword in his hand, and he went to where the dragon was.

It was like a fair there, with the number of riders and coaches and horses and people that were gathered in it. There was a young lady bound to a post on the brink of the sea, and she waiting for the dragon to come to swallow her. It was the King's daughter that was in it, for the dragon would not take any other woman. When the dragon came out of the sea the lad went against him, and they fought with one another, and were fighting till the evening, until the dragon was frothing at the mouth, and till the sea was red with its blood. He turned the dragon out into the sea at last. He went away then, and said that he would return the next day. He left the steed again in the place where he found it, and he took the fine suit off him, and when the other people returned he was before them. When the people came home that night they were all talking and saying that some champion came to fight with the dragon and turned him out into the sea again. That was the story that every person had, but they did not know who was the champion who did it.

HE next day, when his master and the other people were gone, he went to the castle of the three giants again, and he took out another steed and another suit of valour (i.e., armour), and he brought with him the second giant's sword, and he went to the place where the dragon was to come.

The King's daughter was bound to a post on the shore, waiting for him, and the eyes going out on her head looking would she see the champion coming who fought the dragon the day before. There were twice as many people in it as there were on the first day, and they were all waiting till they would see the champion coming. When the dragon came the lad went in face of him, and the dragon was half confused and sickened after the fight that he had made the day before. They were beating one another till the evening, and then he drove away the dragon. The people tried to keep him, but they were not able. He went from them.

When his master came home that evening the lad was in

the house before him. The master told him that another
champion came that day, and that he had turned the dragon
into the sea. But no doubt the lad knew the story better
himself than he did.

On the next day, when the gentleman was gone, he went
to the caher of the giants, and he took with him another steed
and another suit and the sword of the third giant, and when
he came to fight with the dragon the people thought it was
another champion who was in it.

He himself and the dragon were beating each other, then,
and the sorra such a fight you ever saw. There were wings
on the dragon, and when he was getting it tight he rose up
in the air, and he was thrusting and beating the boy in his
skull till he was nearly destroyed. He remembered the
black thong then, and said, "Black thong, bind that one so
hard that they'll be listening to his screeching in the two
divisions of the world with the squeezing that you'll give
him." The black thong leapt away, and she bound him,
and then the lad took the head off him, and the sea was red
with his blood, and the waves of blood were going on the
top of the water.

The lad came to the land, then, and they tried to keep
him; but he went from them, and as he was riding by the
lady snatched the shoe off him.

He went away, then, and he left the horse and the sword
and the suit of armour in the place where he found them,
and when the gentleman and the other people came home he
was sitting before them at the fire. He asked them how
the fight went, and they told him that the champion killed
the fiery dragon, but that he was gone away, and that no one
at all knew who he was.

When the King's daughter came home she said that she would never marry a man but the man whom that shoe would fit.

There were sons of kings, and great people among them, and they saying that it was themselves who killed the dragon; but she said it was not they, unless the shoe would fit them. Some of them were cutting the toes off their feet, and some of them taking off a piece of the heel, and more of them cutting the big toe off themselves, trying would the shoe fit them. There was no good for them in it. The King's daughter said that she would not marry one man of them.

She sent out soldiers, then, and the shoe with them, to try would it fit anyone at all. Every person, poor and rich, no matter where he was from, must try the shoe on him.

HE lad was stretched out lying on the grass when the soldiers came, and when they saw him they said to him, " Show your foot."

" Oh, don't be humbugging me," says he.

" We have orders," said they, " and we cannot return without trying the shoe on everyone, poor and rich, so stretch out your foot." He did that, and the shoe went in on his foot on the moment.

They said to him that he must come with them.

" Oh, listen to me " (i.e., give me time), said he, " till I dress myself."

He went to the caher of the giants, and he got a fine new suit on him, and he went with them then.

That's where the welcome was for him, and he as dressed

up as e'er a man of them. They had a wedding for three days and three nights.

They got the pond and I the lakelet. They were drowned, and I came through. And as I have it (i.e., the story) to-night, that ye may not have it to-morrow night, or if ye have it itself, that ye may only lose the back teeth by it!

DOUGLAS HYDE.

The Demon Cat

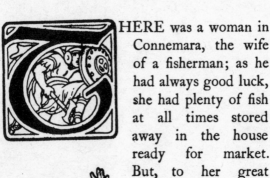

HERE was a woman in Connemara, the wife of a fisherman; as he had always good luck, she had plenty of fish at all times stored away in the house ready for market. But, to her great annoyance, she found that a great cat used to come in at night and devour all the best and finest fish. So she kept a big stick by her, and determined to watch.

One day, as she and a woman were spinning together, the house suddenly became quite dark; and the door was burst open as if by the blast of the tempest, when in walked a huge black cat, who went straight up to the fire, then turned round and growled at them.

"Why, surely this is the devil," said a young girl who was by, sorting fish.

"I'll teach you to call me names," said the cat ; and, jumping at her, he scratched her arm till the blood came. "There, now," he said, "you will be more civil another time when a gentleman comes to see you." And, with that, he walked over to the door, and shut it close to prevent any of them going out, for the poor young girl, while crying loudly from fright and pain, had made a desperate rush to get away.

Just then a man was going by, and, hearing the cries, he pushed open the door, and tried to get in; but the cat stood on the threshold and would let no one pass. On this the man attacked him with a stick, and gave him a sound blow; the cat, however, was more than a match in the fight, for it flew at him, and tore his face and hands so badly that the man at last took to his heels, and ran away as fast as he could.

"Now, it's time for my dinner," said the cat, going up to examine the fish that was laid out on the tables. "I hope the fish is good to-day. Now, don't disturb me, or make a fuss; I can help myself." With that, he jumped up, and began to devour all the best fish, while he growled at the woman.

"Away out of this, you wicked beast!" she cried, giving it a blow with the tongs that would have broken its back, only it was a devil; "out of this; no fish shall you have to-day!"

But the cat only grinned at her, and went on tearing and despoiling and devouring the fish, evidently not a bit the worse for the blows. On this both the women attacked it with sticks, and struck hard blows enough to kill it, on which the cat glared at them and spit fire; then, making a leap, it tore their heads and arms till the blood came, and the frightened women rushed shrieking from the house.

But presently the mistress of the house returned, carrying with her a bottle of holy water; and, looking in, she saw the cat still devouring the fish, and not minding. So she crept over quietly, and threw holy water on it without a word. No sooner was this done than a dense, black smoke filled the place, through which nothing was seen but the two red eyes of the cat burning like coals of fire. Then the smoke gradually cleared away, and she saw the body of the creature burning slowly, till it became shrivelled and black like a cinder, and finally disappeared. And from that time the fish remained untouched and safe from harm, for the power of the Evil One was broken, and the Demon Cat was seen no more.

LADY WILDE.

The Abbot of Inisfalen

(A Legend of Killarney.)

I.

T HE Abbot of Inisfalen
awoke ere dawn of day;
Under the dewy green
leaves went he forth to
pray,
The lake around his island
lay smooth and dark
and deep,
And wrapt in a misty stillness the mountains were all asleep.
Low kneel'd the Abbot Cormac when the dawn was dim
and gray;
The prayers of his holy office he faithfully 'gan to say.
Low kneel'd the Abbot Cormac while the dawn was waxing
red;
And for his sins' forgiveness a solemn prayer he said;
Low kneel'd that holy Abbot while the dawn was waxing
clear;
And he pray'd with loving-kindness for his convent-brethren
dear.

Low kneel'd that blessed Abbot while the dawn was waxing
    bright;
He pray'd a great prayer for Ireland, he pray'd with all his
    might.
Low kneel'd that good old Father while the sun began to
    dart;
He pray'd a prayer for all men, he pray'd it from his heart.
His blissful soul was in Heaven, tho' a breathing man was he;
He was out of Time's dominion, so far as the living may be.

II.

The Abbot of Inisfalen arose upon his feet;
He heard a small bird singing, and O but it sung sweet!
It sung upon a holly-bush, this little snow-white bird;
A song so full of gladness he never before had heard.
It sung upon a hazel, it sung upon a thorn;
He had never heard such music since the hour that he was
    born.
It sung upon a sycamore, it sung upon a briar;
To follow the song and hearken this Abbot could never tire.
Till at last he well bethought him; he might no longer stay;
So he blessed the little white singing-bird, and gladly went
    his way.

III.

But, when he came to his Abbey, he found a wondrous
    change;
He saw no friendly faces there, for every face was strange.
The strange men spoke unto him; and he heard from all and
    each
The foreign tongue of the Sassenach, not wholesome Irish
    speech.

Then the oldest monk came forward, in Irish tongue spake
    he:
"Thou wearest the holy Augustine's dress, and who hath
    given it to thee?"
"I wear the holy Augustine's dress, and Cormac is my name,
The Abbot of this good Abbey by grace of God I am.
I went forth to pray, at the dawn of day; and when my
    prayers were said,
I hearken'd awhile to a little bird that sung above my head."
The monks to him made answer, "Two hundred years have
    gone o'er,
Since our Abbot Cormac went through the gate, and never
    was heard of more.
Matthias now is our Abbot, and twenty have pass'd away.
The stranger is lord of Ireland; we live in an evil day."
"Days will come and go," he said, "and the world will pass
    away,
In Heaven a day is a thousand years, a thousand years are
    a day."

IV.

"Now, give me absolution; for my time is come," said he.
And they gave him absolution as speedily as might be.
Then, close outside the window, the sweetest song they heard
That ever yet since the world began was utter'd by any bird.
The monks look'd out and saw the bird, its feathers all white
    and clean;
And there in a moment, beside it, another white bird was
    seen.
Those two they sang together, waved their white wings,
    and fled;

Flew aloft, and vanished; but the good old man was dead.
They buried his blessed body where lake and greensward
    meet;
A carven cross above his head, a holly-bush at his feet;
Where spreads the beautiful water to gay or cloudy skies,
And the purple peaks of Killarney from ancient woods arise.

WILLIAM ALLINGHAM.

Morraha

(*As told by an Irish Peasant.*)

MORRAHA rose in the morning, and washed his hands and face, and said his prayers, and ate his food; and he asked God to prosper the day for him; and he went down to the brink of the sea, and he saw a currach, short and green, coming towards him; and in it there was but one youthful champion, and he playing hurly from prow to stern of the currach. He had a hurl of gold and a ball of silver; and he stopped not until the currach was in on the shore; and he drew her up on the green grass, and put fastening on her for a day and a year, whether he should be there all that time, or should only be on land for an hour by the clock. And Morraha saluted the young man in words intelligent, intelligible, such as were spoken at that time; and the other saluted him in the same fashion, and asked him would he play a game of cards with him; and Morraha said he had not the wherewithal; and the other answered that he was never without a candle or the making of it; and he put his hand in his pocket and drew out a table and two chairs and a pack of cards, and they sat down on the chairs and went to the card-playing. The first game Morraha won, and the slender red champion bade him make his claim; and he said that the land above him should be filled with stock of sheep in the morning. It was well, and he played no second game, but home he went.

HE next day Morraha went to the brink of the sea, and the young man came in the currach and asked him would he play cards; and they played, and Morraha won. And the young man bade him make his claim; and he said that the land above should be filled with cattle in the morning. It was well, and he played no other game, but went home.

And on the third morning Morraha went to the brink of the sea, and he saw the young man coming. And he drew up his boat on the shore, and asked him would he play cards. And they played, and Morraha won the game; and the young man bade him give his claim. And he said he should have a castle, and of women the finest and fairest; and they were his. It was well, and the young man went away.

On the fourth day the woman asked him how he had found himself, and he told her. "And I am going out," said he, "to play again to-day."

"I cross (forbid) you go again to him. If you have won

so much, you will lose more; and have no more to do with him."

But he went against her will, and he saw the currach coming, and the young man was driving his balls from end to end of the currach. He had balls of silver and a hurl of gold, and he stopped not till he drew his boat on the shore, and made her fast for a year and a day. And Morraha and he saluted each other; and he asked Morraha if he would play a game of cards, and they played and he won. And Morraha said to him, "Give your claim, now."

AID he, "You will hear it too soon. I lay on you the bonds of the art of the Druid not to sleep two nights in one house, nor finish a second meal at the one table, till you bring me the sword of light and news of the death of Anshgayliacht."

He went down to his wife, and sat down in a chair, and gave a groan, and the chair broke in pieces.

"It is the son of a king under spells you are," said his wife; "and you had better have taken my counsel than that the spells should be on you." He said to her to bring news of the death of Anshgayliacht and the sword of light to the slender red champion.

"Go out," said she, "in the morning of the morrow, and take the bridle in the window and shake it; and whatever beast, handsome or ugly, puts the head in it, take that one with you. Do not speak a word to her till she speaks to you; and take with you three pint bottles of ale and three sixpenny loaves, and do the thing she tells you; and when she runs to my father's land, on a height above the court, she will shake herself, and the bells will ring, and my father will say Brown Allree is in the land. And if the son of a king or queen is there, bring him to me on your shoulders; but if it is the son of a poor man, let him come no further."

He rose in the morning, and took the bridle that was in the window and went out and shook it, and Brown Allree came and put her head in it. And he took the three loaves and three bottles of ale, and went riding; and when he was riding, she bent her head down to take hold of her feet with her mouth, in hopes he would speak in ignorance; but he spoke not a word during the time, and the mare at last spoke to him, and said to him to dismount and give her her dinner. He gave her the sixpenny loaf toasted and a bottle of ale to drink. " Sit up, now, riding and take good heed of yourself : there are three miles of fire I have to clear at a leap."

She cleared the three miles of fire at a leap, and asked if he were riding, and he said he was. They went on then, and she told him to dismount and give her a meal; and he did so, and gave her a sixpenny loaf and a bottle; and she consumed them, and said to him there were before them three miles of hill covered with steel thistles, and that she must clear it. And she cleared the hill with a leap, and she asked him if he were still riding, and he said he was. They went on, and she went not far before she told him to give her a meal, and he gave her the bread and the bottleful. And she went over three miles of sea with a leap, and she came then to the land of the King of France; and she went up on a height above the castle, and she shook herself and neighed, and the bells rang; and the King said that it was

Brown Allree was in the land. "Go out," said he, "and if it is the son of a king or queen, carry him in on your shoulders; if it is not, leave him there."

They went out, and the stars of the son of a king were on his breast; and they lifted him high on their shoulders and bore him in to the King. And they passed the night cheerfully with playing and with drinking, with sport and with diversion, till the whiteness of the day came upon the morrow morning.

HEN the young King told the cause of his journey, and he asked of the Queen her counsel and consent, and to give him counsel and good luck, and the woman told him everything she advised him to do. "Go now," said she, "and take with you the best mare in the stable, and go to the door of Rough Niall of the speckled rock, and knock, and call on him to give you news of the death of Anshgayliacht and the sword of light; and let the horse's back be to the door, and apply the spurs, and away with you!"

And in the morning he did so, and he took the best horse from the stable and rode to the door of Niall, and turned the horse's back to the door, and demanded news of the death of Anshgayliacht, and the sword of light; and he applied the spurs, and away with him. And Niall followed him, and as he was passing the gate cut the horse in two. And the mother was there with a dish of puddings and flesh, and she threw it in his eyes and blinded him, and said, "Fool, whatever kind of man it is that's mocking you, isn't that a fine condition you have got into on your father's horse?"

On the morning of the next day Morraha rose and took
another horse from the stable, and went again to the door
of Niall, and knocked and demanded news of the death of
Anshgayliacht, and the sword of light, and applied the spurs
to the horse, and away with him. And Niall followed, and
as he was passing the gate cut the horse in two, and took
half the saddle with him, and his mother met him, and threw
the flesh in his eyes and blinded him.

And on the third day Morraha went also to the door of
Niall; and Niall followed him, and as he was passing the gate
cut away the saddle from under him and the clothes from
his back. Then his mother said to Niall:

"WHATEVER fool it is that's mocking you,
he is out yonder in the little currach,
going home; and take good heed to
yourself, and don't sleep one wink for
three days."

And for three days the little currach
was there before him, and then his
mother came to him and said:

"Sleep as much as you want now. He is gone."

And he went to sleep, and there was heavy sleep on him,
and Morraha went in and took hold of the sword that was
on the bed at his head. And the sword thought to draw
itself out of the hand of Morraha, but it failed. And then
it gave a cry, and it wakened Niall, and Niall said it was
a rude and rough thing to come into his house like that;
and Morraha said to him:

"Leave your much talking, or I will cut the head off
you. Tell me the news of the death of Anshgayliacht."

"Oh, you can have my head."

"But your head is no good to me. Tell me the story."

"Oh," said Niall's wife, "you must get the story."

"Oh," said Morraha, "is the woman your wife?"

"Oh," said the man, "is it not you that have the story?"

"Oh," said she, "you will tell it to us."

"Well," said the man, "let us sit down together till I tell the story. I thought no one would ever get it, but now it will be heard by all."

WHEN I was growing up my mother taught me the language of the birds, and when I got married I used to be listening to their conversation; and I would be laughing; and my wife would be asking me what was the reason of my laughing, but I did not like to tell her, as women are always asking questions. We went out walking one fine morning, and the birds were arguing with one another. One of them said to another:

"Why should you be making comparison with me, when there is not a king nor knight that does not come to look at my tree?"

"Oh, what advantage has your tree over mine, on which there are three rods of magic and mastery growing?"

When I heard them arguing, and knew that the rods were there, I began to laugh.

"Oh," said my wife, "why are you always laughing? I believe it is at myself you are jesting, and I'll walk with you no more."

"Oh, it is not about you I am laughing. It is because I understand the language of the birds."

Then I had to tell her what the birds were saying to one

another; and she was greatly delighted, and she asked me to go home, and she gave orders to the cook to have breakfast ready at six o'clock in the morning. I did not know why she was going out early, and breakfast was ready in the morning at the hour she appointed. She asked me to go out walking. I went with her. She went to the tree, and asked me to cut a rod for her.

"Oh, I will not cut it. Are we not better without it?"

"I will not leave this till I get the rod, to see if there is any good in it."

 CUT the rod, and gave it to her. She turned from me, and struck a blow on a stone and changed it; and she struck a second blow on me, and made of me a black raven, and she went home, and left me after her. I thought she would come back; she did not come, and I had to go into a tree till morning. In the morning, at six o'clock, there was a bellman out, proclaiming that everyone who killed a raven would get a fourpenny bit. At last you would not find man or boy without a gun, nor, if you were to walk three miles, a raven that was not killed. I had to make a nest in the top of the parlour chimney, and hide myself all day till night came, and go out to pick up a bit to support me, till I spent a month. Here she is herself (to say) if it is a lie I am telling.

"It is not," said she.

Then I saw her out walking. I went up to her, and I thought she would turn me back to my own shape, and she struck me with the rod and made of me an old white horse, and she ordered me to be put to a cart with a man to draw stones from morning till night. I was worse off then. She spread abroad a report that I had died suddenly in my bed, and prepared a coffin, and waked me, and buried me. Then she had no trouble. But when I got tired, I began to kill everyone who came near me, and I used to go into the haggard every night and destroy the stacks of corn; and when a man came near me in the morning, I would follow him till I broke his bones. Everyone got afraid of me. When she saw I was doing mischief, she came to meet me, and I thought she would change me. And she did change me, and made a fox of me. When I saw she was doing me every sort of damage, I went away from her. I knew there was a badger's hole in the garden, and I went there till night came, and I made great slaughter among the ducks and geese. There she is herself to say if I am telling a lie.

"Oh, you are telling nothing but the truth, only less than the truth."

When she had enough of my killing the fowl, she came out into the garden, for she knew I was in the badger's hole. She came to me, and made me a wolf. I had to be off, and go to an island, where no one at all would see me, and now and then I used to be killing sheep, for there were not many of them, and I was afraid of being seen and hunted; and so I passed a year, till a shepherd saw me among the sheep, and a pursuit was made after me. And when the dogs came near me, there was no place for me to escape to from them; but I recognised the sign of the King among the men, and I made for him, and the King cried out to stop the hounds. I took a leap upon the front of the King's saddle, and the woman behind cried out, "My King and my lord, kill him, or he will kill you."

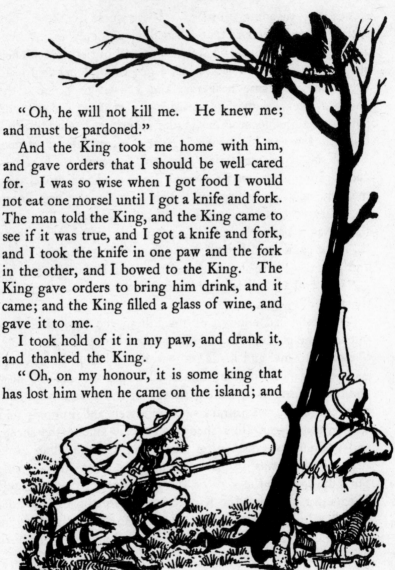

"Oh, he will not kill me. He knew me; and must be pardoned."

And the King took me home with him, and gave orders that I should be well cared for. I was so wise when I got food I would not eat one morsel until I got a knife and fork. The man told the King, and the King came to see if it was true, and I got a knife and fork, and I took the knife in one paw and the fork in the other, and I bowed to the King. The King gave orders to bring him drink, and it came; and the King filled a glass of wine, and gave it to me.

I took hold of it in my paw, and drank it, and thanked the King.

"Oh, on my honour, it is some king that has lost him when he came on the island; and

I will keep him, as he is trained; and perhaps he will serve us yet."

And this is the sort of King he was—a King who had not a child living. Eight sons were born to him and three daughters, and they were stolen the same night they were born. No matter what guard was placed over them, the child would be gone in the morning. The Queen was now carrying the twelfth child, and when she was lying-in, the King took me with him to watch the baby. The women were not satisfied with me. "Oh," said the King, "what was all your watching ever? One that was born to me I have not; and I will leave this one in the dog's care, and he will not let it go."

COUPLING was put between me and the cradle, and when everyone went to sleep I was watching till the person woke who attended in the daytime; but I was there only two nights when, it was near the day, I saw the hand coming down through the chimney, and the hand was so big that it took round the child altogether, and thought to take him away. I caught hold of the hand above the wrist, and, as I was fastened to the cradle, I did not let go my hold till I cut the hand from the wrist, and there was a howl from the person without. I laid the hand in the cradle with the child, and, as I was tired, I fell asleep; and when I awoke I had neither child nor hand; and I began to howl, and the King heard me, and he cried out that something was wrong with me, and he sent servants to see what was the matter with me, and when the messenger came he saw me covered with blood, and he could

not see the child; and he went to the King, and told him the child was not to be got. The King came, and saw the cradle coloured with the blood, and he cried out, "Where was the child gone?" and everyone said it was the dog had eaten it.

The King said, "It is not: loose him, and he will get the pursuit himself."

HEN I was loosed, I found the scent of the blood till I came to a door of the room in which the child was. I went to the King, and took hold of him, and went back again, and began to tear at the door. The King followed me, and asked for the key. The servant said it was in the room of the stranger woman. The King caused search to be made for her, and she was not to be found. "I will break the door," said the King, "as I can't get the key." The King broke the door, and I went in, and went to the trunk, and the King asked for a key to unlock it. He got no key, and he broke the lock. When he opened the trunk the child and the hand were stretched side by side, and the child was asleep. The King took the hand, and ordered a woman to come for the child, and he showed the hand to everyone in the house. But the stranger woman was gone, and she did not see the King; and here she is herself to say if I am telling lies of her.

"Oh, it's nothing but the truth you have."

The King did not allow me to be tied any more. He said there was nothing so much to wonder at as that I cut the hand off, and I tied.

The child was growing till he was a year old, and he was beginning to walk, and there was no one caring for him more than I was. He was growing till he was three, and he was running out every minute; so the King ordered a silver chain to be put between me and the child, so that he might not go away from me. I was out with him in the garden every day, and the King was as proud as the world of the child. He would be watching him every place we went, till the child grew so wise that he would loose the chain and get off. But one day that he loosed it I failed to find him; and I ran into the house and searched the house, but there was no getting him for me. The King cried to go out and find the child, that he had got loose from the dog. They went searching for him, but they could not find him. When they failed altogether to find him, there remained no more favour with the King towards me, and everyone disliked me, and I grew weak, for I did not get a morsel to eat half the time. When summer came I said I would try and go home to my own country. I went away one fine morning, and I went swimming, and God helped me till I came home. I went into the garden, for I knew there was a place in the garden where I could hide myself, for fear she should see me. In the morning I saw my wife out walking, and my child with her, held by the hand. I pushed out to see the child, and, as he was looking about him everywhere, he saw me, and called out, " I see my shaggy papa. Oh," said he; " oh, my heart's love, my shaggy papa, come here till I see you."

I was afraid the woman would see me, as she was asking the child where he saw me, and he said I was up in a tree; and the more the child called me, the more I hid myself. The woman took the child home with her, but I knew he would be up early in the morning.

I went to the parlour window, and the child was within,

and he playing. When he saw me, he cried out, "Oh, my heart's love, come here till I see you, shaggy papa." I broke the window, and went in, and he began to kiss me. I saw the rod in front of the chimney, and I jumped up at the rod and knocked it down. "Oh, my heart's love, no one would give me the pretty rod." I thought he would strike me with the rod, but he did not. When I saw the time was short, I raised my paw, and I gave him a scratch below the knee. "Oh, you naughty, dirty, shaggy papa; you have hurt me so much—I'll give yourself a blow of the rod." He struck me a light blow, and as there was no sin on him, I came back to my own shape again. When he saw a man standing before him he gave a cry, and I took him up in my arms. The servants heard the child. A maid came in to see what was the matter with him. When she saw me she gave a cry out of her, and she said, "Oh, my soul to God, if the master isn't come to life again."

Another came in, and said it was he, really. And when the mistress heard of it, she came to see with her own eyes, for she would not believe I was there; and when she saw me she said she'd drown herself. And I said to her, "If you yourself will keep the secret, no living man will ever get the story from me until I lose my head."

Many's the man has come asking for the story, and I never let one return; but now everyone will know it, but she is as much to blame as I. I gave you my head on the spot, and a thousand welcomes, and she cannot say I have been telling anything but the truth.

"Oh, surely, nor are you now."

When I saw I was in a man's shape I said I would take the child back to his father and mother, as I knew the grief

they were in after him. I got a ship, and took the child
with me; and when I was journeying I came to land on an
island, and I saw not a living soul on it, only a court, dark
and gloomy. I went in to see was there anyone in it.
There was no one but an old hag, tall and frightful, and she
asked me, "What sort of person are you?" I heard someone groaning in another room, and I said I was a doctor,
and I asked her what ailed the person who was groaning.

"Oh," said she, "it is my son, whose hand has been bitten
from his wrist by a dog."

I knew then it was the boy who was taking the child from
me, and I said I would cure him if I got a good reward.

 "HAVE nothing, but there are eight
young lads and three young women, as
handsome as anyone laid eyes on, and
if you cure him I will give you them."

"But tell me in what place his hand
was cut from."

"Oh, it was out in another country
twelve years ago."

"Show me the way, that I may see him."

She brought me into a room, so that I saw him, and his
arm was swelled up to the shoulder. He asked if I would
cure him; and I said I could cure him if he would give me
the reward his mother promised.

"Oh, I will give it, but cure me."

"Well, bring them out to me."

The hag brought them out of the room. I said I would
burn the flesh that was on his arm. When I looked on him
he was howling with pain. I said that I would not leave him
in pain long. The thief had only one eye in his forehead.

I took a bar of iron, and put it in the fire till it was red, and I said to the hag, "He will be howling at first, but will fall asleep presently, and do not wake him until he has slept as much as he wants. I will close the door when I am going out." I took the bar with me, and I stood over him, and I turned it across through his eye as far as I could. He began to bellow, and tried to catch me, but I was out and away, having closed the door. The hag asked me, "Why is he bellowing?"

"Oh, he will be quiet presently, and will sleep for a good while, and I'll come again to have a look at him; but bring me out the young men and the young women."

I took them with me, and I said to her, "Tell me where you got them."

"OH, my son brought them with him, and they are the offspring of the one King."

I was well satisfied, and I had no liking for delay to get myself free from the hag, and I took them on board the ship, and the child I had myself. I thought the King might leave me the child I nursed myself; but when I came to land, and all those young people with me, the King and Queen were out walking. The King was very aged, and the Queen aged likewise. When I came to converse with them, and the twelve with me, the King and Queen began to cry. I asked, "Why are you crying?"

"Oh, it is for good cause I am crying. As many children as these I should have, and now I am withered, grey, at the end of my life, and I have not one at all."

"Oh, belike, you will yet have plenty."

I told him all I went through, and I gave him the child in his hand, and: "These are your other children who were stolen from you, whom I am giving to you safe. They are gently reared."

When the King heard who they were, he smothered them with kisses and drowned them with tears, and dried them with fine cloths, silken, and the hairs of his own head, and so also did their mother, and great was his welcome for me, as it was I who found them all. And the King said to me, "I will give you your own child, as it is you who have earned him best; but you must come to my court every year, and the child with you, and I will share with you my possessions."

"Oh, I have enough of my own, and after my death I will leave it to the child."

I spent a time till my visit was over, and I told the King all the troubles I went through, only I said nothing about my wife. And now you have the story of the death of Anshgayliacht, the hag's son.

And Morraha thanked Rough Niall for the story, and he struck the ground with the Sword of Light, and Brown Allree was beside of him and she said to him, "Sit up, now, riding, and take good heed of yourself," and at one leap she cleared the sea and at the next the three miles of hill covered with steel thistles and at the third the three miles of fire, and then he was home and he told the tale of the death of Anshgayliacht to the Slender Red Champion and gave him the Sword of Light, and he was well pleased to get them, and he took the spells of Morraha, and he had his wife and his castle back again, and by-and-by the five children; but he never put his hand to card-playing with strangers again.

W. LARMINIE.
(From "West Irish Folk Tales.")

The Kildare Pooka

R. H—— R——, when he was alive, used to live a good deal in Dublin, and he was once a great while out of the country on account of the "ninety-eight" business. But the servants kept on in the big house at Rath—— all the same as if the family was at home. Well, they used to be frightened out of their lives, after going to their beds, with the banging of the kitchen door and the clattering of fire-irons and the pots and plates and dishes. One evening they sat up ever so long keeping one another in heart with stories about ghosts and that, when —what would you have of it?—the little scullery boy that used to be sleeping over the horses, and could not get room at the fire, crept into the hot hearth, and when he got tired listening to the stories, sorra fear him, but he fell dead asleep.

Well and good. After they were all gone, and the kitchen raked up, he was woke with the noise of the kitchen door opening, and the trampling of an ass on the kitchen floor. He peeped out, and what should he see but a big ass, sure enough, sitting on his curabingo and yawning before the fire. After a little he looked about him, and began scratching his ears as if he was quite tired, and says he, "I may as well begin first as last." The poor boy's teeth began to chatter in his head, for, says he, "Now he's going to ate me"; but the fellow with the long ears and tail on him had something else to do. He stirred the fire, and then he brought in a pail of water from the pump, and filled a big pot that he put on the fire before he went out. He then put in his hand —foot, I mean—into the hot hearth, and pulled out the little boy. He let a roar out of him with the fright; but the pooka only looked at him, and thrust out his lower lip to show how little he valued him, and then he pitched him into his pew again.

Well, he then lay down before the fire till he heard the boil coming on the water, and maybe there wasn't a plate, or a dish, or a spoon on the dresser that he didn't fetch and put in the pot, and wash and dry the whole bilin' of 'em as well as e'er a kitchen maid from that to Dublin town. He then put all of them up on their places on the shelves; and if he didn't give a good sweepin' to the kitchen, leave it till again. Then he comes and sits fornent the boy, let down one of his ears, and cocked up the other, and gave a grin. The poor fellow strove to roar out, but not a dheeg 'ud come out of his throat. The last thing the pooka done was to rake up the fire and walk out, giving such a slap o' the door that the boy thought the house couldn't help tumbling down.

Well, to be sure, if there wasn't a hullabuloo next morning when the poor fellow told his story! They could talk of nothing else the whole day. One said one thing, another said another, but a fat, lazy scullery girl said the wittiest thing of all. "Musha!" says she, "if the pooka does be cleaning up everything that way when we are asleep, what should we be slaving ourselves for doing his work?" "*Sha gu dheine*," says another, "them's the wisest words you ever said, Kauth; it's meeself won't contradict you."

O said, so done. Not a bit of a plate or dish saw a drop of water that evening, and not a besom was laid on the floor, and everyone went to bed soon after sundown. Next morning everything was as fine as fine in the kitchen, and the lord mayor might eat his dinner off the flags. It was great ease to the lazy servants, you may depend, and everything went on well till a foolhardy gag of a boy said he would stay up one night and have a chat with the pooka. He was a little daunted when the door was thrown open and the ass marched up to the fire.

"And then, sir," says he at last, picking up courage, "if it isn't taking a liberty, might I ax who you are, and why you are so kind as to do half of the day's work for the girls every night?" "No liberty at all," says the pooka, says he: "I'll tell you, and welcome. I was a servant in the time of Squire R——'s father, and was the laziest rogue that ever was clothed and fed, and done nothing for it. When my time came for the other world, this is the punishment was laid on me to come here and do all this labour every night, and then go out in the cold. It isn't so bad in the fine weather; but if you only knew what it is to stand with your head between your legs, facing the storm from midnight to sunrise, on a bleak winter night." "And could we do anything for your comfort, my poor fellow?" says the boy. "Musha, I don't know," says the pooka; "but I think a good quilted frieze coat would help me to keep the life in me them long nights." "Why, then, in troth, we'd be the ungratefullest of people if we didn't feel for you."

To make a long story short, the next night the boy was there again; and if he didn't delight the poor pooka, holding a fine warm coat before him, it's no mather! Betune the pooka and the man, his legs was got into the four arms of it, and it was buttoned down the breast and the belly, and he was so pleased he walked up to the glass to see how it looked. "Well," says he, "it's a long lane that has no turning. I am much obliged to you and your fellow-servants. You have made me happy at last. Good night to you."

So he was walking out, but the other cried, "Och! sure you're going too soon. What about the washing and sweeping?" "Ah, you may tell the girls that they must now get their turn. My punishment was to last till I was thought worthy of a reward for the way I done my duty. You'll see me no more." And no more they did, and right sorry they were for having been in such a hurry to reward the ungrateful pooka.

PATRICK KENNEDY.

The King's Son

WHO rideth through the
driving rain
At such a headlong
speed?
Naked and pale he rides
amain
Upon a naked steed.

Nor hollow nor height his going bars,
His wet steed shines like silk,
His head is golden to the stars
And his limbs are white as milk.

But, lo, he dwindles as the light
That lifts from a black mere,
And, as the fair youth wanes from sight,
The steed grows mightier.

What wizard by yon holy tree
Mutters unto the sky
Where Macha's flame-tongued horses flee
On hoofs of thunder by?

The King's Son

Ah, 'tis not holy so to ban
   The youth of kingly seed:
Ah! woe, the wasting of a man
   Who changes to a steed.

Nightly upon the Plain of Kings,
   When Macha's day is nigh,
He gallops; and the dark wind brings
   His lonely human cry.

THOMAS BOYD.

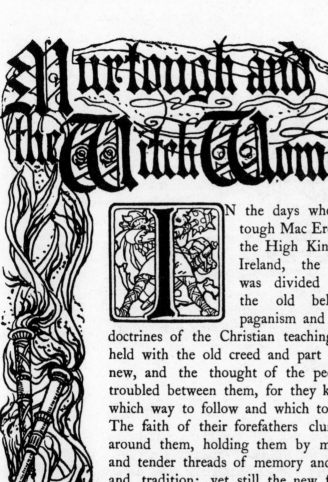

Murtough and the Witch-Woman

IN the days when Murtough Mac Erca was in the High Kingship of Ireland, the country was divided between the old beliefs of paganism and the new doctrines of the Christian teaching. Part held with the old creed and part with the new, and the thought of the people was troubled between them, for they knew not which way to follow and which to forsake. The faith of their forefathers clung close around them, holding them by many fine and tender threads of memory and custom and tradition; yet still the new faith was making its way, and every day it spread wider and wider through the land.

The family of Murtough had joined itself to the Christian faith, and his three brothers were bishops and abbots of the Church, but Murtough himself remained a pagan, for he was a wild and lawless prince, and the peaceful teachings of the Christian doctrine, with its forgiveness of enemies, pleased him not at all. Fierce and cruel was his life, filled with dark deeds and bloody wars, and savage and tragic was his death, as we shall hear.

OW Murtough was in the sunny summer palace of Cletty, which Cormac, son of Art, had built for a pleasure house on the brink of the slow-flowing Boyne, near the Fairy Brugh of Angus the Ever Young, the God of Youth and Beauty. A day of summer was that day, and the King came forth to hunt on the borders of the Brugh, with all his boon companions around him. But when the high-noon came the sun grew hot, and the King sat down to rest upon the fairy mound, and the hunt passed on beyond him, and he was left alone.

There was a witch woman in that country whose name was " Sigh, Sough, Storm, Rough Wind, Winter Night, Cry, Wail, and Groan." Star-bright and beautiful was she in face and form, but inwardly she was cruel as her names. And she hated Murtough because he had scattered and destroyed the Ancient Peoples of the Fairy Tribes of Erin, her country and her fatherland, and because in the battle which he fought at Cerb on the Boyne her father and her mother and her sister had been slain. For in those days women went to battle side by side with men.

She knew, too, that with the coming of the new faith trouble would come upon the fairy folk, and their power and their great majesty would depart from them, and men would call them demons, and would drive them out with psalm-singing and with the saying of prayers, and with the sound of little tinkling bells. So trouble and anger wrought in the witch woman, and she waited the day to be revenged on Murtough, for he being yet a pagan, was still within her power to harm.

O when Sheen (for Sheen or "Storm" was the name men gave to her) saw the King seated on the fairy mound and all his comrades parted from him, she arose softly, and combed her hair with her comb of silver adorned with little ribs of gold, and she washed her hands in a silver basin wherein were four golden birds sitting on the rim of the bowl, and little bright gems of carbuncle set round about the rim. And she donned her fairy mantle of flowing green, and her cloak, wide and hooded, with silvery fringes, and a brooch of fairest gold. On her head were tresses yellow like to gold, plaited in four locks, with a golden drop at the end of each long tress. The hue of her hair was like the flower of the iris in summer or like red gold after the burnishing thereof. And she wore on her breasts and at her shoulders marvellous clasps of gold, finely worked with the tracery of the skilled craftsman, and a golden twisted torque around her throat. And when she was decked she went softly and sat down beside Murtough on the turfy hunting mound. And after a space Murtough perceived her sitting there, and the sun shining upon her, so that the glittering of the gold and of her golden hair and the bright shining of the green silk of her garments, was like the yellow iris-beds upon the lake on a sunny summer's day. Wonder and terror seized on Murtough at

295

her beauty, and he knew not if he loved her or if he hated her the most; for at one moment all his nature was filled with longing and with love of her, so that it seemed to him that he would give the whole of Ireland for the loan of one hour's space of dalliance with her; but after that he felt a dread of her, because he knew his fate was in her hands, and that she had come to work him ill. But he welcomed her as if she were known to him and he asked her wherefore she was come. "I am come," she said, "because I am beloved of Murtough, son of Erc, King of Erin, and I come to seek him here." Then Murtough was glad, and he said, "Dost thou not know me, maiden?" "I do," she answered, "for all secret and mysterious things are known to me and thou and all the men of Erin are well known."

AFTER he had conversed with her awhile, she appeared to him so fair that the King was ready to promise her anything in life she wished, so long as she would go with him to Cletty of the Boyne. "My wish," she said, "is that you take me to your house, and that you put out from it your wife and your children because they are of the new faith, and all the clerics that are in your house, and that neither your wife nor any cleric be permitted to enter the house while I am there."

"I will give you," said the King, "a hundred head of every herd of cattle that is within my kingdom, and a hundred drinking horns, and a hundred cups, and a hundred rings of gold, and a feast every other night in the summer palace of Cletty. But I pledge thee my word, oh, maiden, it were easier for me to give thee half of Ireland than to do

MURTOUGH AND THE
WITCH WOMAN

this thing that thou hast asked." For Murtough feared that when those that were of the Christian faith were put out of his house, she would work her spells upon him, and no power would be left with him to resist those spells.

"I will not take thy gifts," said the damsel, "but only those things that I have asked; moreover, it is thus, that my name must never be uttered by thee, nor must any man or woman learn it."

"What is thy name," said Murtough, "that it may not come upon my lips to utter it?"

AND she said, "Sigh, Sough, Storm, Rough Wind, Winter Night, Cry, Wail, Groan, this is my name, but men call me Sheen, for 'Storm' or Sheen is my chief name, and storms are with me where I come."

Nevertheless, Murtough was so fascinated by her that he brought her to his home, and drove out the clerics that were there, with his wife and children along with them, and drove out also the nobles of his own clan, the children of Niall, two great and gallant battalions. And Duivsech, his wife, went crying along the road with her children around her to seek Bishop Cairnech, the half-brother of her husband, and her own soul-friend, that she might obtain help and shelter from him.

But Sheen went gladly and light-heartedly into the House of Cletty, and when she saw the lovely lightsome house and the goodly nobles of the clan of Niall, and the feasting and banqueting and the playing of the minstrels and all the joyous noise of that kingly dwelling, her heart was lifted within her, and "Fair as a fairy palace is this house of Cletty," said she.

"Fair, indeed, it is," replied the King; "for neither the Kings of Leinster nor the Kings of mighty Ulster, nor the lords of the clans of Owen or of Niall, have such a house as this; nay, in Tara of the Kings itself, no house to equal this house of mine is found." And that night the King robed himself in all the splendour of his royal dignity, and on his right hand he seated Sheen, and a great banquet was made before them, and men said that never on earth was to be seen a woman more goodly of appearance than she. And the King was astonished at her, and he began to ask her questions, for it seemed to him that the power of a great goddess of the ancient time was in her; and he asked her whence she came, and what manner was the power that he saw in her. He asked her, too, did she believe in the God of the clerics, or was she herself some goddess of the older world? For he feared her, feeling that his fate was in her hands.

She laughed a careless and a cruel laugh, for she knew that the King was in their power, now that she was there alone with him, and the clerics and the Christian teachers gone. "Fear me not, O Murtough," she cried; "I am, like thee, a daughter of the race of men of the ancient family of Adam and of Eve; fit and meet my comradeship with thee; therefore, fear not nor regret. And as to that true God of thine, worker of miracles and helper of His people, no miracle in all the world is there that I, by mine own unaided power, cannot work the like. I can create a sun and moon; the heavens I can sprinkle with radiant stars of night. I can call up to life men fiercely fighting in conflict, slaughtering one another. Wine I could make of the cold water of the Boyne, and sheep of lifeless stones, and swine of ferns. In the presence of the hosts I can make gold and silver, plenty and to spare; and hosts of famous fighting men I can produce from naught. Now, tell me, can thy God work the like?"

"Work for us," says the King, "some of these great wonders." Then Sheen went forth out of the house, and she set herself to work spells on Murtough, so that he knew not whether he was in his right mind or no. She took of the water of the Boyne and made a magic wine thereout, and she took ferns and spiked thistles and light puff-balls of the woods, and out of them she fashioned magic swine and sheep and goats, and with these she fed Murtough and the hosts. And when they had eaten, all their strength went from them, and the magic wine sent them into an uneasy sleep and restless slumbers. And out of stones and sods of earth she fashioned three battalions, and one of the battalions she placed at one side of the house, and the other at the further side beyond it, and one encircling the rest southward along the hollow windings of the glen. And thus were these battalions, one of them all made of men stark-naked and their colour blue, and the second with heads of goats with shaggy beards and horned; but the third, more terrible than they, for these were headless men, fighting like human beings, yet finished at the neck; and the sound of heavy shouting as of hosts and multitudes came from the first and the second battalion, but from the third no sound save only that they waved their arms and struck their weapons together, and smote the ground with their feet impatiently. And though terrible was the shout of the blue men and the bleating of the goats with human limbs, more horrible yet was the stamping and the rage of those headless men, finished at the neck.

And Murtough, in his sleep and in his dreams, heard the battle-shout, and he rose impetuously from off his bed, but the wine overcame him, and his strength departed from him, and he fell helplessly upon the floor. Then he heard the challenge a second time, and the stamping of the feet without, and he rose again, and madly, fiercely, he set on them, charging the hosts and scattering them before him, as he thought, as far as the fairy palace of the Brugh. But all his strength was lost in fighting phantoms, for they were but stones and sods and withered leaves of the forest that he took for fighting men.

NOW Duivsech, Murtough's wife, knew what was going on. She called upon Cairnech to arise and to gather together the clans of the children of his people, the men of Owen and of Niall, and together they went to the fort; but Sheen guarded it well, so that they could by no means find an entrance. Then Cairnech was angry, and he cursed the place, and he dug a grave before the door, and he stood up upon the mound of the grave, and rang his bells and cursed the King and his house, and prophesied his downfall. But he blessed the clans of Owen and of Niall, and they returned to their own country.

Then Cairnech sent messengers to seek Murtough and to draw him away from the witch woman who sought his destruction, but because she was so lovely the King would believe no evil of her; and whenever he made any sign to go to Cairnech, she threw her spell upon the King, so that he could not break away. When he was so weak and faint that he had no power left, she cast a sleep upon him, and she went round the house, putting everything in readiness. She called upon her magic host of warriors, and set them round the fortress, with their spears and javelins pointed inwards towards the house, so that the King would not dare to go out amongst them. And that night was a night of Samhain-tide, the eve of Wednesday after All Souls' Day.

 HEN she went everywhere throughout the house, and took lighted brands and burning torches, and scattered them in every part of the dwelling. And she returned into the room wherein Murtough slept, and lay down by his side. And she caused a great wind to spring up, and it came soughing through the house from the north-west; and the King said, "This is the sigh of the winter night." And Sheen smiled, because, unwittingly, the King had spoken her name, for she knew by that that the hour of her revenge had come. "'Tis I myself that am Sigh and Winter Night," she said, "and I am Rough Wind and Storm, a daughter of fair nobles; and I am Cry and Wail, the maid of elfin birth, who brings ill-luck to men."

After that she caused a great snowstorm to come round the house; and like the noise of troops and the rage of battle was the storm, beating and pouring in on every side, so that drifts of deep snow were piled against the walls, blocking the doors and chilling the folk that were feasting within the house. But the King was lying in a heavy, unresting sleep, and Sheen was at his side. Suddenly he screamed out of his sleep and stirred himself, for he heard the crash of falling timbers and the noise of the magic hosts, and he smelled the strong smell of fire in the palace.

He sprang up. "It seems to me," he cried, "that hosts of demons are around the house, and that they are slaughtering my people, and that the house of Cletty is on fire." "It was but a dream," the witch maiden said. Then he slept again, and he saw a vision, to wit, that he was tossing in a ship at sea, and the ship floundered, and above his head a griffin, with sharp beak and talons, sailed, her wings outspread and covering all the sun, so that it was dark as middle-night; and lo! as she rose on high, her plumes quivered for a moment in the air; then down she swooped and picked him from the waves, carrying him to her eyrie on the dismal cliff outhanging o'er the ocean; and the griffin began to pierce him and to prod him with her talons, and to pick out pieces of his flesh with her beak; and this went on awhile, and then a flame, that came he knew not whence, rose from the nest, and he and the griffin were enveloped in the flame. Then in her beak the griffin picked him up, and together they fell downward over the cliff's edge into the seething ocean; so that, half by fire and half by water, he died a miserable death.

When the King saw that vision, he rose screaming from his sleep, and donned his arms; and he made one plunge forward seeking for the magic hosts, but he found no man to answer him. The damsel went forth from the house, and Murtough made to follow her, but as he turned the flames leaped out, and all between him and the door was one vast sheet of flame. He saw no way of escape, save the vat of wine that stood in the banqueting hall, and into that he got; but the burning timbers of the roof fell upon his head and the hails of fiery sparks rained on him, so that half of him was burned and half was drowned, as he had seen in his dream.

The next day, amid the embers, the clerics found his corpse, and they took it up and washed it in the Boyne, and carried it to Tuilen to bury it. And they said, "Alas! that Mac Erca, High King of Erin, of the noble race of Conn and of the descendants of Ugaine the Great, should die fighting with sods and stones! Alas! that the Cross of Christ was not signed upon his face that he might have known the witchdoms of the maiden what they were."

S they went thus, bewailing the death of Murtough and bearing him to his grave, Duivsech, wife of Murtough, met them, and when she found her husband dead, she struck her hands together and she made a great and mournful lamentation; and because weakness came upon her she leaned her back against the ancient tree that is in Aenech Reil; and a burst of blood broke from her heart, and there she died, grieving for her husband. And the grave of Murtough was made wide and deep, and there they laid the Queen beside him, two in the one grave, near the north side of the little church that is in Tuilen.

Now, when the burial was finished, and the clerics were reciting over his grave the deeds of the King, and were making prayers for Murtough's soul that it might be brought out of hell, for Cairnech showed great care for this, they saw coming towards them across the sward a lonely woman, star-bright and beautiful, and a kirtle of priceless silk upon her, and a green mantle with its fringes of silver thread flowing to the ground. She reached the place where the clerics were, and saluted them, and they saluted her.

And they marvelled at her beauty, but they perceived on
her an appearance of sadness and of heavy grief. They asked
of her, " Who art thou, maiden, and wherefore art thou come
to the house of mourning? For a king lies buried here."
" A king lies buried here, indeed," said she, "and I it was
who slew him, Murtough of the many deeds, of the race of
Conn and Niall, High King of Ireland and of the West.
And though it was I who wrought his death, I myself will
die for grief of him."

ND they said, " Tell us, maiden, why you
brought him to his death, if so be that
he was dear to thee? " And she said,
" Murtough was dear to me, indeed,
dearest of the men of the whole world;
for I am Sheen, the daughter of Sige,
the son of Dian, from whom Ath Sigi
or the ' Ford of Sige ' is called to-day. But Murtough slew
my father, and my mother and sister were slain along with
him, in the battle of Cerb upon the Boyne, and there was
none of my house to avenge their death, save myself alone.
Moreover, in his time the Ancient Peoples of the Fairy
Tribes of Erin were scattered and destroyed, the folk of the
underworld and of my fatherland; and to avenge the wrong
and loss he wrought on them I slew the man I loved. I
made poison for him; alas! I made for him magic drink
and food which took his strength away, and out of the
sods of earth and puff-balls that float down the wind, I
wrought men and armies of headless, hideous folk, till all
his senses were distraught. And, now, take me to thee,
O Cairnech, in fervent and true repentance, and sign the Cross
of Christ upon my brow, for the time of my death is come."

Then she made penitence for the sin that she had sinned, and she died there upon the grave of grief and of sorrow after the King. And they digged a grave lengthways across the foot of the wide grave of Murtough and his spouse, and there they laid the maiden who had wrought them woe. And the clerics wondered at those things, and they wrote them and revised them in a book.

ELEANOR HULL.

The Red Pony

(*As told by an Irish Peasant.*)

 HERE was a poor man there. He had a great family of sons. He had no means to put them forward. He had them at school. One day, when they were coming from school, he thought that whichever of them was last at the door he would keep him out. It was the youngest of the family that was last at the door. The father shut the door. He would not let him in. The boy went weeping. He would not let him in till night came. The father said he would never let him in—that he had boys enough.

The lad went away. He was walking till night. He came to a house on the rugged side of a hill on a height, one feather giving it shelter and support. He went in. He got a place till morning. When he made his breakfast in the morning he was going. The man of the house made him a present of a red pony, a saddle, and bridle. He went riding on the pony. He went away with himself.

"Now," said the pony, "whatever thing you may see before you, don't touch it."

They went on with themselves. He saw a light before him on the high road. When he came as far as the light, there was an open box on the road, and a light coming out of it. He took up the box. There was a lock of hair in it.

"Are you going to take up the box?" said the pony.

"I am. I cannot go past it."

"It's better for you to leave it," said the pony.

E took up the box. He put it in his pocket. He was going with himself. A gentleman met him.

"Pretty is your little beast. Where are you going?"

"I am looking for service."

"I am in want of one like you among the stable-boys."

He hired the lad. The lad said he must get room for the little beast in the stable. The gentleman said he would get it. They went home then. He had eleven boys. When they were going out into the stable at ten o'clock each of them took a light with him but he. He took no candle at all with him.

Each of them went into his own stable. When he went into his stable, he opened the box. He left it in a hole in the wall. The light was great. It was twice as much as in the other stables. There was wonder on the boys—what was the reason of the light being so great, and he without a candle with him at all. They told the master they did not know what was the cause of the light with the last boy. They had given him no candle, and he had twice as much light as they had.

"Watch to-morrow night what kind of light he has," said the master.

They watched the night of the morrow. They saw the box in the hole that was in the wall, and the light coming out of the box. They told the master. When the boys came to the house, the King asked him what was the reason why he did not take a candle with him to the stable, as well as the other boys. The lad said he had a candle. The King said he had not. He asked him how he got the box from which the light came. He said he had no box. The King said he had, and that he must give it to him; that he would not keep him, unless he gave him the box. The boy gave it to him. The King opened it. He drew out the lock of hair, in which was the light.

"You must go," said the King, "and bring me the woman to whom the hair belongs."

The lad was troubled. He went out. He told the red pony.

"I told you not to take up the box. You will get more than that on account of the box. When you have made your breakfast to-morrow, put the saddle and bridle on me."

When he made his breakfast on the morning of the morrow, he put saddle and bridle on the pony. He went till they came to three miles of sea.

"Keep a good hold now. I am going to give a jump

over the sea. When I arrive yonder, there is a fair on the strand. Everyone will be coming up to you to ask for a ride, because I am such a pretty little beast. Give no one a ride. You will see a beautiful woman drawing near you, her in whose hair was the wonderful light. She will come up to you. She will ask you to let her ride for a while. Say you will, and welcome. When she comes riding, I will be off."

HEN she came to the sea, she cleared the three miles at a jump. She came upon the land opposite, and everyone was asking for a ride upon the beast, she was that pretty. He was giving a ride to no one. He saw that woman in the midst of the people. She was drawing near. She asked him would he give her a little riding. He said he would give it, and a thousand welcomes. She went riding. She went quietly, till she got out of the crowd. When the pony came to the sea, she made the three-mile jump again, the beautiful woman along with her. She took her home to the King. There was great joy on the King to see her. He took her into the parlour. She said to him she would not marry anyone until he would get the bottle of healing water that was in the eastern world. The King said to the lad he must go and bring the bottle of healing water that was in the eastern world to the lady. The lad was troubled. He went to the pony. He told the pony he must go to the eastern world for the bottle of healing water that was in it, and bring it to the lady.

"My advice was good," said the pony, "on the day you took the box up. Put saddle and bridle on me."

He went riding on her. They were going till they came to the sea. She stood then.

"You must kill me," said the pony. "That, or I must kill you!"

"It is hard to me to kill you," said the boy. "If I kill you, there will be no way to myself."

He cut her down. He opened her up. She was not long opened when there came two black ravens and one small one. The two ravens went into the body. They drank their fill of the blood. When they came out, the little raven went in. He closed up the pony. He would not let the little bird come out till he got the bottle of healing water that was in the eastern world. The ravens were very troubled. They were begging him to let the little bird out. He said he would not let it out till they brought him the bottle. They went to seek the bottle. They came back, and there was no bottle with them. They were entreating him to let the bird out to them. He would not let out the bird till he got the bottle. They went away again for the bottle. They came again at evening. They were tossed and scorched, and they had the bottle. They came to the place where the pony was. They gave the bottle to the boy. He rubbed the healing water to every place where they were burned. Then he let out the little bird. There was great joy on them to see him. He rubbed some of the healing water to the place where he cut the pony. He spilt a drop into her ear. She arose as well as she ever was. He had a little bottle in his pocket. He put some of the healing water into it. They went home.

When the King perceived the pony coming, he rose out. He took hold of her with his two hands. He took her in.

He smothered her with kisses, and drowned her with tears; he dried her with finest cloths of silk and satin.

This is what the lady was doing while they were away. She boiled pitch, and filled a barrel, and that boiling. Now she went beside it. She rubbed the healing water to herself. She came out; she went to the barrel. She gave a jump in and out of the barrel. Three times she went in and out. She said she would never marry anyone who could not do the same. The young King came. He went to the barrel. He fell half in, half out.

E was all boiled and burned. Another gentleman came. He gave a jump into the barrel. He was burned. He came not out till he died. After that there was no one going in or out. The barrel was there, and no one at all was going near it. The lad went up to it. He rubbed the healing water on himself. He came to the barrel. He jumped in and out three times. He was watching her. She came out. She said she would never marry anyone but him.

Came the priest of the pattens, and the clerk of the bells. The pair were married. The wedding lasted three days and three nights. When it was over, the lad went to look at the place where the pony was. He never remembered to go and see the pony during the wedding. He found nothing but a heap of bones. There were two champions and two girls playing cards. The lad went crying when he saw the bones of the pony. One of the girls asked what was the matter with him. He said it was all one to her—that she cared nothing for his troubles.

"I would like to get knowledge of the cause why you are crying."

"It was my pony who was here. I never remembered to see her during the wedding. I have nothing now but her bones. I don't know what I shall do after her. It was she who did all that I accomplished."

The girl went laughing.

"Would you know your pony if you saw her?"

"I would know," said he.

She laid aside the cards. She stood up.

"Isn't that your pony?" said she.

"It is," said he.

"I was the pony," said the girl, "and the two ravens who went in to drink my blood my two brothers. When the ravens came out, a little bird went in. You closed the pony. You would not let the little bird out till they brought the bottle of healing water that was in the eastern world. They brought the bottle to you. The little bird was my sister. It was my brothers were the ravens. We were all under enchantments. It is my sister who is married to you. The enchantments are gone from us since she was married."

W. LARMINIE.

(*From "West Irish Folk Tales."*)

313

King O'Toole and St Kevin

(A Legend of Glendalough.)

HERE was wanst a king, called King O'Toole, who was a fine ould king in the ould ancient times, long ago; and it was him that owned the Churches in the airly days.

"Surely," said I, "the Churches were not in King O'Toole's time?"

"Oh, by no manes, your honor—throth, it's yourself that's right enough there; but you know the place is called 'The Churches' bekase they wor built *afther* by St. Kavin, and wint by the name o' the Churches iver more; and, therefore, av coorse, the place bein' so called, I say that the King owned the Churches—and why not, sir, seein' 'twas his birthright, time out o' mind, beyant the flood? Well, the King (you see) was the right sort—he was the *rale* boy, and loved sport as he loved his life, and huntin' in partic'lar; and from the risin' o' the sun up he got, and away he wint over the mountains beyant afther the deer: and the fine times them wor;

314

for the deer was as plinty thin, aye throth, far plintyer than the sheep is now; and that's the way it was with the King, from the crow o' the cock to the song o' the redbreast. Well, it was all mighty good as long as the King had his health; but, you see, in coorse o' time, the King grewn ould, by raison he was stiff in his limbs, and when he got sthricken in years, his heart failed him, and he was lost intirely for want o' divarshin, bekase he couldn't go a huntin' no longer; and, by dad, the poor King was obleeged at last for to get a goose to divart him. You see, the goose used for to swim acrass the lake, and go down divin' for throut (and not finer throut in all Ireland than the same throut) and cotch fish on a Friday for the King, and flew every other day round about the lake divartin' the poor King that you'd think he'd break his sides laughin' at the frolicksome tricks av his goose; so, in coorse o' time, the goose was the greatest pet in the counthry, and the biggest rogue, and divarted the King to no end, and the poor King was as happy as the day was long. So that's the way it was; and all wint on mighty well antil, by dad, the goose got sthricken in years, as well as the King, and grew stiff in the limbs, like her masther, and couldn't divart him no longer; and then it was that the poor King was lost complate, and didn't know what in the wide world to do, seein' he was gone out of all divarshin by raison that the goose was no more in the flower of her blume.

" Well, the King was nigh broken-hearted and melancholy intirely, and was walkin' one mornin' by the edge of the lake, lamentin' his cruel fate, an' thinkin' o' drownin' himself, that could get no divarshin in life, when all of a suddint, turnin' round the corner beyant, who should he meet but a mighty dacent young man comin' up to him.

"'God save you,' says the King (for the King was a civil-spoken gintleman, by all accounts), 'God save you,' says he to the young man.

"'God save you kindly,' says the young man to him back again; 'God save you, King O'Toole.'

"'Thrue for you,' says the King, 'I am King O'Toole,' says he, 'prince and plennypennytinchery o' these parts,' says he; 'but how kem ye to know that?' says he.

"'Oh, never mind,' says Saint Kavin (for 'twas he that was in it). 'And now, may I make bowld to ax, how is your goose, King O'Toole?' says he.

"'Blur-an-agers, how kem you to know about my goose?' says the King.

"H, no matther; I was given to understand it,' says Saint Kavin.

"'Oh, that's a folly to talk,' says the King, "bekase myself and my goose is private friends,' says he, 'and no one could tell you,' says he, 'barrin' the fairies.'

"'Oh, thin, it wasn't the fairies,' says Saint Kavin; 'for I'd have you know,' says he, 'that I don't keep the likes o' sich company.'

"'You might do worse, then, my gay fellow,' says the King; 'for it's *they* could show you a crock o' money as aisy as kiss hand; and that's not to be sneezed at,' says the King, 'by a poor man,' says he.

"'Maybe I've a betther way of making money myself,' says the saint.

"'By gor,' says the King, 'barrin' you're a coiner,' says he, 'that's impossible!'

"'I'd scorn to be the like, my lord!' says Saint Kavin, mighty high, 'I'd scorn to be the like,' says he.

"'Then, what are you?' says the King, 'that makes money so aisy, by your own account.'

"'I'm an honest man,' says Saint Kavin.

"'Well, honest man,' says the King, 'and how is it you make your money so aisy?'

"'By makin' ould things as good as new,' says Saint Kavin.

"'Is it a tinker you are?' says the King.

"O,' says the saint; 'I'm no tinker by thrade, King O'Toole; I've a betther thrade than a tinker,' says he. 'What would you say,' says he, 'if I made your ould goose as good as new?'

"My dear, at the word o' making his goose as good as new, you'd think the poor ould King's eyes was ready to jump out iv his head, 'and,' says he—'throth, thin, I'd give you more money nor you could count,' says he, 'if you did the like, and I'd be behoulden to you in the bargain.'

"'I scorn your dirty money,' says Saint Kavin.

"'Faith, thin, I'm thinkin' a thrifle o' change would do you no harm,' says the King, lookin' up sly at the ould *caubeen* that Saint Kavin had on him.

"'I have a vow agin it,' says the saint; 'and I am book sworn,' says he, 'never to have goold, silver, or brass in my company.'

"'Barrin' the thrifle you can't help,' says the King, mighty cute, and looking him straight in the face.

"'You just hot it,' says Saint Kavin; 'but though I can't

take money,' says he, 'I could take a few acres o' land, if you'd give them to me.'

" 'With all the veins o' my heart,' says the King, 'if you can do what you say.'

" 'Thry me!' says Saint Kavin. 'Call down your goose here,' says he, 'and I'll see what I can do for her.'

" With that the King whistled, and down kem the poor goose, all as one as a hound, waddlin' up to the poor ould cripple, her masther, and as like him as two *pays*. The minute the saint clapt his eyes on the goose, 'I'll do the job for you,' says he, 'King O'Toole!'

Y *Jaminee*,' says King O'Toole, 'if you do, but I'll say you're the cleverest fellow in the sivin parishes.'

" 'Oh, by dad,' says Saint Kavin, 'you must say more nor that—my horn's not so soft all out,' says he, 'as to repair your ould goose for nothin'; what'll you gi' me if I do the job for you?—that's the chat,' says Saint Kavin.

" 'I'll give you whatever you ax,' says the King; 'isn't that fair?'

" 'Divil a fairer,' says the saint; 'that's the way to do business. Now,' says he, ' this is the bargain I'll make with you, King O'Toole: will you gi' me all the ground the goose flies over, the first offer, afther I make her as good as new?'

" 'I will,' says the King.

" 'You won't go back o' your word?' says Saint Kavin.

" 'Honor bright!' says King O'Toole, howldin' out his fist.

" 'Honor bright,' says Saint Kavin back again, 'it's a bargain,' says he. 'Come here!' says he to the poor ould goose—'come here, you unfort'nate ould cripple,' says he, 'and it's I that'll make you the sportin' bird.'

"With that, my dear, he tuk up the goose by the two wings—'criss o' my crass an you,' says he, markin' her to grace with the blessed sign at the same minute—and throwin' her up in the air, 'whew!' says he, jist givin' her a blast to help her; and with that, my jewel, she tuk to her heels, flyin' like one o' the aigles themselves, and cuttin' as many capers as a swallow before a shower of rain. Away she wint down there, right forninst you, along the side o' the clift, and flew over Saint Kavin's bed (that is, where Saint Kavin's bed is *now*, but was not *thin*, by raison it wasn't made, but was conthrived afther by Saint Kavin himself, that the women might lave him alone), and on with her undher Lugduff, and round the ind av the lake there, far beyant where you see the watherfall—and on with her thin right over the lead mines o' Luganure (that is, where the lead mines is *now*, but was not *thin*, by raison they worn't discovered, *but was all goold in Saint Kavin's time*). Well, over the ind o' Luganure she flew, stout and studdy, and round the other ind av the *little* lake, by the Churches (that is, *av coorse*, where the Churches is *now*, but was not *thin*, by raison they wor not built, but afherwards by Saint Kavin), and over the big hill here over your head, where you see the big clift—(and that clift in the mountain was made by *Finn Ma Cool*, where he cut it acrass with a big swoord that he got made a purpose by a blacksmith out o' Rathdrum, a cousin av his own, for to fight a joyant (giant) that darr'd him an' the Curragh o' Kildare; and he thried the swoord first an the mountain, and cut it down into a gap, as is plain to this day; and faith, sure enough, it's the same sauce he sarv'd the joyant, soon and suddint, and chopped him in two like a pratie, for the glory of his sowl and ould Ireland'—well, down she flew over the clift, and fluttherin' over the wood there at Poulanass. Well —as I said—afther fluttherin' over the wood a little bit, to *plaze* herself, the goose flew down, and bit at the fut o' the King as fresh as a daisy, afther flyin' roun' his dominions, jist as if she hadn't flew three perch.

ELL, my dear, it was a beautiful sight to see the King standin' with his mouth open, lookin' at his poor ould goose flyin' as light as a lark, and betther nor ever she was; and when she lit at his fut he patted her an the head, and '*ma vourneen*,' says he, but you are the *darlint* o' the world.'

"'And what do you say to me,' says Saint Kavin, 'for makin' her the like?'"

"'By gor,' says the King, 'I say nothin' bates the art o' men, 'barrin' the bees.'"

"'And do you say no more nor that?' says Saint Kavin."

"'And that I'm beholden to you,' says the King."

"'But will you gi' me all the ground the goose flewn over?' says Saint Kavin."

"'I will,' says King O'Toole, 'and you're welkim to it,' says he, 'though it's the last acre I have to give.'"

"'But you'll keep your word thrue?' says the saint."

"'As thrue as the sun,' says the King."

"'It's well for you,' says Saint Kavin, mighty sharp—'it's well for you, King O'Toole, that you said that word,' says he; 'for if you didn't say that word, *the divil receave the bit o' your goose id iver fly agin*,' says Saint Kavin."

" ' Oh, you needn't laugh,' said old Joe, ' for it's thruth I'm telling you.'

" Well, whin the King was as good as his word, Saint Kavin was *plazed* with him, and thin it was that he made himself known to the King.

" Well, my dear, that's the way that the place kem, all at wanst, into the hands of Saint Kavin; for the goose flew round every individyial acre o' King O'Toole's property, you see, *bein' let into the saycret* by Saint Kavin, who was mighty *cute*; and so, when he *done* the ould King out iv his property for the glory of God, he was *plazed* with him, and he and the King was the best o' friends iver more afther (for the poor ould King was *doatin'*, you see), and the King had his goose as good as new to divart him as long as he lived; and the saint supported him afther he kem into his property, as I tould you, until the day iv his death—and that was soon afther; for the poor goose thought he was ketchin' a throut one Friday; but, my jewel, it was a mistake he made—and instead of a throut, it was a thievin' horse-eel! and, by gor, instead iv the goose killin' a throut for the King's supper—by dad, the eel killed the King's goose—and small blame to him; but he didn't ate her, bekase he darn't ate what Saint Kavin laid his blessed hands on."

SAMUEL LOVER.

Lament of the last Leprechaun

FOR the red shoon of the Shee,
   For the falling o' the leaf,
   For the wind among the reeds,
      My grief.

For the sorrow of the sea,
For the song's unquickened seeds,
For the sleeping of the Shee,
      My grief.

For dishonoured whitethorn-tree,
For the runes that no man reads
Where the grey stones face the sea,
      My grief.

Lissakeole, that used to be
Filled with music night and noon,
For their ancient revelry,
    My grief.

For the empty fairy shoon,
Hollow rath and yellow leaf,
Hands unkissed to sun or moon,
    My grief—my grief!

NORA HOPPER.

The Corpse Watchers

HERE was once a poor woman that had three daughters, and one day the eldest said, "Mother, bake my cake and kill my cock till I go seek my fortune." So she did, and when all was ready, says her mother to her, "Which will you have—half of these with my blessing, or the whole with my curse?" "Curse or no curse," says she, "the whole is little enough." So away she set, and if the mother didn't give her her curse, she didn't give her her blessing.

She walked, and she walked, till she was tired and hungry, and then she sat down to take her dinner. While she was eating it a poor woman came up, and asked for a bit. "The dickens a bit you'll get from me," says she; "it's all too little for myself." And the poor woman walked away very sorrowful. At nightfall she got lodging at a farmer's, and the woman of the house told her that she'd give her a spadeful of gold and a shovelful of silver if she'd only sit up and watch her son's corpse that was waking in the next room. She said she'd do that, and so, when the family were in their bed, she sat by the fire, and cast an eye from time to time on the corpse that was lying under the table.

All at once the dead man got up in his shroud, and stood before her, and said, "All alone, fair maid?" She gave him no answer; when he had said it the third time he struck her with a switch, and she became a grey flag.

About a week after, the second daughter went to seek her fortune, and she didn't care for her mother's blessing no more *nor* her sister, and the very same thing happened to her. She was left a grey flag by the side of the other.

T last the youngest went off in search of the other two, and she took care to carry her mother's blessing with her. She shared her dinner with the poor woman on the road, and *she* told her that she would watch over her.

Well, she got lodging in the same place as the others, and agreed to mind the corpse. She sat up by the fire, with the dog and cat, and amused herself with some apples and nuts the mistress had given her. She thought it a pity that the man under the table was a corpse, he was so handsome.

But at last he got up, and, says he, "All alone, fair maid?" and she wasn't long about an answer:

> All alone I am not,
> I've little dog Douse, and Pussy, my cat;
> I've apples to roast and nuts to crack,
> And all alone I am not.

"Ho, ho!" says he, "you're a girl of courage, though you wouldn't have enough to follow me. I am now going to

cross the quaking bog, and go through the burning forest.
I must then enter the cave of terror and climb the hill of
glass, and drop from the top of it into the Dead Sea." "I'll
follow you," says she, "for I engaged to mind you." He
thought to prevent her, but she was stiff as he was stout.

Out he sprang through the window, and she followed
him, till they came to the "Green Hills," and then says he:

"Open, open, Green Hills and let the light of the Green Hills through."
"Aye," says the girl, "and let the fair maid too."

THEY opened, and the man and woman
passed through, and there they were
on the edge of a bog.

He trod lightly over the shaky bits
of moss and sod; and while she was
thinking of how she'd get across, the
old beggar appeared to her, but much
nicer dressed, touched her shoes with a stick, and the soles
spread a foot on each side. So she easily got over the shaky
marsh. The burning wood was at the edge of the bog, and
there the good fairy flung a damp, thick cloak over her, and
through the flames she went, and a hair of her head was not
singed. Then they passed through the dark cavern of
horrors, when she'd have heard the most horrible yells, only
that the fairy stopped her ears with wax. She saw frightful
things, with blue vapours round them, and felt the sharp
rocks and the slimy backs of frogs and snakes.

When they got out of the cavern, they were at the mountain of glass; and then the fairy made her slippers so sticky
with a tap of her rod that she followed the young corpse
quite easily to the top. There was the deep sea a quarter

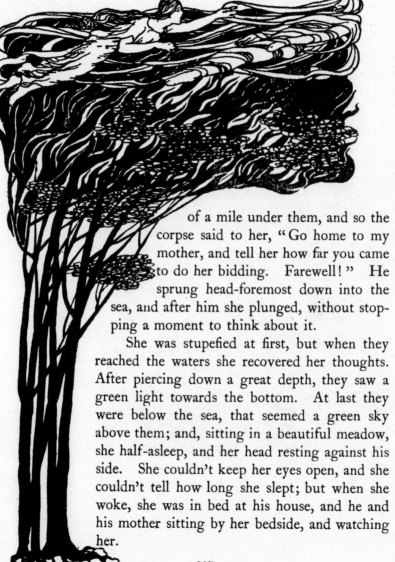

of a mile under them, and so the corpse said to her, "Go home to my mother, and tell her how far you came to do her bidding. Farewell!" He sprung head-foremost down into the sea, and after him she plunged, without stopping a moment to think about it.

She was stupefied at first, but when they reached the waters she recovered her thoughts. After piercing down a great depth, they saw a green light towards the bottom. At last they were below the sea, that seemed a green sky above them; and, sitting in a beautiful meadow, she half-asleep, and her head resting against his side. She couldn't keep her eyes open, and she couldn't tell how long she slept; but when she woke, she was in bed at his house, and he and his mother sitting by her bedside, and watching her.

327

It was a witch that had a spite to the young man because he wouldn't marry her, and so she got power to keep him in a state between life and death till a young woman would rescue him by doing what she had done. So, at her request, her sisters got their own shapes again, and were sent back to their mother, with their spades of gold and shovels of silver. Maybe they were better after that, but I doubt it much. The youngest got the young gentleman for her husband. I'm sure she lived happy, and, if they didn't live happy—*that we may!*

PATRICK KENNEDY.

The Mad Pudding of Ballyboulteen

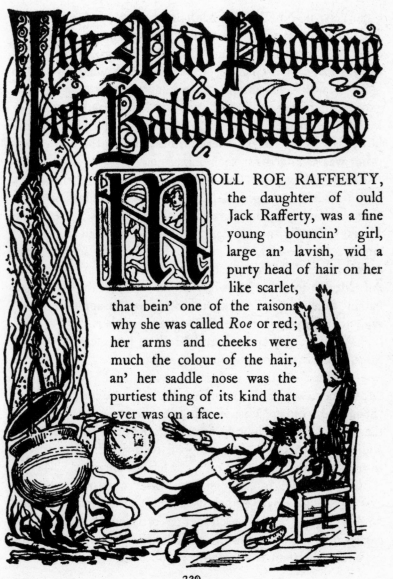

MOLL ROE RAFFERTY, the daughter of ould Jack Rafferty, was a fine young bouncin' girl, large an' lavish, wid a purty head of hair on her like scarlet, that bein' one of the raisons why she was called *Roe* or red; her arms and cheeks were much the colour of the hair, an' her saddle nose was the purtiest thing of its kind that ever was on a face.

" Well, anyhow, it was Moll Rafferty that was the *dilsy*. It happened that there was a nate vagabone in the neighbourhood, just as much overburdened wid beauty as herself, and he was named Gusty Gillespie. Gusty was what they call a black-mouth Prosbytarian, and wouldn't keep Christmas day, except what they call ' ould style.' Gusty was rather goodlookin', when seen in the dark, as well as Moll herself; anyhow, they got attached to each other, and in the end everything was arranged for their marriage.

" Now this was the first marriage that had happened for a long time in the neighbourhood between a Prodestant and a Catholic, and faix, there was one of the bride's uncles, ould Harry Connolly, a fairyman, who could cure all complaints wid a secret he had, and as he didn't wish to see his niece married on sich a fellow, he fought bitterherly against the match. All Moll's friends, however, stood up for the marriage, barrin' him, and, of coorse, the Sunday was appointed, as I said, that they were to be dove-tailed together.

" Well, the day arrived, and Moll, as became her, went to mass, and Gusty to meeting, afther which they were to join one another in Jack Rafferty's, where the priest, Father Mc. Sorley, was to slip up afther mass to take his dinner wid them, and to keep Misther Mc. Shuttle, who was to marry them, company. Nobody remained at home but ould Jack Rafferty an' his wife, who stopped to dress the dinner, for, to tell the truth, it was to be a great let-out entirely. Maybe, if all was known, too, Father Mc. Sorley was to give them a cast of his office over and above the ministher, in regard that Moll's friends were not altogether satisfied at the kind of marriage which Mc. Shuttle could give them. The sorrow may care about that—splice here, splice there—all I can say is that when Mrs. Rafferty was goin' to tie up a big bag pudden, in walks Harry Connolly, the fairyman, in a rage, and shouts out, 'Blood and blunderbushes, what are yez here for?'

"'Arrah, why, Harry? Why, avick?'

"'Why, the sun's in the suds, and the moon in the high Horricks; there's a clip-stick comin' on, and there you're both as unconsarned as if it was about to rain mether. Go out, an' cross yourselves three times in the name o' the four Mandromarvins, for as prophecy says:—"Fill the pot, Eddy, supernaculum—a blazing star's a rare spectaculum." Go out, both of you, an' look at the sun, I say, an' ye'll see the condition he's in—off!'

"Begad, sure enough, Jack gave a bounce to the door, and his wife leaped like a two-year-ould, till they were both got on a stile beside the house to see what was wrong in the sky.

"'Arrah, what is it, Jack?' says she, 'can you see anything?'

"'No,' says he, 'sorra the full of my eye of anything I can spy, barrin' the sun himself, that's not visible, in regard of the clouds. God guard us! I doubt there's something to happen.'

"'If there wasn't Jack, what'd put Harry, that knows so much, in the state he's in?'

"'I doubt it's this marriage,' says Jack. 'Betune ourselves, it's not over an' above religious of Moll to marry a black-mouth, an' only for—; but, it can't be helped now, though you see it's not a taste o' the sun is willin' to show his face upon it.'

"'As to that,' says his wife, winkin' with both her eyes, 'if Gusty's satisfied wid Moll, it's enough. I know who'll carry the whip hand, anyhow; but in the manetime let us ax Harry within what ails the sun?'

" Well, they accordianly went in, and put this question to him, 'Harry, what's wrong, ahagur? What is it now, for if anybody alive knows 'tis yourself?'

"'Ah,' said Harry, screwin' his mouth wid a kind of a dry smile, ' the sun has a hard twist o' the colic; but never mind that, I tell you, you'll have a merrier weddin' than you think, that's all'; and havin' said this, he put on his hat and left the house.

OW, Harry's answer relieved them very much, and so, afther callin' to him to be back for dinner, Jack sat down to take a shough o' the pipe, and the wife lost no time in tying up the pudden, and puttin' it in the pot to be boiled.

" In this way things went on well enough for a while, Jack smokin' away, an' the wife cookin' an' dhressin' at the rate of a hunt. At last, Jack, while sittin', as I said, contentedly at the fire, thought he could persave an odd dancin' kind of motion in the pot that puzzled him a good deal.

"'Katty,' says he, ' what the dickens is in this pot on the fire?'

"'Nerra thing but the big pudden. Why do you ax?' says she.

"'Why,' says he, ' if ever a pot tuck it into its head to dance a jig, and this did. Thundher and sparbles, look at it!'

" Begad, and it was thrue enough; there was the pot bobbin' up an' down, and from side to side, jiggin' it away as merry as a grig; an' it was quite aisy to see that it wasn't the pot itself, but what was inside of it, that brought about the hornpipe.

" ' Be the hole o' my coat,' shouted Jack, ' there's somethin' alive in it, or it would niver cut sich capers! '

" ' Begorra, there is, Jack; somethin' sthrange entirely has got into it. Wirra, man alive, what's to be done?'

" Jist as she spoke the pot seemed to cut the buckle in prime style, and afther a spring that'd shame a dancin' masther, off flew the lid, and out bounced the pudden itself, hoppin' as nimble as a pea on a drum-head about the floor. Jack blessed himself, and Katty crossed herself. Jack shouted, and Katty screamed. ' In the name of goodness, keep your distance; no one here injured you!'

" The pudden, however, made a set at him, and Jack lepped first on a chair, and then on the kitchen table, to avoid it. It then danced towards Katty, who was repatin' her prayers at the top of her voice, while the cunnin' thief of a pudden was hoppin' an' jiggin' it around her as if it was amused at her distress.

" ' If I could get the pitchfork,' says Jack, ' I'd dale wid it—by goxty, I'd thry its mettle.'

" ' No, no,' shouted Katty, thinking there was a fairy in it; ' let us spake it fair. Who knows what harm it might do? Aisy, now,' says she to the pudden, ' aisy, dear; don't harm honest people that never meant to offend you. It wasn't us—no, in troth, it was ould Harry Connolly that bewitched you; pursue *him*, if you wish, but spare a woman like me!'

" The pudden, bedad, seemed to take her at her word, and danced away from her towards Jack, who, like the wife, believin' there was a fairy in it, an' that spakin' it fair was the best plan, thought he would give it a soft word as well as her.

" 'Plase your honour,' said Jack, 'she only spaiks the truth, an' upon my voracity, we both feels much oblaiged to you for your quietness. Faith, it's quite clear that if you weren't a gentlemanly pudden, all out, you'd act otherwise. Ould Harry, the rogue, is your mark; he's jist gone down the road there, and if you go fast you'll overtake him. Be my song, your dancin'-masther did his duty, anyway. Thank your honour! God speed you, and may you niver meet wid a parson or alderman in your thravels.'

" Jist as Jack spoke, the pudden appeared to take the hint, for it quietly hopped out, and as the house was directly on the roadside, turned down towards the bridge, the very way that ould Harry went. It was very natural, of coorse, that Jack and Katty should go out to see how it intended to thravel, and as the day was Sunday, it was but natural, too, that a greater number of people than usual were passin' the road. This was a fact; and when Jack and his wife were seen followin' the pudden, the whole neighbourhood was soon up and afther it.

" ' Jack Rafferty, what is it? Katty, ahagur, will you tell us what it manes?'

" ' Why,' replied Katty, 'it's my big pudden that's be-witched, an' it's out hot foot pursuin' '—here she stopped, not wishin' to mention her brother's name—'*someone* or other that surely put *pishrogues** an it.'

" This was enough; Jack, now seein' that he had assistance, found his courage comin' back to him; so says he to Katty,

* Put it under Fairy influence.

'Go home,' says he, 'an' lose no time in makin' another pudden as good, an' here's Paddy Scanlan's wife, Bridget, says she'll let you boil it on her fire, as you'll want our own to dress the rest of the dinner; and Paddy himself will lend me a pitchfork for purshuin' to the morsel of that same pudden will escape, till I let the wind out of it, now that I've the neighbours to back an' support me,' says Jack.

"This was agreed to, an' Katty went back to prepare a fresh pudden, while Jack an' half the townland pursued the other wid spades, graips, pitchforks, scythes, flails, and all possible description of instruments. On the pudden went, however, at the rate of about six Irish miles an hour, an' sich a chase was never seen. Catholics, Prodestants, and Prosbytarians were all afther it, armed, as I said, an' bad end to the thing, but its own activity could save it. Here it made a hop, there a prod was made at it; but off it went, and someone, as eager to get a slice at it on the other side, got the prod instead of the pudden. Big Frank Farrell, the miller, of Ballyboulteen, got a prod backwards that brought a hullabulloo out of him that you might hear at the other end of the parish. One got a slice of a scythe, another a whack of a flail, a third a rap of a spade, that made him look nine ways at wanst.

"'Where is it goin'?' asked one. 'My life for you, it's on its way to Meeting. Three cheers for it, if it turns to Carntaul!' 'Prod the sowl out of it if it's a Prodestan',' shouted the others; 'if it turns to the left, slice it into pancakes. We'll have no Prodestan' puddens here.'

"Begad, by this time the people were on the point of beginnin' to have a regular fight about it, when, very fortunately, it took a short turn down a little by-lane that led towards the Methodist praychin'-house, an' in an instant all parties were in an uproar against it as a Methodist pudden. 'It's a Wesleyan,' shouted several voices; 'an' by this an' by that, into a Methodist chapel it won't put a foot to-day, or we'll lose a fall. Let the wind out of it. Come, boys, where's your pitchforks?'

"The divle purshuin' to the one of them, however, ever could touch the pudden, and jist when they thought they had it up against the gavel of the Methodist chapel, begad, it gave them the slip, and hops over to the left, clane into the river, and sails away before their eyes as light as an egg-shell.

"NOW, it so happened that a little below this place the desmesne wall of Colonel Bragshaw was built up to the very edge of the river on each side of its banks; and so, findin' there was a stop put to their pursuit of it, they went home again, every man, woman, and child of them, puzzled to think what the pudden was at all, what it meant, or where it was goin'! Had Jack Rafferty an' his wife been willin' to let out the opinion they held about Henry Connolly bewitchin' it, there is no doubt of it but poor Harry might be badly trated by the crowd, when their blood was up. They had sense enough, howaniver, to keep that to themselves, for Harry bein' an ould bachelor, was a kind friend to the Raffertys. So, of coorse, there was all kinds of talk about it—some guessin' this, an' some guessin' that— one party sayin' the pudden was of their side, and another denyin' it, an' insisting it belonged to them, an' so on.

"In the meantime, Katty Rafferty, for 'fraid the dinner

might come short, went home and made another pudden much about the same size as the one that had escaped, an' bringin' it over to their next neighbour, Paddy Scanlan's, it was put into a pot, and placed on the fire to boil, hopin' that it might be done in time, espishilly as they were to have the ministher, who loved a warm slice of a good pudden as well as e'er a gentleman in Europe.

"Anyhow, the day passed; Moll and Gusty were made man an' wife, an' no two could be more lovin'. Their friends that had been asked to the weddin' were saunterin' about in pleasant little groups till dinner-time, chattin' an' laughin'; but above all things, sthrivin' to account for the figaries of the pudden; for, to tell the truth, its adventures had now gone through the whole parish.

"Well, at any rate, dinner-time was drawin' near, and Paddy Scanlan was sittin' comfortably wid his wife at the fire, the pudden boilin' before their eyes, when in walks Harry Connolly in a flutter, shoutin', ' Blood and blunderbushes, what are yez here for?'

"'Arrah, why, Harry—why, avick?' said Mrs. Scanlan.

"'Why,' said Harry, 'the sun's in the suds, an' the moon in the high Horricks! Here's a clipstick comin' on, an' there you sit as unconsarned as if it was about to rain mether! Go out, both of you, an' look at the sun, I say, an' ye'll see the condition he's in—off!'

"'Ay, but, Harry, what's that rowled up in the tail of your cothamore (big coat)?'

"' Out wid yez,' says Harry, ' an' pray aginst the clipstick—the sky's fallin'!'

"Begad, it was hard to say whether Paddy or the wife got out first, they were so much alarmed by Harry's wild, thin face and piercin' eyes; so out they went to see what was wonderful in the sky, an' kep lookin' an' lookin' in every direction, but not a thing was to be seen, barrin' the sun shinin' down wid great good-humour, an' not a single cloud in the sky.

"Paddy an' the wife now came in laughin' to scould Harry, who no doubt was a great wag in his way when he wished. 'Musha, bad scran to you, Harry——' and they had time to say no more, howandiver, for, as they were goin' into the door, they met him comin' out of it, wid a reek of smoke out of his tail like a lime-kiln.

"'Harry,' shouted Bridget, 'my sowl to glory, but the tail of your cothamore's afire—you'll be burned. Don't you see the smoke that's out of it?'

"'CROSS yourselves three times,' said Harry, widout stoppin' or even lookin' behind him, 'for, as the prophecy says, Fill the pot, Eddy——' They could hear no more, for Harry appeared to feel like a man that carried something a great deal hotter than he wished, as anyone might see by the liveliness of his motions, and the quare faces he was forced to make as he went along.

"'What the dickens is he carryin' in the skirts of his big coat?' asked Paddy.

"'My sowl to happiness, but maybe he has stolen the pudden,' said Bridget, 'for it's known that many a sthrange thing he does.'

"They immediately examined the pot, but found that the pudden was there, as safe as tuppence, an' this puzzled them the more to think what it was he could be carryin' about with him in the manner he did. But little they knew what he had done while they were sky-gazin'!

"Well, anyhow, the day passed, and the dinner was ready, an' no doubt but a fine gatherin' there was to partake of it. The Prosbytarian ministher met the Methodist praycher—a divilish stretcher of an appetite he had, in throth—on their way to Jack Rafferty's, an' as he knew he could take the liberty, why, he insisted on his dinin' wid him; for, afther all, in thim days, the clargy of all descriptions lived upon the best footin' among one another, not all at one as now— but no matther. Well, they had nearly finished their dinner, when Jack Rafferty himself axed Katty for the pudden; but, jist as he spoke, in it came, as big as a mess-pot.

"'Gintlemen,' said he, 'I hope none of you will refuse tastin' a bit of Katty's pudden; I don't mane the dancin' one that took to its thravels to-day, but a good solid fellow that she med since.'

"'O be sure we won't,' replied the priest. 'So, Jack, put a thrifle on them three plates at your right hand, and send them over here to the clargy, an' maybe,' he said, laughin'—for he was a droll, good-humoured man—'maybe, Jack, we won't set you a proper example.'

"'Wid a heart an' a half, your riverence an' gintlemen; in throth, it's not a bad example ever any of you set us at the likes, or ever will set us, I'll go bail. An' sure, I only wish it was betther fare I had for you; but we're humble people, gintlemen, an' so you can't expect to meet here what you would in higher places.'

"'Betther a male of herbs,' said the Methodist praycher, 'where pace is——' He had time to get no further, however; for much to his amazement, the priest an' the ministher started up from the table, jist as he was goin' to swallow the first mouthful of the pudden, and, before you could say Jack Robinson, started away at a lively jig down the floor.

"At this moment a neighbour's son came runnin' in, and tould them that the parson was comin' to see the new-married couple, an' wish them all happiness; an' the words were scarcely out of his mouth when he made his appearance. What to think, he knew not, when he saw the ministher footin' it away at the rate of a weddin'. He had very little time, however, to think; for, before he could sit down, up starts the Methodist praycher, an', clappin' his fists in his sides, chimes in in great style along wid him.

"'Jack Rafferty,' says he, and, by the way, Jack was his tenant, 'what the dickens does all this mane?' says he; 'I'm amazed!'

"'The not a particle o' me can tell you,' says Jack; 'but will your reverence jist taste a morsel o' pudden, merely that the young couple may boast that you ait at their weddin'; 'for, sure, if *you* wouldn't, who *would?*'

"'Well,' says he, 'to gratify them, I will; so, just a morsel. But, Jack, this bates Bannagher,' says he again, puttin' the spoonful of pudden into his mouth; 'has there been drink here?'

"'Oh, the divle a spudh,' says Jack, 'for although there's plenty in the house, faith, it appears the gintlemen wouldn't wait for it. Unless they tuck it elsewhere, I can make nothin' o' this.'

"He had scarcely spoken when the parson, who was an

active man, cut a caper a yard high, an' before you could bless
yourself, the three clargy were hard at work dancin', as if for a
wager. Begad, it would be unpossible for me to tell you the
state the whole meetin' was in when they see this. Some were
hoarse wid laughin'; some turned up their eyes wid wondher;
many thought them mad; and others thought they had turned
up their little fingers a thrifle too often.

"'Be goxty, it's a burnin' shame,' said one, 'to see three
black-mouth clargy in sich a state at this early hour!'
'Thundher an' ounze, what's over them at all?' says others;
'why, one would think they were bewitched. Holy Moses,
look at the caper the Methodist cuts! An' as for the Recthor,
who would think he could handle his feet at sich a rate! Be
this, an' be that, he cuts the buckle, an' does the threblin'
step aiquil to Paddy Horaghan, the dancin'-masther himself!
An' see! Bad cess to the morsel of the parson that's not
too hard at *Peace upon a trancher*, and it upon a Sunday, too!
Whirroo, gintlemen, the fun's in yez, afther all—whish!
more power to yez!'

"T HE sorra's own fun they had, an' no
wondher; but judge of what they felt
when all at once they saw ould
Jack Rafferty himself bouncin' in
among them, an' footin' it away like
the best of them. Bedad, no play
could come up to it, an' nothin' could
be heard but laughin', shouts of encouragement, an' clappin'
of hands like mad. Now, the minute Jack Rafferty left the
chair, where he had been carvin' the pudden, ould Harry
Connolly come over and claps himself down in his place, in
ordher to sent it round, of coorse; an' he was scarcely sated

when who should make his appearance but Barney Hartigan, the piper. Barney, by the way, had been sent for early in the day, but bein' from home when the message for him went, he couldn't come any sooner.

"'Begorra,' says Barney, 'you're airly at the work gintlemen! But what does this mane? But divle may care, yez shan't want the music, while there's a blast in the pipes, anyhow!' So sayin' he gave them *Jig Polthogue*, and afther that, *Kiss My Lady*, in his best style.

"IN the manetime the fun went on thick and threefold, for it must be remembered that Harry, the ould knave, was at the pudden; an' maybe, he didn't sarve it about in double-quick time, too! The first he helped was the bride, and before you could say chopstick she was at it hard and fast, before the Methodist praycher, who gave a jolly spring before her that threw them into convulsions. Harry liked this, and made up his mind soon to find partners for the rest; so he accordianly sent the pudden about like lightnin'; an', to make a long story short, barrin' the piper an' himself, there wasn't a pair of heels in the house but was as busy at the dancin' as if their lives depended on it.

"'Barney,' says Harry, 'jist taste a morsel o' this pudden; divle the sich a bully of a pudden ever you ett. Here, your sowl! thry a snig of it—it's beautiful!'

"'To be sure I will,' says Barney. 'I'm not the boy to refuse a good thing. But, Harry, be quick, for you know my hands is engaged, an' it would be a thousand pities not to keep them in music, an' they so well inclined. Thank

you, Harry. Begad, that is a fine pudden. But, blood an'
turnips! what's this for?'

"The word was scarcely out of his mouth when he bounced
up, pipes an' all, and dashed into the middle of the party.
'Hurroo! your sowls, let us make a night of it! The Ballyboulteen boys for ever! Go it, your reverence!—turn your
partner—heel an' toe, ministher. Good! Well done,
again! Whish! Hurroo! Here's for Ballyboulteen, an'
the sky over it!'

"Bad luck to sich a set ever was seen together in this
world, or will again, I suppose. The worst, however, wasn't
come yet, for jist as they were in the very heat an' fury of
the dance, what do you think comes hoppin' in among them
but another pudden, as nimble an' merry as the first! That
was enough; they had all heard of it—the ministhers among
the rest—an' most of them had seen the other pudden, an'
knew that there must be a fairy in it, sure enough. Well, as I
said, in it comes to the thick o' them; but the very appearance
of it was enough. Off the three clargy danced, and off the
whole weddiners danced afther them, everyone makin' the
best of their way home; but not a sowl of them able to break
out of the step, if they were to be hanged for it. Throth,
it wouldn't lave a laff in you to see the parson dancin' down
the road on his way home, and the ministher and Methodist
praycher cuttin' the buckle as they went along in the opposite
direction. To make short work of it, they all danced home
at last wid scarce a puff of wind in them; the bride an' bridegroom danced away to bed; an' now, boys, come an' let us
dance the *Horo Lheig* in the barn widout. But, you see,
boys, before we go, and in order to make everything plain,
I had as good tell you that Harry, in crossin' the bridge of

Ballyboulteen, a couple o' miles between Squire Bragshaw's demesne wall, saw the pudden floatin' down the river—the truth is, he was waitin' for it; but, be this as it may, he took it out, for the wather had made it as clane as a new pin, an' tuckin' it up in the tail of his big coat, contrived to bewitch it in the same manner by gettin' a fairy to get into it, for, indeed, it was purty well known that the same Harry was hand an' glove wid the *good people*. Others will tell you that it was half a pound of quicksilver he put into it, but that doesn't stand to raison. At any rate, boys, I have tould you the adventures of the Mad Pudden of Ballyboulteen; but I don't wish to tell you many other things about it that happened—*for 'fraid I'd tell a lie!*"

WILLIAM CARLETON.

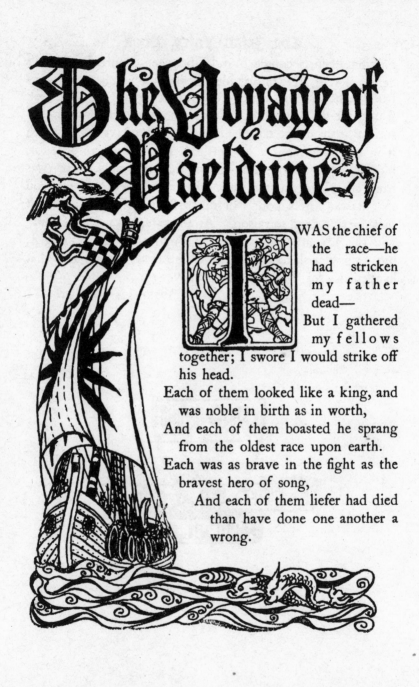

The Voyage of Maeldune

I WAS the chief of the race—he had stricken my father dead—
But I gathered my fellows together; I swore I would strike off his head.
Each of them looked like a king, and was noble in birth as in worth,
And each of them boasted he sprang from the oldest race upon earth.
Each was as brave in the fight as the bravest hero of song,
And each of them liefer had died than have done one another a wrong.

He lived on an isle in the ocean—we sail'd on a Friday
morn—
He that had slain my father the day before I was born.

And we came to the isle in the ocean, and there on the shore
was he.
But a sudden blast blew us out and away through a boundless
sea.

And we came to the Silent Isle that we never had touched
before,
Where a silent ocean always broke on a silent shore,
And the brooks glittered on in the light without sound, and
the long waterfalls
Poured in a thunderless plunge to the base of the mountain
walls,
And the poplar and cypress unshaken by storm flourished up
beyond sight
And the pine shot aloft from the crag to an unbelievable
height,
And high in the heaven above it there flickered a songless
lark,
And the cock couldn't crow, and the bull couldn't low, and
the dog couldn't bark.
And round it we went, and thro' it, but never a murmur, a
breath,
It was all of it fair as life, it was all of it quiet as death,
And we hated the beautiful Isle, for whenever we strove to
speak
Our voices were thinner and fainter than any flittermouse
shriek;

And the men that were mighty of tongue, and could raise
    such a battle-cry
That a hundred who heard it would rush on a thousand lances
    and die—
Oh, they to be dumb'd by the charm!—so fluster'd with
    anger were they
They almost fell on each other; but, after, we sailed away.

And we came to the Isle of Shouting, we landed, a score of
    wild birds
Cried from the topmost summit with human voices and
    words;
Once in an hour they cried, and whenever their voices peal'd
The steer fell down at the plough and the harvest died from
    the field,
And the men dropt dead in the valleys and half of the cattle
    went lame,
And the roof sank in on the hearth, and the dwelling broke
    into flame;
And the shouting of these wild birds ran into the hearts of
    my crew,
Till they shouted along with the shouting, and seized one
    another and slew;
But I drew them the one from the other; I saw that we could
    not stay,
And we left the dead to the birds and we sail'd with our
    wounded away.

And we came to the Isle of Flowers, their breath met us out
    on the seas,

For the Spring and the middle Summer sat each on the lap
    of the breeze;
And the red passion-flower to the cliffs, and the dark-blue
    clematis clung
And starr'd with a myriad blossom, the long convolvulus
    hung;
And the topmost spire of the mountain was lilies in lieu of
    snow,
And the lilies like glaciers winded down, running out below
Thro' the fire of the tulip and poppy, the blaze of gorse, and
    the blush
Of millions of roses that sprang without leaf or thorn from
    the bush;
And the whole isle-side flashing down from the peak without
    ever a tree
Swept like a torrent of gems from the sky to the blue of the
    sea;
And we roll'd upon capes of crocus and vaunted our kith
    and kin,
And we wallowed in beds of lilies, and chanted the triumph
    of Finn,
Till each like a golden image was pollen'd from head to feet
And each was as dry as a cricket, with thirst in the middle-day
    heat.
Blossom, and blossom, and promise of blossom, but never
    a fruit!
And we hated the Flowering Isle, as we hated the isle that
    was mute,
And we tore up the flowers by the million and flung them in
    bight and bay.
And we left but a naked rock, and in anger we sail'd away.

And we came to the Isle of Fruits: all round from the cliffs
and the capes,
Purple or amber dangled a hundred fathom of grapes,
And the warm melon lay, like a little sun, on the tawny sand,
And the fig ran up from the beach, and rioted over the land,
And the mountain arose, like a jewelled throne thro' the
fragrant air,
Glowing with all-coloured plums, and with golden masses
of pear,
And the crimson and scarlet of berries that flamed upon bine
and vine,
But in every berry and fruit was the poisonous pleasure of
wine:
And the peak of the mountain was apples, the hugest that
ever were seen,
And they prest, as they grew, on each other, with hardly a
leaflet between.
And all of them redder than rosiest health, or than utterest
shame,
And setting, when Even descended, the very sunset aflame.
And we stay'd three days, and we gorged and we madden'd
till everyone drew
His sword on his fellow to slay him, and ever they struck
and they slew;
And myself I had eaten but sparsely, and fought till I sun-
der'd the fray,
Then I bade them remember my father's death, and we sail'd
away.

And we came to the Isle of Fire: we were lured by the light
from afar,

For the peak sent up one league of fire to the Northern Star;
Lured by the glare and the blare, but scarcely could stand
  upright,
For the whole isle shudder'd and shook, like a man in a
  mortal affright;
We were giddy, besides, with the fruits we had gorged, and
  so crazed that at last,
There were some leap'd into the fire; and away we sail'd,
  and we past
Over that undersea isle, where the water is clearer than air :
Down we look'd : what a garden !   Oh, bliss, what a Paradise
  there !
Towers of a happier time, low down in a rainbow deep
Silent palaces, quiet fields of eternal sleep !
And three of the gentlest and best of my people, whate'er
  I could say,
Plunged head down in the sea, and the Paradise trembled
  away.

And we came to the Bounteous Isle, where the heavens lean
  low on the land,
And ever at dawn from the cloud glitter'd o'er us a sun-bright
  hand,
Then it opened, and dropped at the side of each man, as he
  rose from his rest,
Bread enough for his need till the labourless day dipt under
  the West;
And we wandered about it, and thro' it.   Oh, never was time
  so good !
And we sang of the triumphs of Finn, and the boast of our
  ancient blood,

And we gazed at the wandering wave, as we sat by the gurgle
of springs,
And we chanted the songs of the Bards and the glories of
fairy kings;
But at length we began to be weary, to sigh, and to stretch
and yawn,
Till we hated the Bounteous Isle, and the sun-bright hand
of the dawn,
For there was not an enemy near, but the whole green isle
was our own,
And we took to playing at ball, and we took to throwing
the stone,
And we took to playing at battle, but that was a perilous play,
For the passion of battle was in us, we slew and we sail'd
away.

And we passed to the Isle of Witches, and heard their musical
cry—
"Come to us, Oh, come, come," in the stormy red of a sky
Dashing the fires and the shadows of dawn on the beautiful
shapes,
For a wild witch, naked as heaven, stood on each of the
loftiest capes,
And a hundred ranged on the rocks, like white sea-birds in
a row,
And a hundred gambled and pranced on the wrecks in the
sand below,
And a hundred splashed from the ledges, and bosomed the
burst of the spray.
But I knew we should fall on each other, and hastily sail'd
away.

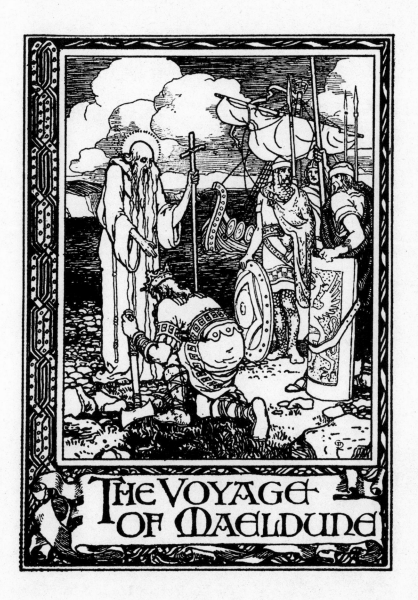

THE VOYAGE
OF MAELDUNE

And we came in an evil time to the Isle of the Double
Towers,
One was of smooth-cut stone, one carved all over with
flowers,
But an earthquake always moved in the hollows under the
dells,
And they shock'd on each other and butted each other with
clashing of bells,
And the daws flew out of the Towers, and jangled and
wrangled in vain,
And the clash and boom of the bells rang into the heart and
brain,
Till the passion of battle was on us, and all took sides with
the Towers,
There were some for the clean-cut stone, there were more for
the carven flowers,
And the wrathful thunder of God peal'd over us all the day,
For the one half slew the other, and, after, we sail'd away.

And we came to the Isle of a Saint, who had sail'd with St.
Brendan of yore,
He had lived ever since on the isle, and his winters were
fifteen score,
And his voice was low as from other worlds, and his eyes
were sweet,
And his white hair sank to his heels, and his white beard fell
to his feet,
And he spake to me, " Oh, Maeldune, let be this purpose of
thine!
Remember the words of the Lord, when He told us ' Ven-
geance is Mine!'

His fathers have slain thy fathers, in war or in single strife,
Thy fathers have slain his fathers, each taken a life for a life,
Thy father had slain his father, how long shall the murder
    last?
Go back to the Isle of Finn and suffer the Past to be Past."
And we kiss'd the fringe of his beard, and we pray'd as we
    heard him pray,
And the Holy Man he assoil'd us, and sadly we sail'd away.

And we came to the Isle we were blown from, and there on
    the shore was he,
The man that had slain my father. I saw him, and let him be.
Oh, weary was I of the travel, the trouble, the strife, and
    the sin,
When I landed again with a tithe of my men on the Island
    of Finn.

ALFRED TENNYSON.